The **GULF REGION**
and **ISRAEL**

OLD STRUGGLES, NEW ALLIANCES

Sigurd Neubauer

KODESH PRESS

The Gulf Region and Israel: Old Struggles, New Alliances
© Copyright Sigurd Neubauer, 2020

Paperback: 978-1-947857-39-1
Hardcover: 978-1-947857-40-7

Published & Distributed Exclusively by
Kodesh Press L.L.C.
New York, NY
www.kodeshpress.com
sales@kodeshpress.com

ABOUT THE AUTHOR

Sigurd Neubauer is a graduate of Yeshiva University in New York where he studied modern Jewish history (MA), political science (BA) and French literature (BA). His decade-long experience covering the Gulf span from the US defense industry to Washington think tanks and Arab media.

CONTENTS

CONTENTS

This book is dedicated to the love of my life,
my wife Hannah, along with our three children.

ACKNOWLEDGMENTS

While the Gulf crisis, which broke out in Summer 2017, has isolated Qatar from its immediate neighbors on the Arabian Peninsula, my book examines the overlooked and widely misunderstood Israeli and Omani roles in this feud.

In addition to my decade-long professional focus on US–Gulf relations, which includes having been affiliated with Emirati- and Qatari-sponsored think tanks in Washington, D.C., as well as regular commentary for Saudi and Qatari media outlets, I covered Israeli defense policies as a Hebrew linguist for a US defense consultancy from 2010 to 2012. Throughout my nine-year tenure with the company—from 2009 to 2018—I used vacations and frequent flier miles to travel extensively to the Gulf region for research and networking purposes.

Because of my overlapping interest in the Gulf region, with a particular focus on US–Arab relations and intra-Gulf dynamics, coupled with that of Israel as a regional actor, I began seeking a better understanding of Gulf–Israel dynamics early on in my career. I quickly discovered, however, that Washington's Middle East policy community was ostensibly divided into two camps: an Arabist roster of Gulf-funded think tanks—with a primary focus on US–Arab relations—and pro-Israel advocacy groups. For Gulf-funded think tanks, Israel–Gulf relations was an off-limits topic, while pro-Israel groups had little of any substance to offer on the topic.

Notwithstanding these dynamics, an Israeli colleague and I attempted to introduce Israel–Gulf relations to the Washington policy discussion. In doing so, we were trying to support then-President

Barack Obama's push for Middle East peace in 2013 and, again, for President Donald Trump's own quest shortly after his electoral victory in November 2016. Both times, our paper was officially declined over technicalities. But, in essence, the topic was too controversial for the Beltway's community of scholars that I had chosen to affiliate with.

Some of that research, which has never been published, has been incorporated into this book.

Although Doha fended off an onslaught from its immediate neighbors in Washington, where United Arab Emirates (UAE)-sponsored surrogates accused Qatar of supporting Hamas and other factions that Washington has classified as terrorist groups, Israel extended Doha a diplomatic lifeline by forging tactical cooperation on reconstruction in Gaza even though Doha and Jerusalem had no bilateral diplomatic agreement in place when the Gulf crisis erupted. Because Israel enjoys strategic cooperation with the UAE and a historic friendship with Oman, the Jewish state played an indirect albeit indispensable role in terms of helping stabilize the Gulf region by upholding the balance of power. Israel also firmly supported Oman during its own standoff with the UAE, which I discuss in great detail in this book.

Thus, within the context of the Gulf-Israel-Iran nexus, I conclude that despite Trump's strategic objective of forging Israel–Gulf ties, the Gulf crisis was never about collectively confronting Iran. Instead it was about attempting to establish hegemony over the Arab region.

But beyond the shifting sands of the Middle East and a new set of geopolitical dynamics triggered by Trump's presidency, this book is also dedicated to my late friend, Jamal Khashoggi. We had made plans to meet in Washington, where he went into his self-imposed exile in 2017, after his planned return from Istanbul. We were going to discuss him possibly endorsing this book. Jamal was, as it is widely

ACKNOWLEDGMENTS

known, brutally murdered at his own country's consulate in Istanbul, Turkey, on October 2, 2018. Khashoggi was an extraordinary, kind, and humble person who was always willing to share his insights about a changing Saudi Arabia and Gulf region with anyone who was interested, myself included. My fond memories of our many conversations and outings will remain with me forever.

The research for this book is based primarily on Qatari, Omani, and Israeli diplomatic sources. Given the sensitivity of the subject matter, all sources—over four dozen—requested that their comments and insights be referenced without attribution so I have omitted names and affiliated organizations from the text. However, any mistakes made are entirely my own.

I am particularly grateful to Ambassador (Ret.) Patrick Nickolas Theros for reviewing my manuscript and several other distinguished colleagues, who requested anonymity, for sharing their insights and comments with me. It is my sincere objective to provide a balanced and informed account about a one-sided conflict.

Last but not least, I would like to thank Rabbi Alec Goldstein of Kodesh Press for making the publishing process a seamless and enjoyable one.

THE ARABIAN PENINSULA
AND THE PERSIAN GULF REGION

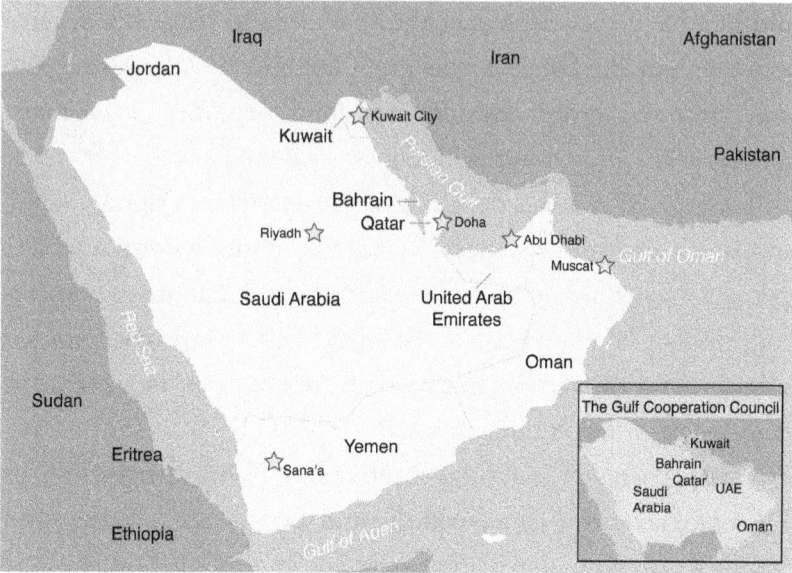

Iraq
Afghanistan

Jordan
Iran

Kuwait City
Kuwait

Pakistan

Bahrain
Qatar — Doha
Riyadh
Abu Dhabi
Muscat
Gulf of Oman

Saudi Arabia
United Arab
Emirates

Red Sea

Oman

Sudan

The Gulf Cooperation Council

Eritrea
Yemen
Sana'a

Kuwait
Bahrain
Qatar
Saudi
Arabia
UAE

Ethiopia
Gulf of Aden
Oman

ABBREVIATIONS

Al Jazeera Media Network (AJ)

AJ is the Doha-based Pan-Arab television network founded in 1996.

Al Udeid Air Base (AUAB)

The AUAB is the largest overseas US military base and is located southwest of Doha, Qatar. It houses Qatar Air Force, US Air Force, Britain's Royal Air Force, and other Gulf War Coalition personnel and assets. The base was inaugurated in 2001.

American-Israel Public Affairs Committee (AIPAC)

AIPAC is America's preeminent pro-Israel lobbying group founded in 1963.

Gulf Cooperation Council (GCC)

The GCC is s a sub-regional intergovernmental political and economic union comprised of Bahrain, Kuwait, Oman, Qatar, Saudi Arabia, and the United Arab Emirates. The organization was founded in 1981.

Foundation for the Defense of Democracies (FDD)

FDD is a neoconservative and pro-Israel research organization founded in 2001.

Hudson Institute (HI)

HI is a neoconservative research organization founded in 1961.

Jewish Institute for National Security of America (JINSA)

JINSA is a neoconservative activist organization founded in 1976.

Middle East Forum (MEF)

MEF is a neoconservative activist organization founded in 1990.

Middle East Strategic Alliance (MESA)

MESA, as a concept, is a security partnership between the six GCC member-states, Egypt, and Jordan. MESA was announced in May 2017.

Muslim Brotherhood (MB)

The MB is a transnational Sunni Islamist organization founded in Egypt by Islamic scholar Hassan Al Banna in 1928.

North Atlantic Treaty Organization (NATO)

NATO is an intergovernmental military alliance between 29 North American and European countries. The organization was founded in 1949.

Qatar News Agency (QNA)

QNA is a Doha-based Qatari state-run news organization.

United Against a Nuclear Iran (UANI)

UANI is a not-for-profit, bipartisan, educational, and advocacy group that seeks to prevent Iran from obtaining nuclear weapons.

United States Central Command (USCENTCOM)

USCENTCOM is a Tampa, Florida–headquartered division within the US Department of Defense. CENTCOM's area of responsibility includes the Middle East (but not Israel), Central Asia, and Afghanistan.

Notes on the
Main Characters

BAHRAIN

Hamad bin Isa Al Khalifa

King of Bahrain since 2002.

Khalid bin Ahmed Al Khalifa

Foreign Minister of Bahrain from 2005 to 2020.

KUWAIT

Sabah Al Ahmad Al Jaber Al Sabah

Amir of Kuwait since 2006.

OMAN

Qaboos bin Said Al Said

Sultan of Oman from 1970 to 2020.

Sayyid Fahd Al Said

Deputy Prime Minister of Oman.

Yusuf bin Alawi

Foreign Minister of Oman.

QATAR

Tamim Bin Hamad Al Thani

Appointed Amir of Qatar on June 25, 2013. He is the fourth son of the previous Amir, Hamad bin Khalifa Al Thani, and second son of Sheikha Moza bint Nasser, Hamad's second wife.

Mohammed Bin Abdulrahman bin Jassim Al Thani

Deputy Prime Minister and Minister of Foreign Affairs. He has been foreign minister since 2016.

Hamad Bin Khalifa Al Thani (HBK)

Often referred to as Father Amir, Hamad served as Amir of Qatar from 1995- 2013.

Khalifa bin Hamad Al Thani

Served as Amir of Qatar from 1972 to 1995.

Sheikha Mozah Al Thani

Amir Tamim's mother and Hamad's wife.

Hamad Bin Jassim Bin Jabr Al Thani (HBJ)

Prime Minister of Qatar from 2007 to 2013 and foreign minister from 1992 to 2013.

Abdullah bin Ali Al Thani

Son of deposed Qatari Amir Sheikh Ali Bin Abdullah Al Thani.

Khalid Al Attiyah

Deputy Prime Minister and Minister of Defense. He previously served as foreign minister from 2013 to 2016.

Nasir Al Aziz Al Nasir

Former permanent representative of Qatar to the United Nations. His tenure at the UN includes President of the Security Council in 2006.

Yusuf Al Qaradawi

Egyptian Islamic theologian based in Doha, Qatar.

SAUDI ARABIA

Salman bin Abdulaziz Al Saud

King of Saudi Arabia since 2015.

Mohammed bin Salman bin Abdulaziz Al Saud (MbS)

Crown Prince of Saudi Arabia and de-facto ruler. He is also King Salman's son.

Muhammad Bin Nayef Al Saud (MbN)

Prominent member of the Saudi royal family and served as crown prince from January 2015 until June 2017 when King Salman replaced him with his son, MbS.

Adel Bin Ahmed Al Jubair

Saudi Arabia's Minister of State for Foreign Affairs. He served as foreign minister from 2015 to 2018 and from 2007 to 2015 as the Saudi ambassador to Washington.

Saud Al Qahtani

Prominent advisor to Crown Prince Muhammad of Saudi Arabia.

Jamal Khashoggi

Saudi journalist—October 13, 1958 to October 2, 2018—who was murdered at the Saudi Consulate in Istanbul, Turkey.

UNITED ARAB EMIRATES

Mohammed bin Zayed Al Nahyan (MbZ)

Crown Prince of Abu Dhabi and the UAE's de-facto ruler. In 2005, he was appointed Deputy Supreme Commander of the UAE Armed Forces and was accordingly promoted to Lieutenant General.

Tahnoun bin Mohammed Al Nahyan

UAE's intelligence chief and MbZ's younger brother.

Sheikh Abdullah bin Zayed bin Sultan Al Nahyan

UAE's Foreign Minister and MbZ's younger brother.

Yousuf Al Otaiba

UAE Ambassador to the United States, a post he has held since 2008.

Alaa Al Seddiqi

Emirati national and married to an Emirati dissident living in exile in London, United Kingdom.

YEMEN

Abdrabbuh Mansur Hadi

Has been the president of Yemen since 2012.

ISRAEL

Benjamin Netanyahu

Prime Minister of Israel since 2009. He also served as Prime Minister from 1996 to 1999.

Notes on the Main Characters

Yossi Cohen

Director of Israel's foreign intelligence organization, the Mossad, since 2016.

Ron Dermer

Israeli Ambassador in Washington, a post he has had since 2013.

IRAN

Hassan Rouhani

President of the Islamic Republic of Iran since 2013.

Muhammad Javad Zarif

Foreign Minister of the Islamic Republic of Iran since 2013. From 2002 to 2007, he served as ambassador to the United Nations.

EGYPT

Abdel Fattah El Sisi

President of Egypt since 2014.

Mohamed Morsi

Former president of Egypt from 2012 to 2013.

JORDAN

Abdullah II bin Al Hussein

King of Jordan since 1999.

SYRIA

Bashar Al Assad

President of Syria since 2000.

TURKEY

Recep Tayyip Erdogan

President of Turkey since 2014. He served as Prime Minister from 2003 to 2014 and as Mayor of Istanbul from 1994 to 1998.

LIBYA

Muammar Al Ghaddafi

Commonly known as Colonel Gaddafi, was the head of the Great Socialist People's Libyan Arab Jamahiriya from 1977 to 2011. From 1969 to 1997, he was the head of the Libyan Arab Republic.

UNITED STATES

Donald J. Trump

Forty-fifth President of the United States.

Rex W. Tillerson

Served as the 69th US Secretary of State from February 1, 2017, to March 31, 2018, under President Trump. Prior to his government service, Tillerson was chairman and chief executive officer of ExxonMobil, holding that position from 2006 until 2017.

James N. Mattis

Served as the 26th US Secretary of Defense from January 2017 through December 2018 under President Trump. Prior to that appointment, Mattis had retired as a US Marine Corps general who had served in the Persian Gulf War, the War in Afghanistan, and the Iraq War.

Notes on the Main Characters

Michael R. Pompeo

Serves as the 70th US Secretary of State and replaced Tillerson. Prior to that role, he served as President Trump's director of the Central Intelligence Agency. From 2011 to 2017, Pompeo served in the US House of Representatives, where he represented Kansas's 4th congressional district.

Jared Kushner

Trump's son in-law and senior advisor to the President at the White House.

Stephen K. Bannon

Bannon was appointed chief executive officer of Trump's 2016 presidential bid in August 2016. Upon his inauguration, Trump appointed Bannon to be his chief strategist, a newly created position, where he served until August 2017.

Sebastian Gorka

Served as Deputy Assistant to President Trump from January 2017 until August 25, 2017.

Barack Obama

Forty-fourth President of the United States, from 2009 to 2017.

FOREWORD

The political history of the Middle East is turbulent, with instances of violence and intrigue, and the development of new alliances that often reverse. Regional instability creates anxiety in small and weaker states by forcing them to seek protection from foreign powers. This dependency on foreign help combined with the desire from regional players to extend their hegemonic reach, creates permanent tensions and conflicts in the Middle East.

The Gulf Region and Israel: Old Struggles, New Alliances by Sigurd Neubauer masterly depicts the complex regional strategic environment. The book examines one of the most interesting and yet neglected diplomatic dynamics of the Persian Gulf where the intrigue and behaviour of the Islamic Republic of Iran, coupled with inter-Arab / GCC conflicts have produced an unexpected dynamic where Israel gets the opportunity to collaborate with the regional countries in security issues.

Sigurd is a passionate observer of the events unfolding in the Persian Gulf and the Middle East. He uses the Qatar crisis as an example to show how Saudi Arabia and the United Arab Emirates seek to establish their power over the Arab region in order to build a viable wall against the hegemonic behaviour of the Islamic Republic of Iran (IRI) in the Persian Gulf. The book is a fascinating account of inter-Arab relations in the Persian Gulf and reveals the permanent sabotage of each country's efforts which in actuality, only serve to weaken the GCC.

It is ironic that the old and the new enemies of the majority of the GCC countries, Israel and IRI respectively, are benefiting the most from the inter-Arab divide. Therefore, the rehabilitation of Israel is mainly due to three important factors: First, the inter-Arab division which hinders Arab cohesion— a union that has historically been weak and fragile. Second, the structural military weakness of the small GCC states which forces them to turn directly to Washington or to call on the offices of Israel, hoping the country will put pressure on Washington to protect them against threats from neighbouring nations. Finally, the behaviour of the Islamic Republic of Iran in the region, which exacerbates inter-Arab divisions and forces the small states of the GCC to turn to Israel for protection and support.

And so, Israel's task of gaining acceptance and participating in the Arab concert against the IRI has been greatly facilitated by factors other than its own efforts. From a pariah state, Israel has become an indispensable ally for some of the GCC states.

The triangular strategic hostilities of the GCC-Israel-IRI have created increasingly favourable conditions for military confrontation between IRI and a coalition led by Saudi Arabia, UAE and their allies. The parties harden their positions and lock themselves in a posture which leaves no chance for the peaceful outcome of hostilities.

Even the mediation of Oman, which champions pacifism and the peaceful resolution of conflicts, risks not being able to bridge the gap between the two shores of the Persian Gulf.

The Israeli-Arab rapprochement creates a certain strategic balance in favour of Israel, which since the 1980s has been surrounded first by Lebanese Hezbollah, an IRI client organization in the North, and more recently by Palestinian groups in the South.

Thanks to recent developments, Israel is becoming a neighbour of the IRI and considerably decreasing the distance between itself and the IRI.

FOREWORD

As for relations between GCC (with the exception of Oman, Qatar and Kuwait to a certain degree) and IRI, they remain very tense and will likely not improve because of, among other things, the territorial issues which make any compromise on both sides unthinkable. If during forty years of existence and spending billions of dollars, the IRI tried to threaten the existence of Israel by its Lebanese-Palestinian allies, thanks to the inter-Arab crises and the strategic changes at regional and global level, Israel consolidates its presence south of the IRI border. Tel Aviv has succeeded in considerably reducing the existential Islamic danger to its own survival by making the most of Tehran's mistakes in its troubled relations with the GCC and by exploiting inter-Arab divisions.

Geo-economic and geostrategic interests have forced the United Arab Emirates and Qatar to forge and strengthen their relations with Israel and to use these relations as a moderating instrument in their strained relations with the United States Congress.

The book has skillfully illustrated how Israel's diplomacy combined with the weakness of the GCC has enabled Tel Aviv to instrumentalize its influence in Washington to achieve tangible results in the region of the Persian Gulf which seemed highly improbable, until recently. It is an important read for experts on strategic issues in the Middle East and those interested in the complexities of interstate relations in the troubled waters of the Persian Gulf.

Professor Houchang Hassan-Yari,
Sultan Qaboos University, Muscat, Oman.

LIST OF MAPS

1

QATAR AND THE CRISIS OF 2017

Three years have passed since Saudi Arabia, the United Arab Emirates (UAE), Bahrain, and Egypt severed diplomatic relations with Qatar on June 5, 2017, over allegations that Doha is supporting terrorism and that it embraces Iran and its regional agenda. Often referred to as the "Quartet," these four Arab states imposed an air and land blockade on Qatar on the first day of the crisis. The Quartet sought to justify the siege of Doha on the grounds that Qatar was a state sponsor of terrorism and too embracive of the Islamic Republic of Iran's regional agenda.

In tandem with the blockade, Saudi Arabia, the UAE, and Bahrain's governments expelled all Qatari citizens from their countries and provided their citizens living in Qatar a 14-day deadline to leave the blockaded emirate. Egypt, however, has not placed any travel restrictions on its estimated 200,000 citizens residing in Qatar or expelled Qataris living in Egypt or imposed an economic embargo on Doha.[1] Saudi Arabia and its regional partners, namely the blockading states, including Egypt, have closed down all air routes to and from Doha from their respective countries. Yet Qatar has not expelled any citizens from the blockading countries.

Qatar has repeatedly rejected the allegations leveled against it as baseless, insisting instead that the blockading countries' diplomatic assault is part of an international smear campaign that ultimately

1

seeks to cripple Qatar's sovereignty and turn it into a vassal state. Notwithstanding these dynamics, since the eruption of the crisis, Doha has called for dialogue to resolve the dispute.

The dispute is not only the most significant of its kind since the establishment of the Gulf Cooperation Council (GCC) in 1981. The Arabian feud has effectively eroded President Trump's initial foreign policy success, which rested on his historic address before the US-Arab-Islamic Summit in Riyadh, which took place on May 20 and 21, 2017. While addressing dozens of leaders in the Saudi capital, Trump called for Arab unity against Iran's regional agenda and joint efforts to defeat terrorism and extremism. Given the severity of the restrictions imposed, from the expulsion of Qatari citizens from the blockading countries to the air and land blockade imposed on Qatar, it was immediately clear to Washington that this dispute was far more serious than the GCC spat of 2014.

The Trump administration tried to immediately resolve the crisis. Then-US Secretary of State Rex Tillerson and then-US Secretary of Defense James Mattis spearheaded these efforts. The two collaboratively sought to advance a diplomatic process that would end the crisis while ensuring that US military operations throughout the broader Middle East, particularly in the Gulf, would face minimal disruption over the standoff.

Both Mattis and Tillerson enjoyed longstanding professional ties to Qatar and other Gulf states prior to their service in the Trump administration. Mattis had also served as Commander of US Central Command (USCENTCOM) from 2010 to 2013.[2]

Prior to becoming America's 69th Secretary of State in February 2017, Tillerson had served as CEO of ExxonMobile, which acquired an $80 billion investment in Qatar in 1999.[3] The original agreement with Qatar had been signed in 1995 by Lucius Noto, the Chairman and CEO of Mobil Oil, and Hamid Bin Khalifa Al Thani (HBK), who at the time was Crown Prince and Prime Minister.[4] In November 1999, the US Securities and Exchange Commission approved Exxon's merger with Mobile, giving the new combined company, ExxonMobil, control of the investment.[5] At the time, Tillerson served as Executive Vice President while Lee Raymond served as CEO from 1999 to 2005. During Tillerson's tenure as CEO (2006 to 2017), Exxon Mobile's venture in Qatar rose to providing 40 percent of the company's worldwide profits.

Qatar is also home to the Al Udeid Air Base (AUAB), USCENTCOM's forward headquarters, from where the US-led coalition carried out its military campaigns against the Islamic State in Iraq and Syria (ISIS) and from where it continues to manage a direct line to Russia to manage Syria's crowded skies.

Bahrain is the home of the US Navy's 5th Fleet and a crucial base for its campaign against ISIS, as well as the war in Afghanistan. The UAE hosts a US Air Force contingency at its Al Dhafra Air Base, where it provides logistical support. The Emiratis also provide logistics support for US Navy operations at the Fujairah and Jebel Ali ports. The Global Center for Excellence in Countering Violent Extremism (Hedayah) is also headquartered in the Emirates.[6]

From a US perspective, the GCC is not only a strategic partner, but as a bloc it has significant potential when it comes to strengthening both economic and security cooperation. Together, the six nations have the potential to strengthen counter-terrorism cooperation and the GCC members have the financial resources to raise funds for the strategic effort to stabilize Iraq in the post-ISIS environment. Preserving the stability of the GCC – both economically and in terms of security – became key objectives for Tillerson and Mattis in their engagements with the feuding parties, particularly Saudi Arabia and the UAE.

Tensions between Qatar and its neighbors, however, are long-standing and run deep. Qatar, because of its vulnerable geography, faces Bahrain to the north, which historically was richer and more populous; Saudi Arabia to the west; and Iran to the east.

Before the ruling Al Thani family consolidated power in the 1800s, the Qatar Peninsula served as a frontier where a poor community of pearl fishermen resided without being fully absorbed into neighboring states, which were more powerful.[7] At that time, the Qataris would pay Bahrain and King Abdelaziz bin Saud Al Saudi of Saudi Arabia protection money in exchange for preserving Qatar's independent status.[8]

But Emirati animus – represented by the sheikhs of Abu Dhabi – with Qatar arguably stretches back to 1868 to the Qatari–Bahraini War, which is also known as the Qatari War of Independence. The conflict pitted Bahrain and Abu Dhabi against the people of Qatar, who were ruled by the Al Thani family. Bahrain, whose ruling Al Khalifah family had been expelled from Qatar a decade earlier, invaded the peninsula in concert with Abu Dhabian forces. Responding in kind, the Qataris resoundingly defeated the invading forces and even counterattacked into Abu Dhabi.

Qatar's rise from obscurity to securing British protection for its independence through the Anglo-Qatar treaty of 1916 ushered in the modern era for the country. Once Qatar achieved independence from Britain in 1971, the country attempted to establish a direct relationship with the United States, which Washington initially rejected. At the time, Washington made it clear that Qatar should work through Saudi Arabia. In 1972, Khalifa bin Hamad Al Thani assumed power through a coup d'état, but throughout much of his tenure Qatar remained a vassal state of Saudi Arabia. Under that arrangement, Saudi Arabia provided Qatar with protection while Riyadh adopted a position of neutrality vis-à-vis Qatar and Bahrain's dispute over the Hawar island. The Hawar Islands are an archipelago of Bahraini desert islands situated off the west coast of Qatar in the Gulf of Bahrain. In 1986, however, Saudi Arabia prevented hostilities between Qatar and Bahrain over the territorial dispute.[9]

Iraq's invasion of Kuwait in August 1990 profoundly changed Qatar's security calculus as Doha concluded that Saudi Arabia was incapable of defending the smaller GCC countries, including Qatar, without US support. Doha thus concluded that in order to obtain the security it needed, it would appeal to Washington directly without Riyadh as its intermediary, a move which infuriated Saudi Arabia.

In June 1995, the Al Thani family deposed Sheikh Khalifa and brought Hamad Bin Khalifa Al Thani (HBK) to power. Among his strategic objectives was to cement Qatari independence from Saudi Arabia.

But even before HBK took power, during the reign of his father, Amir Khalifa Bin Hamad Al Thani, Qatar had taken practical steps to preserve its independence through building global alliances, which included the controversial step of establishing diplomatic relations with the Soviet Union in 1988. The decision to do so provoked Saudi Arabia, which in turn contributed to heightened tensions culminating in the 1992 clashes along their disputed border, which left two Qatari soldiers dead.[10] The border dispute erupted after Saudi Arabia build a highway along the un-demarcated Saudi–Qatari border, triggering violent clashes in the border town of Al Khafus. The newly constructed highway effectively deprived Qataris of their free movement into the UAE.[11]

Prior to Britain's withdrawal, Qatar and the Emirate of Abu Dhabi shared a disputed land border. In the early 1970s, Saudi Arabia and Abu Dhabi negotiated a border agreement granting the Kingdom control of the disputed coastline (roughly 100 kilometers in length), granting Riyadh access to the Gulf east of Qatar in exchange for Saudi recognition of Emirati control over territory in the Buraimi/Al-Ain region. The agreement was kept secret until Saudi Arabia cut the road linking Qatar and Abu Dhabi, which in turn triggered the clashes of 1992.

5

The border incident occurred despite Saudi Arabia and Qatar having both accepted a British-brokered demarcation agreement in 1965. Qatar maintained that Saudi Arabia had attacked its border post at Khafus, while Saudi Arabia countered that the clash was on Saudi territory and had occurred between Bedouins from the two sides.[12]

Adding to the longstanding tensions between Qatar and Saudi Arabia was Riyadh's decision in 1991 to abandon its initial neutrality over Qatar's own territorial dispute with Bahrain by siding with Manama. At that time, Doha had referred its border dispute with Bahrain over the Hawar Islands to the United Nations' International Court of Justice (ICJ). The two Gulf countries disputed the sovereignty of Zubara (a town located on mainland Qatar), the Janan Islands, and a number of reefs. The ICJ ruled that Bahrain had sovereign rights over the Hawar Islands and one of the reefs, while Qatar was awarded the other reef, Zubara, and the Janan Islands.

Although much literature has already been published about the shifting tribal alliances on the Arabian Peninsula and about the power dynamics between Saudi Arabia's dominant Al Saud family and the sheikhs of the smaller littoral Gulf states—all of whom had historically enjoyed British protection—the root cause of the present crisis can arguably be traced back to February 1996.

During the month of Ramadan that year, Saudi Arabia, the UAE, Bahrain, and Egypt attempted to unseat HBK through a coup d'état. HBK, as we shall later discuss, was widely accredited—both at home and abroad—for having transformed Qatar from a small and inward-looking state on the periphery of the Arabian Peninsula to a leader of Arab affairs, which in turn provoked the ire of its larger and mightier neighbors.

Another parallel between the present crisis and the 1996 coup attempt, also known as the so-called Operation Abu Ali, was that they were both triggered during the holy Muslim month of Ramadan. Another similarity is that the UAE's *de facto* ruler, Crown Prince Mohammed bin Zayed Al Nahyan (MbZ) of Abu Dhabi (who in 1996 was the Chief of the General Staff of the UAE's Armed Forces) spearheaded both operations.

When HBK seized power, his first step, unsurprisingly, was to seal the border with Saudi Arabia, put his forces on high alert, and dispatch troops south to the disputed border area.[13] In November 1996, the Amir oversaw the launch of the Al Jazeera Media Network, which quickly developed into the Arab world's most influential satellite television network. Al Jazeera's coverage of Arab affairs has ever since remained a subject of controversy.

Since its inception, Al Jazeera has prodded fellow Arab governments about sensitive issues, including the role of political Islam, corruption, Arab states' support for the US/UK-led invasion and occupation of Iraq, and the lack of democracy across the Arab world. It has also provided Israeli officials with a platform to express their views and government positions.

While generally progressive on Arab issues, when it comes to the coverage of Qatar, Al Jazeera's coverage is muted (which falls in line with the rest of the GCC state media, which prohibits criticizing royal families and government policies in general). Al Jazeera is fully state owned, which explains why Qatar's neighbors have long considered it to be a tool of Doha's foreign policy.

These underlying dynamics set the stage for the present crisis.

The subject of Israel, which we will examine in great detail throughout this book, exacerbated Saudi–Qatari tensions and triggered a crisis in bilateral relations in 2002. That year Riyadh withdrew its ambassador to Qatar, Hamad Al Tuwaymi, over Al Jazeera's coverage and in particular over a televised debate in June of that year in which participants had criticized then-Crown Prince Abdullah Bin Abdulaziz Al Saud's peace initiative, known as the

Arab Peace Initiative (API). Riyadh timed its ambassadorial recall to coincide with Qatar's National Day.[14]

Oman played a key role in the API as it had passed a message from Saudi Arabia to then-Israeli Prime Minister Ariel Sharon requesting that Israel not reject the initiative outright. Sharon accepted the request.[15]

While Qatar and all other GCC members endorsed the API at the 2002 Arab League Summit, then-Palestinian leader Yasser Arafat, then-Egyptian President Hosni Mubarak, and King Abdullah II of Jordan all decided to boycott the meeting.[16]

The API was endorsed by the Arab League in 2002 at the Beirut Summit and re-endorsed at the 2007 Arab League Summit and at the 2017 Arab League Summit.[17]

Under the API, all members of the Arab League would recognize Israel provided that the Jewish state withdrew from all territories occupied since June 1967. The plan also called for the implementation of Security Council Resolutions 242 and 338, reaffirmed by the Madrid Conference of 1991. According to the land-for-peace principle and Israel's acceptance of an independent Palestinian state with East Jerusalem as its capital, Arab states would grant full normalization of relations within the context of a comprehensive peace with Israel. The API also calls for a "just settlement" of Palestinian refugees based on Security Council resolution 194.

In September 2007, the Saudi–Qatar rapprochement, which US–Iran tensions significantly contributed to, was finalized after HBK, who was accompanied by then Prime Minister and Foreign Minister Shaikh Hamad Bin Jassim Bin Jabr Al Thani (HBJ), traveled to Jeddah for talks with King Abdullah.[18]

The Riyadh-Doha rapprochement lasted from 2007 to 2013. In June 2013, HBK abdicated in favor of his son, Amir Tamim Bin Hamad Al Thani, and tensions between Saudi Arabia, the UAE, and Bahrain on one side and Qatar on the other broke out within the first year of the current Qatari leader's time on the throne. On March 5, 2014, Abu Dhabi, Manama, and Riyadh withdrew their ambassadors from Doha because of Qatar's alleged interference in the affairs of other Arab states via support for the MB.

Following Kuwaiti mediation, which Amir Sabah Al Ahmad Al Jaber Al Sabah spearheaded, the three countries announced on November 17, 2014, that their ambassadors would return to Qatar and that their differences would be put behind them. This time, the Qatar–Saudi rapprochement lasted until the eruption of the Gulf crisis on June 5, 2017.

The Gulf crisis of 2014 set precedence for the feud that broke out in 2017. Ultimately, the present crisis is anchored in decades of acrimony between the rival sheikhdoms of the Gulf.

But beyond personality conflicts between the ruling royal families of the Gulf Cooperation Council (GCC), Qatar's mixture of religious conservatism with modernism and economic liberalization also threatens the ideological makeup of the UAE, which has banned political Islam and adopted an ideological framework rooted in a secularized top-down national identity coupled with a laissez faire capitalist approach toward governance and society at large. Between Saudi Arabia's arch conservatism and the UAE's authoritarian modernism, the Qatari model of religious conservatism married with economic liberalism and Al Jazeera's soft power as the Arab world's most popular television network has contributed to Riyadh and Abu Dhabi's longstanding grievances with Doha as they respectively compete for regional influence and prestige.

Another factor guiding Qatar's independent streaks, both in terms of domestic reforms and Doha's controversial foreign policy, is the country's ethnic and religious composition. Unlike its fellow GCC members, Qatar's population is relatively ethnically and religiously homogeneous, which eliminates a potential source of opposition to the country's ruling family.[19] Thus, Qatar's demographic composition enables Doha to craft its own foreign policy while celebrating its own exceptionalism at home through rigorous reform initiatives.

These dynamics partially explain why the Quartet made Al Jazeera and Doha's support for the MB focal points in its dispute with Qatar.

From the outset of the crisis, analysts close to Abu Dhabi, such as experts at UAE-sponsored think tanks in Washington, portrayed the standoff as an ideological choice for the Middle East between secularism, as presented by the UAE model, and political Islam as embodied by the MB, which Doha has backed.[20, 21, 22, 23]

This analysis is an oversimplification. Most of the Islamist groups (with the notable exception of the MB's Tunisian branch) that Qatar once backed during the immediate aftermath of the Arab Spring have failed to cement their positions in Arab governments.

Indeed, the Syrian regime's resilience and the Egyptian military's ouster of the democratically elected Muslim Brotherhood President Mohamed Morsi in 2013 marked major setbacks for Doha's foreign policy agenda.[24]

Morsi was president from 2012 to 2013 but died from a heart attack in July 2019 during a court appearance in Cairo. Morsi, a diabetic, had been denied the necessary medical treatment throughout his incarceration.[25]

Qatar also provided up to an estimated $10 billion in assistance and investment to prevent Egypt's economy from collapsing during Morsi's tenure. Toward that end, Doha planned to sell Egypt's gas and invest in infrastructure projects such as the redevelopment of the Suez Canal.[26]

During Morsi's presidency, his regional critics and domestic detractors accused Qatar of using Al Jazeera as a pro-Islamist platform for the MB, in which the fiery cleric Yusuf Al Qaradawi played an outsized role.[27]

Qaradawi, who had his own show on Al Jazeera from its inception in 1996 until the Gulf crisis of 2014, when he was taken off air as part of a Qatari concession toward its neighbors, has long been considered a controversial figure in the Gulf and Egypt.[28] The Egyptian-born cleric, who became a naturalized Qatari citizen, has been residing in exile in Doha since 1961.

Under the 2014 GCC agreement, however, Qatar agreed to close down one of Al Jazeera's affiliates, Al Jazeera Mubasher Misr (or Al Jazeera Live Egypt) and Qaradawi would no longer appear on screen.[29] Qaradawi's harsh criticism of Israel and negative commentary about Jews in general, including on Al Jazeera Arabic, explains his controversial standing in Israel and among American Jews.[30] Qaradawi has since become largely irrelevant figure in Qatar and in the Arab world in general.

Under the 2014 GCC agreement, Al Jazeera Arabic also removed the station's two top programming executives as part of a concession to Saudi Arabia.

Thus, Qatar's experiences in Egypt and Syria and the Gulf spat of 2014 taught Amir Tamim important lessons. For Doha to maintain some of its hard-won regional influence, strengthening ties with Saudi Arabia would be paramount. Such lessons subsequently helped inform the Amir's decision to move closer to Riyadh's orbit following the 2014 crisis.[31]

His decision to do so, including adopting part of Riyadh's foreign policy agenda by participating in its war against Yemen's Houthi rebels, illustrate why Qatar considered its relationship with Saudi Arabia to be excellent prior to the blockade that went into effect in 2017.

Qatar's assessment was also based on its close cooperation with Saudi Arabia and Turkey on the Syria file when Doha was fully supporting the uprising against President Bashar Al Assad's Ba'athist government with the support of the Obama administration.

Then the Gulf crisis of May/June 2017 erupted. Despite the blockade, which was arguably designed to cripple Qatar's economy, Doha appears confident regarding its economic performance as growth remains resilient, according to the International Monetary Fund.[32] As part of an effort to boost its liquidity, Qatar injected about $40 billion into its banking system relatively early on in the blockade.[33]

Thus, the direct economic and financial impact of the diplomatic rift has been manageable, especially during the first year of the crisis, which was its hardest given that an estimated 60 percent of its imports came from Saudi Arabia, the UAE, and Bahrain. Because prior to the blockade the Qataris were dependent on Saudi Arabia for milk and dairy supplies, a month into the blockade, thousands of cows were flown into the country via Qatar Airways in order for the country to become food secure and self-reliant.[34]

Prior to the crisis, however, Qatar had set up a committee on food security and had several months of food supplies in storage or readily available.

And in September 2017, Qatar officially opened the $7.4 billion deep-water Hamad Port, which enabled the country to receive much larger cargo ships.[35]

In 2018, Qatar's economy grew 1.4 percent, down from 1.6 percent in 2017.[36] Qatar's initial economic recovery was tied to its robust relationship with Turkey, which began to gain momentum in the pre-crisis period. Ultimately, these ties with Turkey enabled Doha to swiftly deepen its trade relations with Ankara once the standoff erupted.

Turkey has arguably become the big winner on the economic front as Doha and Ankara have moved closer throughout the crisis.[37] The strength of the bilateral relationship, however, was formed during the immediate Arab Spring environment when the two countries supported Islamist movements in Tunisia, Libya, Egypt, and Syria, which in turn strengthened Doha's standing as a regional player.[38]

Regarding Qatari–Iranian relations, it has become clear that Amir Tamim made an initial strategic decision to limit political or diplomatic ties with Tehran beyond strengthening economic ties during the initial phase of the blockade. The Quartet, however, has since the onset of the crisis accused Qatar of embracing Tehran's regional agenda.

Since its eruption, the crisis swiftly moved beyond policy and philosophical differences pertaining to the post–Arab Spring environment. The accusations against Qatar have evolved from the Quartet castigating Doha over its alleged support of terrorism and fomentation of regional instability to politically motivated attacks on Qatar for having secured the hosting rights of the 2022 FIFA World Cup.[39]

But beyond these accusations, Doha's principal challenge throughout the crisis has been focusing all of Qatar's diplomatic energy on fighting a media war dominated by a steady flow of manufactured allegations. In the mix, Qatar has also had to defend the honor of its royal family through a constant avalanche of insults, including of Amir Tamim's mother, Sheikha Mozah Al Thani. The insults against Qatari women and members of the royal family in particular are unprecedented within the socially conservative cultural framework of the Gulf region.

Since the crisis began, no inter-GCC activity has taken place without persistent US diplomatic pressure, and despite these efforts, nearly three years later, no resolution appears in sight.

In 2017, when the crisis broke out, Qatar's population consisted of 2.7 million people, of which only an estimated 300,000 were citizens.[40] While the remaining 2.3 million are expatriates, Qatar does not publish statistics breaking down population by nationality.[41]

In 2017, Qatar enjoyed the highest GDP per capita in the world, which was $129,726.[42]

Qatar's wealth is directly tied to its natural gas reserves. As the world's largest exporter of liquefied natural gas, Qatar shipped 81 million tons in 2017, or 28 percent of the global total. Qatar also exports 600,000 barrels of oil a day, but it left the Organization of the Petroleum Exporting Countries (OPEC) in early 2019 to focus more on gas.[43] The subject of Qatar's wealth was never publicly broached by the blockading states throughout the crisis.

The majority of Qatar's natural gas is located in the massive offshore North Field, which spans an area roughly equivalent to Qatar itself. A part of the world's largest non-associated natural-gas field, the North Field is a geological extension of Iran's South Pars / North Dome Gas-Condensate field, which holds an additional 450 trillion cubic feet (13 trillion cubic meters) of recoverable natural gas reserves.

Until recently, Qatar was the only Gulf country to have established a formal treaty with Iran. Doha and Tehran signed this treaty in 1969, demarcating the thalweg (the midpoint in the Gulf) and thus the gas field.

Therefore, according to the US–Qatar Business Council,

Qatar is the second largest exporter of natural gas in the world (about 4.3 trillion cubic feet, worth roughly $35 billion annually) of which 70% goes to Asia. Japan, South Korea, and India are the top three consumers of Qatari fuel exports, accounting for 55% of the total. Of Qatar's natural gas exports, almost a quarter goes to Europe. Qatar exports about 12% of total natural gas in international trade globally.[44]

QATAR AND THE BLOCKADING STATES

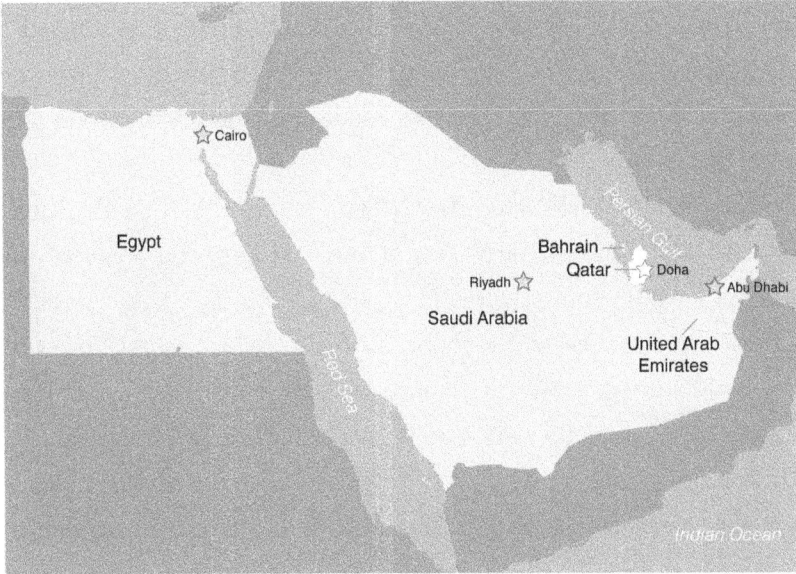

GULF AIRSPACES

KEY EVENTS LEADING UP TO THE CRISIS

On May 2, 2017, Secretary Tillerson hosted Saudi counterpart Adel Al Jubair at the State Department to discuss the upcoming Riyadh Summit. The subject of Qatar or Saudi grievances with Doha was never brought up.[45]

Almost two weeks later, the Crown Prince of Abu Dhabi, MbZ, paid Trump a visit at the White House to discuss the preparations for the Riyadh Summit, including the UAE's diplomatic push to help secure the President's support for MbS's reform agenda in Saudi Arabia.[46] During the White House meeting, MbZ also put out feelers regarding Trump's stance on Qatar by outlining the alleged MB threat to regional stability and to the broader fight against radicalism. But the topic of Qatar as such was not raised this time, either.

On May 23, 2017, the Foundation for the Defense of Democracies (FDD), a neo-conservative and pro-Israel think tank in Washington, hosted a conference in the US capital titled "Qatar and the Muslim Brotherhood's Global Affiliates: New US Administration Considers New Policies." The conference's primary focus was to advocate for a US withdrawal from Qatar's Al Udeid Air Base (AUAB) while castigating Qatar over its traditional support for the MB. The FDD conference, which the UAE bankrolled, took place only days after the Riyadh Summit.[47]

FDD describes itself as conducting "in-depth research, produc[ing] accurate and timely analyses, identif[ying] illicit activities, and provid[ing] policy options—all with the aim of strengthening US national security and reducing or eliminating threats posed by adversaries and enemies of the United States and other free nations."[48]

At the FDD conference, then-Chairman of the US House of Representatives Ed Royce, a Republican from California, announced that he would introduce House Resolution 2712.

HR 2712, also known as "Palestinian International Terrorism Support Act of 2017," sought to essentially classify Qatar as a state sponsor of terrorism because of Doha's links to Hamas. Royce introduced his resolution to Congress on May 25, 2017, two days after the FDD conference. Also, on the same day as the FDD conference, the UAE blocked the Al Jazeera and Qatari News Agency (QNA) websites in the Emirates.

In the months leading up to the FDD event, American foreign policy experts published 14 op-eds in various US media outlets that castigated Qatar as a supporter of terrorism and called for Washington to withdraw its military from AUAB. Some of them were paid $10,000 per article to publish anti-Qatar op-eds focusing on Qatar–Iran relations and Al Jazeera while they were encouraged to recruit other "likeminded" individuals to publish similar articles.[49] Many of these influencers, who had penned anti-Qatar op-eds, continued to play prominent roles throughout the crisis, including speaking at various anti-Qatar conferences hosted in Washington.[50, 51, 52, 53, 54, 55, 56, 57, 58, 59, 60, 61, 62, 63, 64, 65, 66, 67, 68, 69, 70]

On May 24, a day after the FDD conference, the QNA website was hacked. The hackers falsely attributed a fake statement to Amir Tamim, saying that Iran is an "Islamic power" and that Qatar enjoys "good" relations with Israel. The statement also quoted the Amir calling Hamas "the legitimate representative of the Palestinian people," as well as saying that Qatar had "strong relations" with Iran and the United States. (The QNA was penetrated by the initial cyberattack on April 25).[71]

The QNA Twitter account was also hacked and posted fake reports that Qatar had withdrawn its ambassadors from several countries in the region, which Doha denied.[72]

Days after the QNA hack, Turkish President Recep Tayyip Erdogan dispatched one of his top advisors, Ibrahim Kalin, along with his son-in-law, then-Energy Minister Berat Albyrak, on an unannounced visit to Riyadh to assess the mounting tensions between Qatar and Saudi Arabia. The Turkish delegation, however, returned without any clear answers.[73]

On May 25, Saudi Arabia and UAE blocked Qatari TV broadcasts, including Al Jazeera. Qatar began to investigate the source of the hack and requested assistance from US and British authorities, who agreed to provide such help.[74] The following day, Kuwaiti Amir Sabah Al Ahmad Al Jaber Al Sabah began his mediating efforts in order to ease tensions.

A team from the US Federal Bureau of Investigation (FBI) arrived in Doha on June 2 to investigate the QNA hack.

On June 5, Bahrain, Egypt, Saudi Arabia, and the UAE began blockading Qatar. The blockade was announced at 5:00 am (Doha time), and Bahrain was the first country to sever diplomatic relations with Qatar, followed by Saudi Arabia, UAE, and finally Egypt.[75]

On June 6, Qatar's Foreign Minister Mohammed Bin Abdulrahman Al Thani called for dialogue in a televised speech. He stated, "For us the strategic choice of the State of Qatar is to solve any dispute through dialogue."[76]

THE SAUDI–QATAR RELATIONSHIP: FROM FRIEND TO FOE

On December 6, 2016, Saudi Arabia's King Salman Bin Abdulaziz Al Saud visited Doha as part of his regional tour to thank his GCC counterparts for participating in the Saudi-led coalition against Yemen's Houthi rebels.[77] He visited every GCC country except for

Oman.[78] The Saudi king's brother, Fahd Bin Abdulaziz Al Saud, joined him. During his meeting with Amir Tamim, King Salman was feted with the traditional Arab sword dance, and the meeting appeared free of tensions.

Adding to the symbolic importance of King Salman's visit to Doha was the fact that during the reign of his immediate predecessor, Abdullah Bin Abdulaziz Al Saud, King Abdullah had never visited Qatar for a bilateral meeting.

King Salman's visit to Doha in December 2016 was officially attributed to Qatar's participation in the war against Yemen's Houthi rebels. As part of an effort to celebrate the strong bilateral relationship, Amir Tamim gifted King Salman a sword, known as the Sheikh Jassim bin Muhammad sword, which was named after the founder of the State of Qatar, Sheikh Jassim Bin Mohammed Al Thani. The symbolism of the sword was meant to demonstrate the strong Qatari–Saudi relationship, united in war and peace.[79]

In 2017, several months after King Salman's historic visit to Doha but after a string of anti-Qatar op-eds began appearing throughout various US media outlets, Amir Tamim departed for Riyadh on May 1 for talks with the Saudi monarch to discuss perceived tensions mounting in the region.

By the time he arrived in Riyadh, the 14 op-eds had been published. These hit pieces featured nearly identical talking points about Qatar's alleged double dealings, from hosting the AUAB to supporting terrorist groups and fomenting regional extremism.

The op-eds all concluded that Washington should withdraw its presence from the AUAB. These arguments became the central theme of the aforementioned FDD conference but continued to be relegated throughout the crisis, particularly in Washington.

During Amir Tamim's May 2017 meetings in Riyadh, he met King Salman, Crown Prince Muhammad Bin Nayef (MbN), and Deputy Crown Prince Muhammad Bin Salman (MbS). All three assured Qatar's head of state that Doha-Riyadh relations were flourishing. Amir Tamim appeared to believe them, notwithstanding the string of anti-Qatar op-eds that had begun to proliferate. At the time, Qatar had no intelligence about the impending Gulf crisis and how a well-organized public relations campaign against Doha was about to kick off in Washington.

Two weeks after Amir Tamim's visit, then-Saudi Foreign Minister Jubair attended the 2017 Doha Forum, held on May 14 to 15. At this event, the Qataris hosted him as the guest of honor at the Annual Qatari Ambassadors' conference. The conference presented all of Qatar's ambassadors the opportunity to meet their Amir and foreign minister. During his address before the Qatari diplomatic establishment, which included the Amir, Jubair praised the state of Qatari–Saudi relations but also warned that the two countries faced similar reputational challenges stemming from their decades-long support for Wahhabi Islamic causes, constructions of mosques abroad, and the roles of Islamic charities.

Jubair added in his remarks that strengthening regional counter terrorism cooperation was essential and that this applied to all GCC countries.

On May 16, 2017, Amir Tamim received Jubair, where the parties touted the excellent state of bilateral ties.

Capturing the moment's mood, Jubair tweeted a picture of himself sitting next to his Qatari counterpart, saying, "I met in Doha with my brother and colleague Sheikh Mohammad Bin Abdulrahman Al Thani Foreign Minister of the sister #Qatar and discussed together topics of common interest." Foreign Minister Al Thani retweeted it immediately.[80]

The following day, Jubair hosted Foreign Minister Al Thani, along with their other four GCC counterparts in Riyadh. In light of Jubair's positive rhetoric during his Doha visit, it remains unclear whether or not he was aware of the behind-the-scenes planning leading up to the eruption of the siege of Qatar and ensuing Gulf crisis.

From a Qatari vantage point, even though Doha's bilateral relationship with Saudi Arabia had gone through ups and downs since the attempted coup d'état plot of 1996, relations had, overall, steadily improved.

But the relationship between Saudi Arabia and Qatar had not been limited to close coordination in Yemen only. The two neighbors had in fact been coordinating closely on Syria policy since 2012, including with Turkey and the United States. This was particularly evident during the Geneva I and II diplomatic processes as well as for Vienna I and II.

The Saudi–Qatari relationship had indeed come a long way since the events of 1996. When Qatar chaired the GCC Summit in January 2016, it was, along with Saudi Arabia, concerned about how the Joint Comprehensive Plan of Action (JCPOA) between Iran and the international community would provide Tehran with additional funding for its regional activities, which Doha and Riyadh considered destabilizing. In fact, at the time, Qatar shared Saudi Arabia's concerns about the Obama administration's regional policies. Both Gulf states feared that they, along with the rest of the GCC, would face a more influential Iran without strong American support as Washington appeared to be withdrawing from the Middle East.[81]

Images of Amir Tamim bin Hamad Al Thani receives King Salman Al Saud of Saudi Arabia. Courtesy of the Qatari Amiri Diwan.

Amir Tamim bestows King Salman with the Sheikh Jassim sword. Courtesy of the Qatari Amiri Diwan.

QATAR AND LIBYA

On March 19, 2011, a North Atlantic Treaty Organization (NATO)-led multinational coalition began a military intervention in Libya. This purpose was ostensibly to implement United Nations Security Council (UNSC) resolution 1973. At that point, Qatar chaired the Arab League presidency and called on the UNSC to impose a no-fly zone over Libya. Qatar's Arab League resolution was supported by all members, save Syria and Algeria.[82]

Following the passing of UNSC resolution 1973, Qatar and the UAE began to ready themselves to engage militarily in Libya. Towards that end, a squadron from the Qatar Emiri Air Force of Mirage fighters became the first ones to arrive at the Suda Bay base in Crete, Greece.

While Qatar was enthusiastic about overthrowing Libyan strongman Col. Muammar Al Ghadhafi, it considered the intervention "an opportunity to protect a peaceful popular movement calling for social justice and socio-economic change after Al Ghadhafi [had] sent troops to the gates of Benghazi, the birthplace of the revolution," Anas El Gomati argues in *Divided Gulf: The Anatomy of a Crisis*.[83]

Only months earlier, Qatar became the first country to officially endorse the Tunisian revolution of late 2010 and early 2011.

Meanwhile, with the goal of providing international support for an indigenous revolution, Qatar's military involvement in Libya was spearheaded by Major General Hamad Bin Ali Al Attiyah, the chief of staff, who eventually became responsible for overseeing NATO's land operation in Libya. Under that mandate, Qatar also became the first Arab state to set up a patrol zone within Libya's western Nafusa mountain region.

Qatar's operations in Libya, however, were overseen by Qatar Special Forces Commander General Hamad Al Afutis, who during the Gulf crisis of 2017 was added by the UAE to its terrorism list for allegedly providing the Houthis with military intelligence. Al Afutis was responsible for planning and training the initial set of groups that had been cleared by the United States and NATO on behalf of Qatar's 17 Brigade but did not command or oversee any military operations.

Under that arrangement, the United Kingdom, France, Qatar and the UAE "organized shipments of weapons and led training and equipment missions into Libya in support of the most powerful armed groups in the country," writes Gomati.[84]

Qatar and the UAE, in cooperation with the US intelligence services, vetted all these groups. In tandem with these efforts, Qatar had also established humanitarian camps in neighboring Tunisia, where thousands of Libyans fled after the fighting intensified.

From the beginning of the Libya intervention, the initial coalition consisted of Belgium, Canada, Denmark, France, Italy, Norway, Qatar, Spain, the United Kingdom, the United States, and the UAE. But the coalition eventually expanded into 19 participating countries with newer states mostly enforcing the no-fly zone and naval blockade or providing military logistical assistance.

The Qatar Armed Forces contributed with six Mirage 2000-5EDA fighter jets and two C-17 strategic transport aircraft to coalition no-fly zone enforcement efforts. The Qatari aircraft were stationed on the Greek island of Crete. At later stages in the operation, Qatari Special Forces had been assisting in operations, including the training of the Tripoli Brigade and rebel forces in Benghazi and the Nafusa mountains. Qatar also brought small groups of Libyans to Qatar for small-unit leadership training in preparation for the rebel advance on Tripoli in August 2011.

The states that entered during the latter stage were mostly responsible for enforcing the no-fly zone and naval blockade or providing military logistical assistance. Qatar and the UAE were the only GCC countries to participate.

For its part, the UAE placed its national contributions under US command. On March 24, 2011, Abu Dhabi dispatched six F-16 Fighting Falcon and six Mirage 2000 fighter jets to join the NATO mission. This was also the first combat deployment of the Desert Falcon variant of F-16, which is the most sophisticated F-16 variant. The planes were based at the Italian Decimomannu Air Base in Sardinia.

As the Arab League president, the organization tasked Qatar with helping the Libyan people against Ghaddafi. Additionally, the United States and NATO assigned Doha to carry out humanitarian operations and thus began its first operation in March 2011. During that mission, it dispatched its C-17 Globemaster III military transport aircraft to Benghazi and Tobruk to establish safe zones. Initially, Qatar was not present in Benghazi because of the fighting but as fighting on the ground eased, Qatar established a presence in the eastern city where it brought in food and medicine for the civilian population.

In Tobruk, Qatar refurbished a hospital and provided the necessary equipment required for all operations and oversaw and financed its management for the first two months. From the hospital, Qatar would transport injured civilians from western Libya to the safe zones established in the eastern part of the country. These operations were carried out as part of a joint effort with NATO.

Qatar also rented commercial ships from Turkey and Greece on behalf of the Qatari Navy to move civilians out of the battle sites in western Libya and transport them eastward to Benghazi and Tobruk. Foreign nationals, including Egyptians, were also among those transferred to these eastern safe zones, which were established in cooperation with the International Red Crescent.

However, NATO had to clear all ships participating in the evacuation efforts, whether it was of wounded fighters or civilians. Qatar coordinated this aspect of the operation directly with the United States and France. As part of that effort, Qatari officers were onboard French ships to participate in the coordination efforts.

Qatar also trained Libyan nationals to guard their oil fields. US intelligence services vetted all of these Libyans. Their training focused on providing the guards with knowledge on how to protect critical infrastructure while preventing looters from selling oil on the black market. The Qatari training also focused on preventing looting from other infrastructure sites, mainly in Tobruk, and included water facilities, electricity, and food storage sites. Protecting roads and bridges, however, was beyond Qatar's scope, which is why Doha did not participate in these efforts.

Qatar did, however, provide basic combat training. The training focused on self-defense. Qatar did not carry out any combat operations on behalf of the fighters trained by Doha.

All of these matters were carried out in coordination with NATO, whose Libya headquarters were established in Benghazi and were popularly dubbed "the great man-made river project." From there, Qatar, along with its NATO partners, cooperated on issues ranging from air operations such as air reconnaissance (also known as spotters) to establishing weapon depots.

Qatar also had a presence at NATO's principal operation center in Paris and at a separate operation center in Milan. The Forward Operating Center was on Crete, where Qatar also enjoyed a presence. The Qataris were also present at the Utmost Forward Operation Center in Benghazi, Libya.

From the Forward Air Control, the Qatari Air Force carried out flying missions with its various NATO partners, which included selecting targets. These operations were supported on the ground by Qatari ground forces in cooperation with their US and UK counterparts.

From that point on, Doha's narrow focus was on strengthening Libya's economy with the goal of ensuring that tankers could deploy and dock at ports in order to provide oil to global markets.

Qatar provided rebels with small firearms, rifles, and guns. Several NATO members had also provided these types of weapons to the Libyan rebels. Doha, however, declined to provide rebels with anti-tank rockets, which they were ultimately unable to secure but had requested. Qatar's decision to deny the rebels these weapons was directly tied to NATO's presence in Libya.

In July 2011, Qatar stopped providing weapons, a decision that Doha also carried out in coordination with NATO. At that point, Qatar participated in a buyback program of the weapons the Gulf country had introduced while Doha continued to simultaneously advise Libyan forces on how to move forward with a political process.

The buyback program also included anti-aircraft/chemical weapons from the Ghaddafi-era stockpiles. The US and Qatari militaries dispatched chemical-biological radiological teams to secure the chemical stockpiles, which were at that point removed quickly by the United States. The anti-aircraft weapons were almost empty. At the time, around November 2011, the United States had paid $1,500 per launcher and $1,200 per Milan, and Washington had financed the buyback program.

Once Tripoli fell in August 2011, Qatar's focus became security sector reform. As part of that effort, the Qataris established fire brigades, police, and operations centers in northern Libya. Several factions were taking up and dividing Libyan parts among themselves. Toward the end of 2011, Libya's various rebel factions began fighting each other, and Qatar exited the country.

SAUDI AND QATARI COOPERATION IN SYRIA

By 2012, Qatar and the Obama administration had, to a significant extent, aligned in relations to the Syrian conflict. Washington had requested Doha's assistance to support the Free Syrian Army (FSA) as well as cooperating with Syria's MB faction whom Washington had armed under a program managed by the Central Intelligence Agency (CIA).[85] The US request came after the two countries had successfully cooperated in Libya during a NATO-led military campaign to oust Ghaddafi. The United States requested that Qatar, along with other regional partners, use its deep pockets to arm the FSA.

Qatar carried out its involvement in Syria via its Ministry of Defense. Once Qatar entered the Syrian theater, Washington, Riyadh, and Ankara had already been cooperating on Syria. While Ankara was providing support for the FSA in northern Syria, Qatar had its operations in the war-torn country's southern areas. Saudi Arabia, for its part, operated from the Jordanian/Saudi border with the strategic objective of planning the advance of the FSA toward Damascus. Qatar did not initially support regime change in Syria, unlike Ankara and Riyadh, but as it moved closer to Saudi Arabia, Doha's position changed.

US intelligence services vetted all anti-Assad groups—whether supported by Turkey, Saudi Arabia, or Qatar.

All of Qatar's training of the FSA took place outside of Syria in Jordan and Qatar. But the emphasis was on peacekeeping operations as Doha lacked sufficient combat experience to train the FSA for combat. From the Jordanian Operation Center in Amman, Qatar and Saudi Arabia carried out their respective involvements in the Syrian civil war. Qatar also operated from an undisclosed base within Turkey.

In addition to receiving training in Jordan and Turkey, Abu Dhabi dispatched FSA fighters to the UAE to participate in additional training. The UAE operated out of Jordanian Operation Center in Amman but maintained training sites in the UAE as well.

Qatar punched above its weight in Syria for reasons that largely pertained to the Gulf country's interest in strengthening the Doha–Washington partnership. Qatar's increased involvement in Syria was also meant to counterbalance its principal regional rival, the UAE, which at the time was widely referred to in Washington as "Little Sparta."[86]

At the same time, Qatar's close cooperation with Washington and Riyadh was also about countering Tehran's hand in Syria. Along with seeking to change facts on the ground, Qatar, Saudi Arabia, and Washington sought to shape the diplomatic process in favor of its objectives through the Geneva I and II and Vienna I and II processes.

The Vienna Communiqué, which all members of the International Syria Support Group (ISSG) signed on to, stipulated that ISIS, the Al Nusra Front, and other terrorist groups, as designated by the UN Security Council, must be defeated.[87] The ISSC members included Qatar, the Arab League, China, Egypt, the European Union, France, Germany, Iran, Iraq, Italy, Jordan, Lebanon, Oman, Russia, Saudi Arabia, Turkey, UAE, the United Kingdom, the United Nations, and the United States.

During this process, Qatar began to suspect that the UAE was seeking to undermine Doha's close cooperation with Saudi Arabia vis-à-vis Syria by pushing for a greater Russian role in that theater. Because Egypt has been a de-facto ally of the Syrian government since the toppling of the Morsi administration, it pushed for the Vienna Communiqué of 2015, which in turn allowed for Iranian forces to operate in Lebanon. At this point, Abu Dhabi began capitalizing on its partnership with Cairo along with its close relationship with Washington while also moving closer to Moscow's geopolitical orbit. Toward that end, Abu Dhabi began to push for the establishment of additional working groups through the Friends of Syria framework, as well as within the Geneva and Vienna diplomatic processes.[88]

The ISSG developments began in November 2015, one year after the first GCC crisis ended, and lasted until May 2016. During that time, the Qatari and Saudi foreign ministers held regular coordination meetings on Syria and Libya.

RIYADH SUMMIT: US–OMAN TENSIONS

On May 20, 2017, a day before Trump presided over the Arab Islamic American Summit in Riyadh, MbZ and MbS hosted a private dinner for the president's son-in-law and Senior White House Advisor, Jared Kushner, and senior White House official Stephen K. Bannon. During the dinner, the two Arabian princes divulged their plans about the forthcoming blockade of Qatar and secured Kushner and Bannon's support for the campaign against Doha.[89]

MbZ and MbS's rationale for the blockade, as made to Kushner, was to prevent Qatar's Al Jazeera television network and its Arabic channel in particular from becoming a potential spoiler of Kushner's proposed peace plan for Israel/Palestine by providing what the Saudi prince argued would be "damaging" coverage of what later was popularly referred to as the "Deal of the Century." Tillerson, who had accompanied Trump to the Summit, was not informed about the alleged understanding between MbZ/MbS and Kushner/Bannon about the impending blockade of Qatar.

During Trump's address before the Arab Islamic American Summit, he praised every GCC member, save Oman, for their counterterrorism efforts. President Trump also met Amir Tamim, where he touted proposed US arms sales to Qatar even as the Emirati/Saudi preparations for the impending blockade of Qatar were underway.

In his meeting with the Qatari Amir, Trump said, "One of the things that we will discuss is the purchase of lots of beautiful military equipment because nobody makes it like the United States. And for us that means jobs, and it also means frankly great security back here, which we want."[90]

Trump praising Qatar suggested that the president had authored his speech, and that it had been reviewed by Tillerson and Mattis, prior to his arrival in Riyadh and that the issue of the blockade had only been divulged to Kushner and Bannon the previous night. Because Trump praised Qatar during his subsequent meeting with the Amir, in which he touted the weapons sale, it appears unlikely that Trump was informed about the siege during the Riyadh Summit.

Following Trump's address, he inaugurated a Counter Terrorism Center, which all GCC members signed on to despite Qatar, Kuwait, and Oman not being informed about the center prior to the Riyadh Summit.[91] It is also unclear whether Bahrain was informed in advance about the matter.

The UAE, however, through its ambassador to Washington, Yousuf Al Otaiba, had not only spearheaded the diplomatic efforts to secure Trump's decision to pay Saudi Arabia his first visit abroad as president, but the ambassador also played a key role in planning for the Riyadh Summit.

Otaiba was the first GCC ambassador to engage with Trump's incoming national security team immediately after his presidential victory, which paved the way for MbZ's visit to Trump Tower in December 2016.[92]

The American businessman Thomas Barack Jr., a close confidant of Trump and longstanding friend of Otaiba, introduced Otaiba to Kushner.[93] It was Otaiba, along with his Israeli counterpart, Ambassador Ron Dermer, who jointly sought to influence Kushner's thinking about Middle East security issues because of his close proximity to Trump and lack of foreign policy experience. Dermer and Otaiba remain close.

During the Summit, however, evidence emerged that the US–Oman relationship was facing turbulence as Trump held bilateral talks with every GCC leader except for Oman's deputy prime minister, Sayyid Fahd Bin Mahmoud Al Said, who had his meeting canceled at the last moment with no public explanation. Prior to the Summit, no bilateral meeting had been requested by Washington for a meeting between Trump and Oman's deputy prime minister, who represented Sultan Qaboos Al Said. At the Summit itself, however, Tillerson requested a meeting with Oman's deputy prime minister, which was accepted, but the top US diplomat subsequently informed him that the meeting had been canceled because of scheduling issues. The move was followed by Tillerson canceling his meeting with Omani counterpart Yusuf bin Alawi without any explanation provided.

These developments suggested at the time that Washington was revaluating its relationship with Muscat.

Adding to what appeared at the time to be mounting tensions between Oman and the Trump administration was the fact that Oman became the last GCC country to receive invitations from the White House for meetings pertaining to Trump's quest to revitalize the Israel/Palestinian peace process and efforts to accelerate Gaza reconstruction. Qatar, however, actively pushed behind the scenes for Oman's participation.

But tensions between the UAE and Oman had been culminating for years, including in Washington. Otaiba had instructed his staff, in addition to all Emirati nationals residing in the US capital, not to fraternize with their Omani counterparts in either a professional or social capacity. Amid these dynamics, the UAE began hacking the personal devices of senior Omani officials, both in Muscat and in Washington, to obtain access to official correspondence and private emails.

Although the UAE's adverse relationship with Oman never played out in public, at least not in Washington, it helped set the stage for Oman's initial isolation from the Trump administration given that it was Otaiba who had helped organize the summit in Riyadh and had capitalized on his relationships with Kushner and Bannon, who lacked familiarity with Gulf dynamics, to freeze out Oman over its ties with Tehran.

But irrespective of the trajectory of the US–Oman relationship before and immediately after the Riyadh Summit, the relationship between Saudi Arabia and Qatar remained strong during the Riyadh Summit. This was later confirmed by Kuwait's Amir Sabah Al Ahmad Al Jaber Al-Sabah, who said, "We met in Riyadh, in the presence of President Trump, and there was no one to say that there was a dispute between us. But suddenly, this dispute came into existence." [94]

Via Bannon, MbZ encouraged Trump to raise the issue of Qatar's traditional support for MB groups during his bilateral meeting with Tamim at the Riyadh Summit. The two leaders agreed on a unified approach toward fighting radicalism. Kushner played a key role when it came to encouraging Trump to address the MB issue with Tamim. MbZ and MbZ interpreted the Trump–Tamim meeting as a sign that the Trump administration would accept, in principal, the forthcoming blockade imposed on Qatar.

Two days after the Summit, the campaign for the US withdrawal from Qatar's Al Udeid Air Base (AUAB) culminated during the aforementioned full-day FDD conference. But immediately after the anti-Qatar conference, Doha deported Saudi human rights activist Mohammad Al Otaibi to Saudi Arabia on May 25, 2017, as he was about to depart for Norway, where he had been granted political asylum.[95]

The official Saudi request for Al Otaibi's extradition was made during the Riyadh Summit. Al Otaibi's extradition was included in the US State Department's report on Qatar, which criticized Qatar for this decision.[96]

In January 2018, the Saudi human rights activist received a 14-year prison sentence after being found guilty of setting up an organization before receiving authorization, spreading chaos, inciting public opinion, and publishing statements harmful to the Kingdom and its institutions.[97]

While Bahrain, Egypt, Saudi Arabia, and the UAE have long accused Qatar of interfering in their respective domestic affairs, including by hosting dissidents and providing them with a platform to express their views on Al Jazeera, Al Otaibi's deportation to Riyadh underscored to what great length Qatar was willing to go to preserve Doha's relationship with Saudi Arabia. Put simply, the Qataris were determined to avoid a crisis in Doha–Riyadh relations at any cost.

The UAE has similarly requested the release of the wife of an unidentified dissident, currently in exile in the United Kingdom. The woman, Alaa Al Seddiqi, and her husband moved to Qatar after leaving the UAE in 2013. Her husband subsequently moved to the UK, but Ms. Seddiqi, a mother of six, remained in Qatar because of family ties. When Seddiqi attempted to renew her passport, the

Emirati Embassy in Doha refused her application and demanded her extradition.[98] Siddiqi's father is a prominent MB leader in the UAE. In 2019, she and her children left for the UK to reunite with her husband.

The Seddiqi issue was also discussed during Tamim's visit to Riyadh on May 1, 2017, and the topic was revisited again by the Saudi leadership during the Riyadh Summit. But other than Al Otaibi (who had already been deported) and Seddiqi, Qatar is not hosting any other dissidents from the Quartet countries, and neither has it received any extradition requests. In fact, Amir Tamim had sought to assure MbZ that Seddiqi would not issue any public statements while in Qatar, including through media appearances.

This changed in July 2018 when the UAE's Sheikh Rashid Bin Hamad Al Sharqi, the second son of the Amir of Fujayrah, one of the smaller and less wealthy of the seven monarchies that form the UAE, fled to Qatar, where he asked for asylum.[99] In an interview with *The New York Times*, Al Sharqi alleged that the rulers of Abu Dhabi had not consulted "the emirs of the other six Emirates before committing their troops to the [Yemen] war...But soldiers from smaller emirates, such as Al Fujayrah, have filled the front lines and accounted for most of the war deaths, which Emirati news reports have put at a little more than 100... I am the first in a royal family going out of the UAE and telling everything about them," the newspaper quoted him as saying.[100]

Qatar, which did not arrest or detain any individuals based upon political activity during 2017, quickly appeared to begin regretting its initial decision to extradite Al Otaibi to Saudi Arabia and is thus actively deliberating whether to become a signatory of the 1953 UN Convention of Refugees as part of its own reform agenda.[101]

As part of that effort, in September 2018 Qatar adopted the so-called Asylum Law, which guarantees political asylum by implementing article 58 of the Qatari constitution.[102] This policy change coincided with the abolishment of the exit visa requirement for the vast majority of foreign workers and formalizing the process of applying for permanent residency in Qatar, making Qatar the first Arab Gulf country to do so.

Qatar has supported refugees, most notably from Syria, having already provided $1.6 billion in humanitarian aid. Qatar has also coordinated with a UN General Assembly initiative to provide education and professional development for Syrian children and youth, a program that has benefited over 400,000 Syrians over five years.[103] Additionally, Qatar hosts more than 57,000 Syrians.[104]

The risks related to Qatar becoming a signatory of the UN Convention of Refugees, formally known as the Travaux Préparatoires, are significant given that political dissidents from across the GCC may seek refuge in Doha, which in turn will inevitably aggravate existing tensions between Qatar and the Quartet. But the Travaux Préparatoires issue could also threaten Qatar's fragile relationship with Iran should Iranian dissidents seek refuge in Doha. In light of the present geopolitical environment, it remains unclear whether Qatar would become the first GCC country to sign onto the Travaux Préparatoires.

The issue of political dissidents is particularly sensitive as it became one of the 13 demands issued by the Quartet on June 23, 2017. The Quartet issued this list nearly three weeks after the crisis erupted, and it came after Washington had deployed extensive diplomatic pressure on the Quartet to clarify its position vis-à-vis Qatar.

In addition to its strong relationship with Saudi Arabia, Qatar had sought to improve its relationship with the UAE by replacing its longtime ambassador to Abu Dhabi, Faris Al Nuaimi, following the Gulf crisis of 2014. As part of that effort, Qatar dispatched Prime

Minister Abdullah Bin Nasser Bin Khalifa Al Thani to attend the inauguration of UAE's Smart City, although the diplomatic representation was only on the undersecretary level. The decision to dispatch the prime minister was directly attributed to the fact that the personal relationship between MbZ and Amir Tamim had never recovered from the GCC's spat in 2014. Since the eruption of the 2017 crisis, Qatar has reassigned Al Hajri as Doha's ambassador to Poland.

Prime Minister Al Thani's participation at the Smart City inauguration was therefore a signal to Abu Dhabi about Doha's desire to improve relations. Despite these efforts, the groundwork for the Gulf crisis of 2017 was set by MbZ's visit to Trump Tower in December 2016.[105]

In light of these dynamics, Qatar did not initially understand that the blockade was supported by Saudi Arabia as it had suspected that it was an Emirati initiative but only understood that Riyadh was behind it once Saudi state media began broadcasting anti-Qatar segments immediately after the blockade went into effect on June 5, 2017.

Neither President Erdogan nor his Iranian counterpart, Hassan Rouhani, participated at the Riyadh Summit. Ankara, however, was represented by Turkey's chief diplomat, Mevlut Cavusoglu.

THE MILITARY THREAT AGAINST QATAR

When the crisis erupted, US secretaries of state and defense Tillerson and Mattis were traveling in Australia.[106] While it is unclear whether the timing of the crisis had been adjusted to when they would be abroad, the two secretaries returned immediately to Washington when they learned about the unfolding developments. They arrived during the evening of June 5, 2017.

The following morning, at 8:06 am, Trump weighed in on the dispute by posting the following message on Twitter:

"During my recent trip to the Middle East I stated that there can no longer be funding of Radical Ideology. Leaders pointed to Qatar—look!"

He swiftly followed up with another two tweets at 9:36 and 9:44 am, which gave little ambiguity of his stance vis-à-vis Qatar:

"So good to see the Saudi Arabia visit with the King and 50 countries already paying off. They said they would take a hard line on funding extremism, and all reference was pointing to Qatar. Perhaps this will be the beginning of the end to the horror of terrorism!"[107]

Immediately after Trump put out these tweets, Saudi Arabia's ambassador to Washington, Khalid Bin Salman bin Abdulaziz Al Saud (KbS), MbS's younger brother, requested an urgent meeting with Mattis at the Pentagon to seek US permission for a military invasion of Qatar. The Saudi ambassador arrived unaccompanied at the Pentagon.[108] The Saudi ambassador had deliberately sought to circumvent Tillerson as he concluded that he held favorable views of Qatar from his tenure at Exxon Mobile.[109]

KbS's quest to secure US permission for a military invasion was directly tied to Saudi Arabia's military objective to seize Qatar's North Dome Gas field. Taking control of Qatari fields would have made Saudi Arabia the world's second-biggest LNG exporter overnight.[110]

Mattis's rejection of the proposed Saudi invasion of Qatar, however, surprised the Saudi leadership, especially given that Kushner and Bannon had already approved the Quartet's proposal to blockade Qatar during the lead up to the Riyadh Summit. MbS and King Salman, along with the Emirati ambassador to Washington and MbZ, assumed that Mattis would support their quest to take direct military action against Qatar, which was partially based on Trump's tweets, but also about how well Saudi Arabia and the UAE appeared to be doing with the Trump administration at the time.

These dynamics, with the FDD conference, the plethora of op-eds penned by several prominent members of the Washington foreign policy establishment castigating Qatar as a supporter of terrorism, and MbZ's White House visit the week before the Riyadh Summit, had led Riyadh and Abu Dhabi to believe that US support would be guaranteed.

The fact that Trump had paid Saudi Arabia his first visit abroad as president before traveling to Israel also gave Riyadh and Abu Dhabi a sense of confidence. Contributing to Riyadh's confidence in its standing in Washington, including for its proposed military invasion, was how Saudi Arabia and the UAE had generously supported various think tanks in Washington, which provided them with multiple platforms to propagate their views.

Bannon influenced Trump's decision to tweet against Doha. Arguably, it was the UAE's immediate outreach following the 2016 presidential election that influenced Bannon's negative views about Doha.

It appears that Bannon endorsed the UAE narrative about Qatar, which centers on the premise that Washington had a choice to make between supporting "moderate" states (i.e., the UAE, Saudi Arabia, Bahrain, and Egypt) against "extremist" states (i.e., Qatar, Turkey, and Iran).

Prior to the Gulf crisis, while addressing Washington think tanks and the Middle East policy community in general, Otaiba would often drive home the point that Washington had to make a choice between supporting "moderate" states and Iran. But he did not publicly mention Qatar during his regular appearances leading up to the GCC crisis. Nonetheless, his US surrogates would routinely disparage Qatar in private conversations. Thus, the consistent message was clear: The UAE was not just Washington's partner. Instead, the UAE was the United States' principal regional ally. Otaiba framed the US–UAE relationship in moral terms: The Emiratis were "the good guys" and the Qataris were not.

This narrative, along with the apocalyptic notion that the Trump Presidency presented a historic opportunity to align Israel with "moderate" Arab states against Iran, which Qatar had a pragmatic relationship with, may have influenced Bannon's thinking when he advised Trump to tweet against Qatar.

Following Trump's anti-Qatar tweets, but immediately after Mattis had rejected KbS's request for US support for a military invasion of Qatar, Mattis and Tillerson rushed to the White House to block the impending Saudi military moves vis-à-vis Doha. Immediately after briefing Trump about the Saudi request, which Mattis and Tillerson relayed to the President, Trump called King Salman to warn him against a military invasion.[111] Trump also requested that the Quartet lift the blockade. During the call, however, King Salman sought to deflect Trump's request to lift the blockade—and perhaps also save face as his son's high-stakes proposal had been outright rejected—by flattering the US president, and the nature of the conversation changed but the military move was successfully blocked.

Prior to the Trump–Salman call, Saudi Arabia and the UAE had planned an invasion of Qatar, which was prepared for during the nightfall of June 6 (the day Trump tweeted against Qatar). In the days before the blockade, Saudi Arabia had deployed a large number of troops to a military base near the eastern city of Dhahran in the

40

Eastern Province, from where they could be deployed to the Saudi–Qatari border while awaiting further instructions. However, no Saudi troops were visibly positioned along the Saudi–Qatari border during the first days of the Gulf crisis.

In addition to the mobilization of Saudi ground troops to a military base near Dhahran, the UAE had maintained sixteen F-16 fighter jets on high alert to provide air support for the Saudi ground troops as part of a joint plan for invasion. The 16 fighter jets remained on alert for two consecutive weeks after the siege of Qatar began.

Even after the Trump–Salman call on June 6, 2017, Saudi Arabia and the UAE continued to test the waters with military maneuvers along the border. It was at this point that Qatar called upon Turkey for assistance as Doha feared that Trump would pull US troops out of AUAB. The push to encourage Trump to withdraw his support for AUAB was never actually about removing the US military presence from Qatar. Rather it was about pressuring Amir Tamim to abdicate.

The day after Trump had called off the proposed military invasion, on June 7, 2017, the Turkish Parliament passed legislation to dispatch its troops to a Turkish military base in Qatar.

Fearing a Saudi military invasion during the initial phase of the blockade, the Qatari leadership dispersed from the Amiri Diwan to several secure locations throughout the country as they feared the decision-making process could be paralyzed in the event of air strikes launched by either Saudi Arabia or the UAE.

On June 9, 2017, after Tillerson called upon the Quartet to ease its blockade of Qatar, Trump publicly contradicted his top diplomat by announcing hours later during a press conference at the White House that "the nation of Qatar, unfortunately, has historically been a funder of terrorism." Bannon instigated Trump's decision to undercut Tillerson.

Whatever intention Trump had vis-à-vis the GCC dispute, his tweets followed up by the June 9 press conference clearly had a destabilizing impact. The reaction was perceived as Trump supporting the Saudis as well as a "green light" for a Saudi military invasion, even after he had called it off only days prior. But Mattis and Tillerson intervened once again.

Given that the US Secretaries of State and Defense actively and consistently opposed any military moves against Qatar, coupled with the fact the Saudi ambassador's initial request had been rejected, Saudi Arabia and the UAE had concluded that if only Trump could be swayed, the government of Qatar could still be brought to its knees.

With that objective in mind, Otaiba published an op-ed in *The Wall Street Journal* on June 12, 2017 (three days after the June 9 press conference) seeking to keep the pressure on the president to withdraw from AUAB.[112] A US withdrawal, the UAE believed, would trigger the downfall of Qatar's Al Thani dynasty and force Amir Tamim to abdicate or even go into exile.

At the time, Trump's anti-Qatar tweets were based on the anti-Qatar allegations repeatedly relegated by UAE, and by Otaiba in particular, via Bannon and his deputy, Deputy Assistant to the President Sebastian Gorka. Both were at the White House at the time.

During the initial stage of the crisis, when there was a lingering uncertainty over where the White House stood, the Qatari monarch spearheaded Doha's engagement with Washington, as did Doha's Foreign Minister Al Thani and Minister of State for Defense Khalid Al Attiyah, who were in close contact with Tillerson and Mattis. During this phase, Qatar had also relied on its institutional and decades-old relationships with the Pentagon and State Department while Trump's initial White House was staffed by political outsiders and nonexperts, which only contributed to Bannon and Gorka's outsized influence over Trump.

During this phase, Mattis made several phone calls to King Salman and to Defense Minister Al Attiyah to de-escalate tensions, which included forcing Saudi Arabia to withdraw its troops from close proximity to the Qatari border.

In parallel with the Qatari leadership's engagement with Mattis and Tillerson, on June 14, 2017, Al Attiyah signed a deal in Washington to buy as many as seventy-two F-15 fighters jets valued at $21 billion.[113] The F-15 transaction had been planned for over three years, and the timing of the agreement was coincidental. There was no Congressional opposition against the F-15 agreement, even though anti-Qatar legislation had been introduced on May 25, 2017. The military threat against Qatar, however, remained in place.

For example, in August 2017, Saudi Arabia continued to pressure Qatar when it introduced Abdullah Bin Ali Al Thani, the son of deposed Qatari Amir Sheikh Ali Bin Abdullah Al Thani, to represent Qatar on issues pertaining to the Hajj. Abdullah met with King Salman on August 18, 2017, at his guest residence in the Moroccan city of Tangier. The two discussed the opening of the Salwa border crossing for Qatari pilgrims, which was widely understood as a veiled military threat against the Qatari leadership given that Riyadh had closed the border and banned Qataris from participating in the Hajj.[114]

Amir Sheikh Ali Bin Abdullah Al Thani ruled from 1960 to 1972. Abdullah, however, has had an ambiguous position in the Qatari royal family since his father was deposed by Khalifa bin Hamad Al Thani.[115] Sheikh Khalifa deposed Sheikh Ali in 1972 because of an agreement within the Al Thani family.

Qatar's Al Thani Dynasty

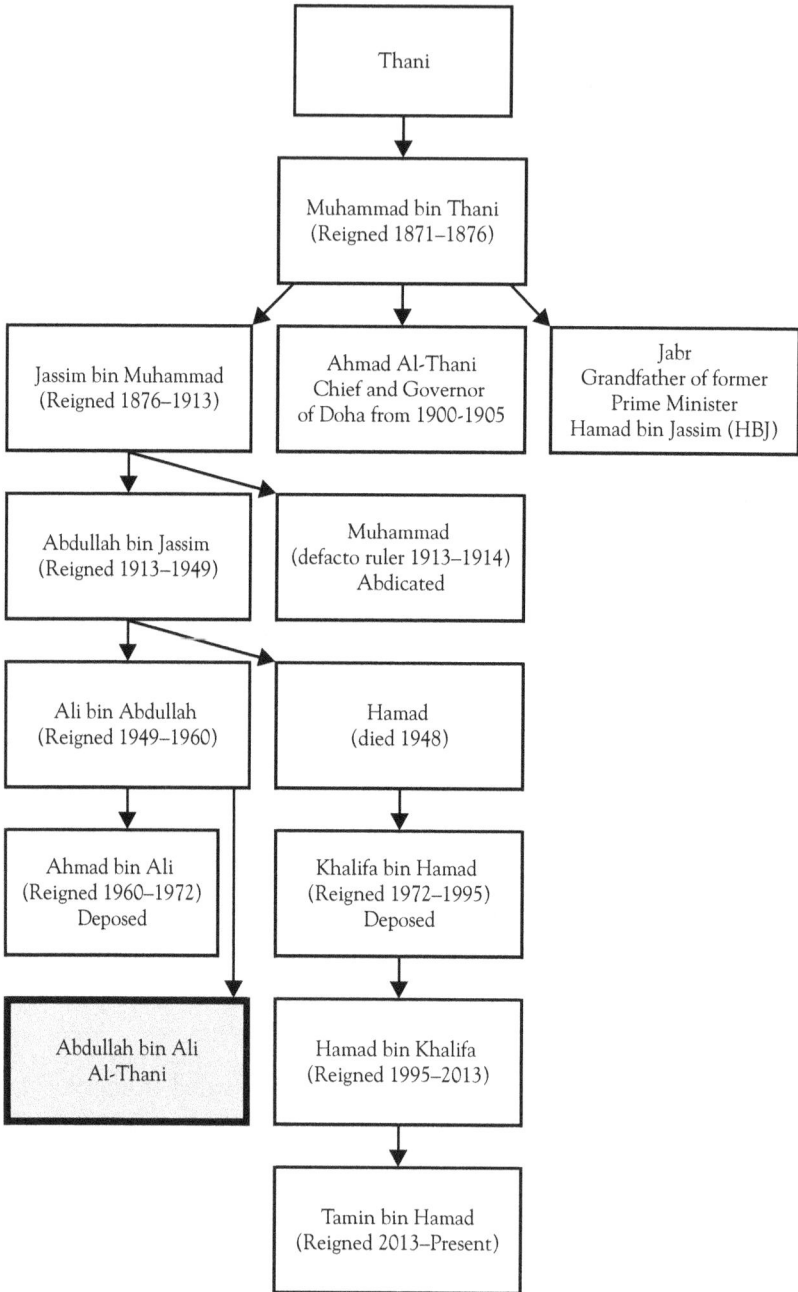

Thani

Muhammad bin Thani
(Reigned 1871–1876)

Jassim bin Muhammad
(Reigned 1876–1913)

Ahmad Al-Thani
Chief and Governor
of Doha from 1900-1905

Jabr
Grandfather of former
Prime Minister
Hamad bin Jassim (HBJ)

Abdullah bin Jassim
(Reigned 1913–1949)

Muhammad
(defacto ruler 1913–1914)
Abdicated

Ali bin Abdullah
(Reigned 1949–1960)

Hamad
(died 1948)

Ahmad bin Ali
(Reigned 1960–1972)
Deposed

Khalifa bin Hamad
(Reigned 1972–1995)
Deposed

Abdullah bin Ali
Al-Thani

Hamad bin Khalifa
(Reigned 1995–2013)

Tamin bin Hamad
(Reigned 2013–Present)

Thus, the idea of introducing Abdullah as an alternative, Saudi-backed Amir who would return to Doha via the Salwa border crossing among Qatari pilgrims was extremely threatening and inflammatory from the Qatari government's perspective.

Following the introduction of Sheikh Abdullah, Saud Al Qahtani, an adviser to the Saudi Royal Court and the Supervisor General of the Center for Studies and Information Affairs, sought to keep up the pressure on Qatar on September 14, 2017, by posting the following Twitter thread[116]:

> Today is a lesson in our unity for the #Ghaddafi of the Gulf [a reference to Amir Tamim's father who is also known as Sheikh Hamad], who funded what he called the Nostalgia Revolution, the gathering spots announced by Al Faqeeh (in reference to Shiite Imams), Ramadan sit in and today's joke #against the September 15 conspiracy.
>
> I repeat in the name of every Gulf national, warning the #two Hamads regime against using foreign Iranian or other forces to suppress the peaceful movements by the brotherly people of Qatar. This is a war crime.
>
> KSA is a lofty mountain that won't shake the conspiracies of the little. Yet, do the little afford their transgression against the big? I leave the answer to you.
>
> You are indebted to each Saudi. We will defend our homeland with ourselves, children and money.
>
> Tell your father, #Ghaddaffi of the Gulf and your brother, #scarecrow, that using the support of foreign forces in Qatar against the Qatari people is a war crime that you will be held accountable for. This is your warning. You have been warned.

Al Qahtani "is considered one of the most influential figures on the Saudi Twitter scene," according to *Arab News*, a Jeddah-based Saudi newspaper close to the royal Al Saud family.[117] He was credited with not only speaking on behalf of MbS, at least throughout the social media sphere, but was also responsible for establishing an online army of trolls that would not only attack Qatar but also Saudi journalist Jamal Khashoggi.[118] Washington has accused Al Qahtani of having been the mastermind behind Khashoggi's murder and later had his Twitter account suspended by Twitter.[119, 120]

Al Qahtani's tweets were largely seen across the Gulf as an attempt to mobilize the tribes of Ajman, Shammar, Mutair, and Otaiba, which have cousins and extended families on both sides of the border against Qatar's royal Al Thani family.[121]

Minute 1:00 from Al-Arabia video:

Saudi analyst: The aims of previous Iran-loyalist cells was to gather information and report intelligence on specific military targets. This cell is totally different in terms of methodology, objectives, actions, formation and support. I believe there is a new factor. I believe when the names are revealed, it will be shocking for the Saudi people.

Question: According to our security sources and information, we were informed that this group is regularly active in participating in suspicious conferences, seminars and meetings. It is also active in attracting and recruiting the youth in antagonistic activities. To what extent does this explain the involvement of Saudis in this cell that was arrested and how did they manage to recruit them?

Answer: As I mentioned, when the names are revealed, the Saudi people will be shocked. Some wore the cloaks of preachers and reformers. They were recruited by one of the countries of the region, specifically, Qatar. They were provided with funds and great services. Hence, I believe this cell is different as it aimed to undermine the Saudi state, vis-à-vis the previous cells mainly working to obtain military information.

On September 26, 2017, Saudi Arabia's *Okaz Newspaper* published an editorial titled, "Is it Time for Change in Qatar?!," which cited Abdullah's reference to "the anger of the Qatari people" against the "Two Hamads" over their "support for terrorism." The editorial concluded with a warning for Qatar: "The four countries, especially Saudi Arabia, have grown impatient thwarting the 'Hamad' conspiracies one after the other. When the grand grow impatient, the Two Hamads have to bear the consequences, as grave as they might be!"[122]

Immediately after the editorial in question was published, the founder of the Saudi American Public Relation Affairs Committee, or SAPRAC, Salman Al Ansari, piled on by threatening Qatar with a military invasion on Twitter. "If it is proved that #Qatar is involved in terms of intelligence in the recent terrorist operations in #Egypt, it might be a declaration of war, and a call to close exits and navy channels for Doha."[123] Al Ansari had also established The Qatar Insider (TQI), an anti-Qatar entity in Washington.

On December 18, 2017, the UAE deployed two or three F-16 fighter jets to Saudi Arabia, near the Qatari border. Qatar filed a complaint with the United Nations about the issue. The UAE fighter jets violated Qatar's airspace en route to Saudi Arabia, which at the time sent a clear message: the military threat against Qatar remained in place.

In April 2018, Riyadh's efforts to stoke tribal tensions along the Saudi–Qatari border resurfaced when Saudi authorities arrested Qatari national Mohsen Saleh Saadoun Al Karbi, a Qatari national, upon his return from Yemen, where he visited relatives.[124] On April 24, 2018, the Saudi Press Agency (SPA) posted a string of Twitter messages accusing Al Qurabi, along with 23 other unidentified individuals, of seeking to inflame sectarian tensions in the northwestern Saudi city of Ha'il.

The SPA posted the following Twitter messages:

> Breaking News: 24 arrested for attempting sectarian tensions in Ha'il. Statement from State Security and Ministry of Interior.
>
> State Security Agency announces it arrested 22, including a Qatari citizen.
>
> More briefings soon from the Ministry of Interior.
>
> Breaking News: The Ministry of Interior confirms it stands firmly against all these practices and the spreading of falsehoods and jeopardy to security.
>
> Investigations are underway to know their roles, goals and will continue to pursue all the involved.
>
> The person who designed a logo for this purpose has been arrested.
>
> One of the arrested is a Qatari citizen and the rest are Saudi.
>
> State Security managed to identify the owners of these footages and arrested 22.
>
> The footage tracked incite directly and indirectly for illegitimate and anti-state acts.
>
> Video footage has been circulating on social media inciting against public order regarding certain issues at hand.
>
> State security warns against getting involved in such practices and confirms it will be very firm with any perpetrators.
>
> Investigations are underway regarding the motives and connections of the arrested.

All the arrested will be under investigations until the Public Prosecution identifies their roles and charges. Ministry of Interior spokesperson: The crimes at hand fall under the cope of combatting cyber crimes.

Ministry of Interior spokesperson: Some individuals should bear in mind that resorting to social media to commit violations will not be unnoticed.

Ministry of Interior spokesperson: Security agencies are professionally and technically equipped to track cyber crimes.[125]

Saudi authorities eventually released Al Karbi in July 2019. Two additional Qatari citizens, Ahmad Khalid Moqbel and Nawaf Talal Al-Rasheed, received their freedom in December 2018 and April 2019, respectively. Yet one more Qatari, a student named Abdulaziz Saeed Abdulla, remains imprisoned at the Haer prison, located south of Riyadh. The Saudi authorities have been holding him since July 2018.[126] Yet the Saudi government has not filed charges against Abdulla, and neither has he received a trial. Qatar has filed a complaint with the United Nations and international organizations to conduct extensive investigations into "the gross and systematic violations and discriminatory measures against Qatari nationals by Saudi authorities."[127]

On June 2, 2018, ahead of the one-year anniversary of the Gulf crisis, Saudi Arabia once again threatened military action against Doha when the London-based *Asharq Al-Awsat* newspaper, which is close to Riyadh, published an article encouraging a military coup against Qatar.[128]

Coinciding with the *Asharq Al-Awsat* editorial marking the one-year anniversary of the crisis, the French newspaper *Le Monde* obtained a letter that King Salman sent to French President

Emmanuel Macron in which the Saudi monarch threatened to take military action against Qatar should it acquire the Russian-manufactured S-400 system.[129]

THE IRAN TRAP AND THE QATAR–TURKISH RELATIONSHIP IN CONTEXT

Qataris widely perceived the Quartet's ultimatum, which required Doha to "scale down" ties with Tehran, as a trap. Officials in Doha anticipated that Saudi Arabia would have pressed Trump to take additional diplomatic steps to isolate Qatar further from his administration if Doha would turn to Tehran for protection during the blockade's initial phase.

During this phase, Erdogan engaged leaders from the Organization of Islamic Cooperation (OIC) through phone calls and shuttle diplomacy while urging them not to be drawn into the crisis by submitting to the allegations the Quartet was leveling against Qatar.

In addition to these efforts, Ankara provided Doha with assistance in various forms, including an airlift to break the economic blockade on Qatar, which included ensuring that Turkish Airlines and Turkish cargo flights to Doha were dispatching Turkish goods, such as fruits and vegetables, along with dairy products to the Qatari capital. Turkey also established a separate terminal for Qatar Airways at Istanbul Sabiha Gökçen International Airport to facilitate the airlift.[130]

As previously mentioned, the Turkish Parliament accelerated procedures on June 7, 2017, to deploy Turkish troops to Qatar. Erdogan signed the legislation the following day. On June 22, 2017, Ankara dispatched a new detachment of forces comprising 5 armored vehicles and 23 soldiers who joined the 88 Turkish soldiers already deployed to the Tariq bin Ziyad base.[131]

Although Qatar initially announced that 3,000 Turkish troops would arrive, Ankara only dispatched 180. Turkey assigned these troops to train and advise their Qatari counterparts. Qatar and Turkey deliberately decided to inflate the numbers of Turkish troops set to arrive in Doha in public statements as part of a deterrence strategy vis-à-vis Saudi Arabia and the UAE.

Prior to the crisis of 2017, Turkey and Qatar had signed a bilateral defense agreement in 2014, which followed the first Gulf crisis. The two countries later signed supplementary defense agreements in 2015 and 2016.[132] These initial agreements enabled the fast-tracking of the additional Turkish troops on June 7, 2017.

Following the Turkish troop deployment, Qatari Minister of State for Defense Al Attiyah arrived in Ankara on June 30, 2017, to secure additional Turkish diplomatic and military support. On the diplomatic front, Tukey dispatched Foreign Minister Mevlut Çavuşoglu to Qatar, Kuwait, and Saudi Arabia on June 14, 2017. Nine days later, Erdogan visited the same three countries, but he traveled first to Riyadh, then to Kuwait City and Doha.[133] By the time Erdogan arrived in Riyadh, his public support for Doha was crystal clear, which contributed to his inability to ease GCC tensions.

At the request of Qatar's Attorney General Ali Bin Fetais Al Marri, Turkish authorities arrested five hackers behind the QNA hack on August 25, 2017.[134]

During the immediate aftermath of the failed coup against Turkey's government of July 15, 2016, Qatar and Turkey established the strategic nature of their bilateral relationship. On the night of the failed coup, while developments were still unfolding and everything seemed uncertain, Tamim called Erdogan to pledge his support.[135] The Qatari foreign minister also became the first foreign official to visit Turkey following the botched coup plot. Notable was the fact that the leader of Qatar (not any leader of a NATO member) was the first head of state to express solidarity with his Turkish counterpart.

At the time, Ankara accused Abu Dhabi of having tacitly supported the failed coup as Turkish–Emirati relations deteriorated. Sky News Arabia, a UAE-based media outlet, covered the coup plot in ways which were sympathetic to the putschists and also claimed that Erdogan had fled to Germany amid the dramatic events of July 15, 2016. Such media coverage triggered Ankara and did much to contribute to the Turkish government's conclusion that the UAE had a hand in the coup plot. For its part, Saudi Arabia's Al Arabiya television network had hosted Fethullah Gulen, the very man whom Erdogan had accused of having spearheaded the coup attempt from the US state of Pennsylvania.[136]

At the time, Doha offered to mediate between Ankara and Abu Dhabi with the twin objective of repairing Qatar's relationship with the UAE and strengthening its ties with Turkey. The UAE, however, rejected the Qatari mediation offer.

QATAR AND IRAN

Qatar's bilateral relationship with Iran is primarily tied to economic and diplomatic agreements relating to the extraction of natural gas from the South Pars/North Dome field, which is by far the largest of its kind in the world. This shared gas field links the two countries strategically. Diplomatically, Doha engages Iran based on the view that a non-confrontational relationship with the Islamic Republic best advances Qatar's interests. These dynamics contributed to the establishment of the Gas Exporting Countries Forum (GECF), alongside Russia, in 2001. In 2010, the two countries signed a security pact similar to those signed between Iran and Oman, as well as

Kuwait and Saudi Arabia, which arguably proved to be more symbolic than substantial.[137]

Despite these agreements, there was always a limit to Qatar and Iran's diplomatic and political closeness because Doha had always sought to operate within the GCC consensus vis-à-vis Tehran, which in practical terms often meant supporting Riyadh's position. For example, on January 2, 2016, Qatar sided with Saudi Arabia against Iran after an angry mob attacked the Saudi embassy in Tehran and its consulate in Mashhad in response to the Kingdom's execution of the Saudi Shiite cleric Nimr Al Nimr at the start of that year. Before attacking the Saudi embassy with Molotov cocktails and petrol bombs, thousands of protestors stormed the premises, climbing over its surrounding fences. In Mashhad, demonstrators also set the consulate ablaze while tearing down the Saudi flag. Qatar responded by pulling its envoy back from Tehran in order to demonstrate solidarity with its GCC neighbor and to make it clear that Doha did not tolerate such actions on the part of Iranians. While the attacks were swiftly condemned by a unified GCC, Saudi Arabia and Bahrain severed relations. Kuwait and Qatar withdrew their ambassadors while UAE downgraded relations. Oman, for its part, took no diplomatic action besides condemning the attacks.[138]

Qatar only returned its ambassador to Tehran in August 2017 as a direct result of the GCC crisis. Before doing so, Qatar had not received any Iranian officials on the ministerial level in Doha. The highest-ranking Iranian official to visit Doha during the initial phase of the blockade was Iran's Deputy Foreign Minister for Arab and African Affairs Hossein Jaberi Ansari, who visited Doha on June 18, 2017.

Iran's Foreign Minister Javad Zarif made his first trip to blockaded Doha on October 3, 2017. During this visit he met with Amir

Tamim.[139] Their meeting took place well after the Quartet blocked Washington's initial push for GCC reconciliation and after the Trump–Tamim relationship had solidified. This topic will be discussed in further detail in the next chapter of this book, which covers American and Kuwaiti diplomacy in relation to the GCC crisis.

Nonetheless, there was a Qatari–Iranian rapprochement after Tehran delivered 350 tons of food supplies to Doha during the first few days of the blockade.[140] Iran also opened up its airspace for Qatar Airways, which was another significant gesture and sign of Tehran's quest to capitalize the Gulf dispute to the Islamic Republic's advantage.

Regardless of Tehran's own interests and motivations, by opening up its airspace for Qatar, Iran played a critical role in preventing the Quartet from strangling Qatar's economy. In this regard, Iran played a stabilizing role in the Gulf-dispute from a Qatari perspective. Yet the blockading states would come to see the significant improvements in Qatari–Iranian relations as nothing but confirmation of Doha's keenness to abandon fellow GCC capitals in favor of good relations with the Islamic Republic.

UNITED STATES AND KUWAIT

In light of what appeared to be Tillerson's diminishing personal rapport with Trump and strained relationships with various figures within the White House, particularly Bannon and Kushner, Tillerson sought to reach the President through Mattis in order to prevent further escalations, including during the aforementioned threat of a Saudi military invasion during the first 24 to 48 hours of the crisis.

These dynamics explain why Tillerson's first public statement on the crisis came on 9 June 2017, three days after Trump's anti-Qatar tweet and four days after the blockade began. In his statement, the top US diplomat called for the blockade to be lifted while stressing that it was "hindering US military actions in the region and the campaign against ISIS." Tillerson also called on the parties to adhere to the principles agreed to at the Riyadh Summit while expressing support for Kuwaiti mediation efforts.[141]

Adding to the confusing state of US foreign policy vis-à-vis Qatar at the time, Trump openly contradicted Tillerson after his initial statement on the crisis. Trump said,

> We had a decision to make: do we take the easy road or do we finally take a hard but necessary action? We have to stop the funding of terrorism. I decided, along with secretary of state Rex Tillerson...the time had come to call on Qatar to end its funding...and its extremist ideology in terms of funding.[142]

Despite this initial set of contradictory statements, Tillerson sought to reach Trump via Mattis as they jointly sought to block Saudi Arabia from moving ahead with further escalatory measures against Qatar, including by reiterating that Washington would not tolerate any military measures against Doha.

Amid these developments, Kuwait began its mediation efforts, which the country's head of state spearheaded with the full backing of Washington.

The Kuwaiti Amir had also mediated during the 2014 Gulf crisis, which explains why Tillerson and Mattis sought to boost his efforts.

Even though tensions between the Quartet and Qatar had simmered below the surface ever since Doha began supporting

Islamist groups during the Arab Spring, the crisis of 2017 surprised Washington's Middle East policy community as many analysts had concluded that inter-GCC tensions had been resolved following the 2014 standoff.

Toward that end, then US State Department spokeswoman Heather Nauert issued a statement on June 20, 2017, that endorsed Kuwaiti mediation efforts and requested clarity from the Quartet about what they wanted from Qatar.

"We see this as long-simmering tensions that have been going on for quite some time, and that is why we believe that this can be resolved peacefully among the parties without the United States having to step in in some sort of formal mediation role, that they can do this on their own, and we're asking them to 'Let's move this along,'" Nauert said.[143] She added that Tillerson had held more than 20 phone calls and meetings with leaders from the Gulf and elsewhere.

Three days later the Quartet responded to the US statement with 13 official demands for Qatar, including a 10-day deadline to comply with the demands.[144]

2

US and Kuwaiti Diplomacy

THE 13 DEMANDS IN FULL

1. Curb diplomatic ties with Iran and close its diplomatic missions there. Expel members of Iran's Revolutionary Guards and cut off any joint military cooperation with Iran. Only trade and commerce with Iran that complies with US and international sanctions will be permitted.

2. Sever all ties to "terrorist organizations," specifically the Muslim Brotherhood, Islamic State, Al Qaida, and Lebanon's Hezbollah. Formally declare those entities as terrorist groups.

3. Shut down Al Jazeera and its affiliate stations.

4. Shut down news outlets that Qatar funds, directly and indirectly, including Arabi21, Rassd, Al Araby Al Jadeed, and Middle East Eye.

5. Immediately terminate the Turkish military presence in Qatar and end any joint military cooperation with Turkey inside Qatar.

6. Stop all means of funding for individuals, groups or organizations that have been designated as terrorists by Saudi

Arabia, the UAE, Egypt, Bahrain, the US, and other countries.

7. Hand over "terrorist figures" and wanted individuals from Saudi Arabia, the UAE, Egypt, and Bahrain to their countries of origin. Freeze their assets, and provide any desired information about their residency, movements, and finances.

8. End interference in sovereign countries' internal affairs. Stop granting citizenship to wanted nationals from Saudi Arabia, the UAE, Egypt, and Bahrain. Revoke Qatari citizenship for existing nationals where such citizenship violates those countries' laws.

9. Stop all contacts with the political opposition in Saudi Arabia, the UAE, Egypt, and Bahrain. Hand over all files detailing Qatar's prior contacts with and support for those opposition groups.

10. Pay reparations and compensation for loss of life and other financial losses caused by Qatar's policies in recent years. The sum will be determined in coordination with Qatar.

11. Consent to monthly audits for the first year after agreeing to the demands, then once per quarter during the second year. For the following 10 years, Qatar would be monitored annually for compliance.

12. Align itself with the other Gulf and Arab countries militarily, politically, socially, and economically, as well as on economic matters, in line with an agreement reached with Saudi Arabia in 2014.

13. Agree to all the demands within 10 days of it being submitted to Qatar, or the list becomes invalid.

In addition to the 13 demands, Saudi Arabia delivered an oral message to Kuwait, demanding that Qatar close down the Brookings Doha Center, Georgetown School of Foreign Service, Northwestern University School of Journalism, and all the churches. Saudi Arabia denies that this stipulation had been included.

US–QATAR MEMORANDUM OF UNDERSTANDING

As part of Washington's efforts to defuse the crisis, Tillerson's first step was to reduce the dispute from centering on terrorism allegations to differences pertaining to Qatar's foreign policy priorities during the immediate post–Arab Spring environment.

Thus, Washington's objective became to narrow the scope of the dispute so that it could be resolved within the GCC through Kuwaiti mediation.

With that objective in sight, Tillerson began his first round of shuttle diplomacy in the Gulf by visiting Kuwait on July 10, 2017. In Kuwait he met with Amir Sabah and Deputy Prime Minister and Foreign Minister Sabah Al Khalid Al Sabah.[145]

From Kuwait, Tillerson traveled to Doha to sign a bilateral Memorandum of Understanding (MoU) aimed at combating the financing of terrorism.[146] The process leading up to the MoU, which Tillerson and his Qatari counterpart signed on July 10, started in February 2017 as part of an effort to strengthen cooperation between the US Transportation Security Administration (TSA) and Qatar Airways on issues pertaining to airport and aviation security.

But, because of the crisis, Washington accelerated the MoU process, which was turned into a comprehensive document focusing on counterterrorism measures, in order to send a message to the Quartet, particularly Saudi Arabia.

The message was clear. Washington took the allegations about terrorism financing seriously but wanted to frame the crisis as an inter-GCC dispute as opposed to one that centered on Qatar's alleged support for terrorism. In the process, the MoU had a stabilizing impact on shielding the US–Qatar strategic partnership from politically motivated attacks in Washington by Qatar's regional adversaries.

The TSA–Qatar Airways process had initially been launched by the US and Qatari ambassadors, and the initiative had been requested by Doha. Qatar did not at the time meet the capacity of enhanced airport and aviation security.

Washington's principal objective with the MoU was to ensure that Doha is competent to carry out the technical aspects of the MoU, and that Qatari citizens do not join terrorist organizations.

The concept of a bilateral MoU on Counter Terrorism Financing (CTF) was conceived in Washington weeks after the crisis erupted as part of an effort to demonstrate the US government's concern with terrorism financing and that it took allegations about sponsoring terrorist organizations seriously.

From a US vantage point, the crisis presented an opportunity to expand the CTF cooperation with Qatar and formalize it with an MoU.

Washington has also called upon the remaining GCC countries to sign bilateral CTF MoUs with the United States.

After signing the MoU, Tillerson traveled to Riyadh for talks with King Salman where he called for the lifting of the blockade and measures to resolve the standoff.[147]

During Tillerson's first round of shuttle diplomacy in the Gulf, he omitted Abu Dhabi and Manama, which suggested that the solution to the crisis was in Riyadh and that UAE and Bahrain would follow if the parties achieved a breakthrough.

Since the MoU was signed, Washington and Doha have been moving forward on CTF cooperation, an issue not unique to Doha but a challenge for all the GCC countries.

THE POLITICS OF AL-UDEID AIR BASE (AUAB)

In his previously mentioned *Wall Street Journal* op-ed, UAE Ambassador Yusuf Al Otaiba called for a US withdrawal from AUAB. But his message arguably had the opposite impact because it helped inform Trump about the seriousness of the crisis, which in turn accelerated his administration's quest to solve it.[148]

Experts widely understood that if the United States had withdrawn from either AUAB or from its second military facility in that country, As Sayliyah Army Base, Qatar would have invited Russia to establish a military presence in the country in order to preserve its sovereignty and independence.

The Trump administration, however, never contemplated evacuating the US military presence in Qatar.

But prior to the establishment of Qatar's AUAB, the UAE had unsuccessfully placed its own bid to host US CENTCOM forward headquarters—which moved from Saudi Arabia's Prince Sultan Air Base to Qatar's AUAB in 2003.[149]

After Tillerson's initial round of shuttle diplomacy between Kuwait, Doha, and Riyadh had failed, Trump became personally involved. His involvement suggested that the standoff between Washington's key Gulf partners had begun to disrupt the White House's regional agenda, which explained Trump's decision to intervene. The Quartet responded in kind—but after Tillerson had already left the region following his initial round of shuttle diplomacy—by revising its position vis-à-vis Qatar by moving away from the 13 Demands to embracing its so-called 6 Principles.

THE 6 PRINCIPLES

1. Commitment to combat extremism and terrorism in all its forms and to prevent their financing or the provision of safe havens.

2. Prohibiting all acts of incitement and all forms of expression which spread, incite, promote or justify hatred and violence.

3. Full commitment to Riyadh Agreement 2013 and the supplementary agreement and its executive mechanism for 2014 within the framework of the Gulf Cooperation Council (GCC) for Arab States.

4. Commitment to all the outcomes of the Arab-Islamic-US Summit held in Riyadh in May 2017.

5. To refrain from interfering in the internal affairs of States and from supporting illegal entities.

6. The responsibility of all States of international community to confront all forms of extremism and terrorism as a threat to international peace and security.[150]

While Tillerson sought to narrow differences between the Quartet and Qatar, Washington never played any role in seeking to bridge the 13 Demands or use them as a basis of negotiations between the parties. This was also the case for the 6 Principles.

The reduction from the 13 Demands to 6 Principles, nonetheless, had a stabilizing impact on Qatar as the 6 Principles could theoretically provide the opposing parties with face-saving mechanisms for negotiation purposes.

The Quartet's evolving position vis-à-vis Qatar away from the 13 Demands to embracing the 6 Principles was directly attributed to Kuwait's mediation efforts.

Internal White House dynamics shaped by Bannon and Gorka's departure from the White House in August 2017 strengthened Tillerson and Mattis's influence on Trump with respect to Qatar, which in turn boosted Kuwaiti mediation efforts.[151, 152]

In August 2017, the White House chose General (Ret.) Anthony Zinni to help contribute to US shuttle diplomacy and was dispatched to the Gulf later that month. This choice had much to with Zinni's longstanding relationship with the UAE. Zinni, through his DC Capital Partners, a venture capital firm, oversees three Emirati investment funds. Zinni returned to the Gulf a second time in March 2018.

Immediately after Zinni's return to Washington in August 2017, Saudi Arabia's Al Arabiya television channel launched an animated video purporting to show the shooting down of a Qatar Airways commercial airliner by an unidentified fighter jet, which was presumably Saudi because Al Arabiya is a Saudi television network.

In a tweet referencing the video and posted on August 14, 2017, Al Arabiya English (@AlArabiya_Eng), said: VIDEO: Understanding why the ban on #QatarAirways exists https://t.co/mrhRhlApWT pic. twitter.com/DFuMu0Hew8[153]

According to the video, the blockading countries would have two options in the event that Qatar enters their airspace. The first would be to dispatch a fighter plane to force the commercial [Qatar Airways] aircraft to land. "After which, its members may be prosecuted for several crimes, such as breaching national security and exposing civilians to danger," the video said, depicting a plane with Qatar Airways' logo on it as an example. The second option would be to "bring down any plane entering its atmosphere which is identified as an enemy target, especially in military bases, where Air Defense is unrestrained," the video added.[154]

The Al Arabiya video, which was not only meant as an outright rejection of Zinni's mediation efforts, was also a redline for Washington as it instead crystalized the urgency of Trump's quest to accelerate the GCC reconciliation process.[155]

Immediately after the Al Arabiya video, Saudi Arabia continued to pressure Qatar when it introduced Abdullah Bin Ali Al Thani, the son of deposed Qatari Amir Ali Bin Abdullah Al Thani, to represent Qatar on issues pertaining to the hajj.

KUWAITI MEDIATION

Between June 5 and July 21, 2017, Qatar had engaged with Kuwait 23 times. During that period, Saudi Arabia, the UAE, and Bahrain had engaged with Kuwait 13, 7, and 5 times, respectively.

The Amir of Qatar, along with his foreign minister, met with the Kuwaiti Amir six times. King Salman met with the Kuwaiti Amir twice. MBZ met with the Kuwaiti Amir only once.

Between June 5 and July 21, 2017, Qatar engaged with Kuwait on average twice a month through official meetings, but that does not include the dozens of phone calls which the Qatari Amir and his foreign and defense ministers made to their Kuwaiti counterparts.

AMIR TAMIM'S ADDRESS BEFORE THE NATION

On July 21, 2017, two days after the Quartet revised its demands to the 6 Principles, Amir Tamim delivered his first address to the nation since the crisis had erupted.

The Amir emphasized that the unprecedented smear campaign in the media, which was filled with innuendo and fake news, had targeted Qatar. He added that he valued Kuwait's mediation and the support of the United States, Turkey, and Germany for their efforts to resolve the crisis. With the full support of his people, the Amir delivered this speech, which became a turning point in the Gulf dispute.

The Amir declared:

All those who live in this country have become spokespersons for Qatar. Here I would like to recognize, with great pride, the high moral standard exercised by this people despite the campaign of incitement as well as the siege. They combined the solidity of stance and magnanimity of behavior that has always characterized the Qatari people. They have amazed the world by maintaining a high level of tenacity in tackling the situation, despite the unprecedented incitement in tone and language, the honor-related prejudices, and the unparalleled blockade in the relations between our countries.

This was tantamount to a true moral test where our society has achieved great success, as we have proved that there are basic principles and norms that we observe even in times of conflict and dispute, because we respect ourselves first and foremost. I call upon all to continue this approach, and not slip into what is inappropriate for us, nor for our principles and our values. The sons and daughters of this country have realized, with common sense and political awareness, the seriousness of this campaign against their homeland, and the goals of the siege imposed on it.[156]

The Amir's measured response may have influenced the Qatari people to close rank behind their ruler.

His speech also set the stage for Qatar's diplomatic engagement with the Quartet. The Amir articulated that Doha was open for dialogue with the blockading countries but that it would not compromise its sovereignty. Qatar would "fight terrorism relentlessly without compromise" and reform its economy and public policy, he added.

The Amir's commitment to noninterference in other Arab states' internal affairs was arguably an olive branch to the Quartet as he sought to dispel allegations of meddling in their affairs, which was a major part of the anti-Qatar narratives pushed by the blockading states. The Amir said, "Qatar does not try to impose its opinion on anyone."[157]

Similarly, it can be argued that the Amir's acknowledgement of Qatar's past "mistakes" could be interpreted as another olive branch to the Quartet as he alluded to Doha's fallout with its neighbors and Egypt in particular over its initial post–Arab Spring foreign policy.

The past "mistakes" acknowledgement may have been an effort to deliver the Quartet a tangible concession, which potentially could serve as a baseline for future negotiations via Kuwaiti mediators.

However, the UAE responded to the Qatari leader's speech by waging an attempted cyberattack against the Al Jazeera Media Network's website and digital platforms.

KUWAITI MEDIATION—AGAIN

The Al Arabiya flight simulation followed by the introduction of Abdullah Bin Ali Al Thani had a decisive impact on Washington's approach towards the crisis, leaving Trump with little choice but to once again step up his personal involvement as part of an effort to resolve the standoff.

As part of that effort, Trump hosted the Kuwaiti Amir at the White House on September 6, 2017, where he publicly and unequivocally reiterated Washington's support for GCC reconciliation through Kuwaiti mediation.

Standing next to Trump, Kuwait's head of state said, "We met in Riyadh, in the presence of President Trump, and there was no one to say that there was a dispute between us. But suddenly, this dispute came into existence. Thank God, now, what is important is that we have stopped any military action."[158]

The Amir's reference to the Saudi and Emirati military threats against Qatar was the first public acknowledgement by a world leader about the military threat against Doha, which up until that point, was widely considered to be a rumor only.

It is, of course, unclear whether the Amir was familiar with the exact details about how Trump had personally rejected the Saudi request to invade Qatar on 6 June 2017.

Following the Trump-Sabah meeting, the President consistently called for an end to the dispute while at the same time praising the steadily improving state of US–Qatar relations.

Two days after the Trump–Sabah meeting, Trump brokered a telephone call between Amir Tamim and MbS. The détente generated by the Trump-initiated phone call between Qatar and Saudi Arabia lasted for about an hour before it collapsed over the interpretation of a Qatari statement and how to proceed with a reconciliation process.

Only a few days before the call, however, the Quartet, particularly Saudi Arabia, actively sought to topple the government of Qatar. The Trump-mediated phone call failed to bring the parties together apparently because the UAE saw itself as skipped over in the resolution that had been formed, so Abu Dhabi concluded that it needed a face-saving gesture.

On September 19, 2017, Amir Tamim addressed the United Nations General Assembly (UNGA) in New York. Before the entire international community, he reiterated his call for a peaceful resolution of the Gulf crisis. Qatar's leader also praised Kuwaiti mediation efforts.

Additionally, the Amir criticized Qatar's public relations war. He said:

> Despite the disclosure of the hacking and falsification of quotes of the Amir of a sovereign State, the blockading countries did not back down or apologize for lying, but rather intensified their campaign, in the hope that the blockade would cause a cumulative effect on the economy and the society of my country, after it failed to bring about any direct impact. The perpetrators of the hacking and the falsification of the quotes have committed an assault against a sovereign State. The crime was deliberately committed for political aims, and was followed by a list of political dictations which contravene sovereignty, and caused worldwide astonishment. This disgraceful act has once again raised international queries about digital security and the unruliness in cybercrime and electronic piracy.[159]

A day after delivering his UNGA address, the Amir met with Trump in New York. The meeting came about after Saudi Arabia had threatened to bring Abdullah Bin Ali Al Thani, who the Quartet and Riyadh in particular were actively promoting through state media outlets as an alternate Amir for Qatar, to the UNGA to join MbS. But MbS had not left Saudi Arabia at that point as he had not yet fully consolidated his power domestically and was widely considered unable to travel.

Washington, however, rejected Riyadh's proposal to have Abdullah Bin Ali Al Thani represent Qatar during the UNGA.

In the end, Saudi Foreign Minister Jubair represented Riyadh at the UNGA, but the Trump–Tamim meeting also signaled to the Quartet that Washington would not tolerate any efforts to threaten regime change in Qatar.

During the Trump–Tamim meeting, the parties discussed the President's proposal for a US–GCC Summit at Camp David in Maryland. The initial concept for the proposed US–GCC Summit was that its agenda would be follow-on to the US–Arab Summit held in Riyadh in 2017 where Trump convened the Arab-Islamic Summit. Within this context, the proposed Summit could have focused on regional issues such as stabilizing operations in post-ISIS Iraq, Iran, and Libya.

GCC MILITARY DRILLS AND US SHUTTLE DIPLOMACY

In parallel with Washington and Kuwait City's efforts to solve the crisis diplomatically, the Quartet has attempted to isolate Qatar from various military exercises, but Washington rejected these measures as part of an effort to signal support for Doha while at the same time strengthening the US–Qatar bilateral relationship.

As Washington was pushing ahead with its agenda to normalize relations between the Quartet and Doha, Mattis made an unannounced visit to the Qatari capital on September 28, 2017. While in Doha, the then-Pentagon chief met with Amir Tamim and his Qatari counterpart, Al Attiyah, at AUAB.

Following Mattis's visit, the US military halted some exercises with its Gulf partners over the ongoing diplomatic crisis, including a US–UAE exercise titled "Iron Union 5." [160]

On October 19, 2017, Tillerson returned from his second round of shuttle diplomacy in the Gulf. This time Washington's top diplomat began in Riyadh before traveling to Doha. Prior to his departure, Tillerson criticized the Quartet for being unwilling to engage with Qatar, and he held the anti-Qatar bloc responsible for prolonging the dispute.[161] Officials in Riyadh disapproved of his interview with *Bloomberg News*. In fact, MbS snubbed the top US diplomat during his visit because Tillerson had made such calls for Quartet–Qatar dialogue.[162]

Washington's decision to cancel the joint exercises came after the blockading states failed to respond to Tillerson's diplomatic initiatives and Trump's, which pushed for a negotiated political solution to the GCC crisis.

By scaling back on the military exercises with its Gulf partners, Washington signaled that it is willing and able to deliver tangible pressure on the various parties to bring about an end to the standoff. Mattis also warned Saudi Arabia and the UAE that if they continued to escalate military tensions against Qatar, Washington would significantly reduce US intelligence and military cooperation on Yemen, which would be considered an incremental escalation by Washington and could run in parallel with the suspension of future exercises.

Washington's message was clear, and such clarity enabled Qatar to participate in the US–GCC multilateral Gulf Shield exercise, which took place from March 21 to April 16, 2018, in the eastern Saudi city of Ras Al Khair, north of Jubail.

A number of officers from the Qatari Armed Forces, led by Brigadier General Khamis Mohamed Deblan, participated in the exercise, along with land, sea, and air forces from 25 other countries. The exercise featured a number of stages, including a command center drill and field training. It concluded with the implementation of the exercise of regular and non-regular fire with live ammunition, in addition to a military parade.[163]

GULF COOPERATION COUNCIL SUMMIT IN KUWAIT

On the eve of the 2017 GCC Summit in Kuwait, which took place on December 5, it was far from certain who among the respective monarchs would attend as only Amir Tamim had confirmed his attendance. There were speculations, until the last moment, that Amir Sabah would not have pushed ahead with the summit without tacit approval from King Salman of Saudi Arabia, who was expected to arrive. At the time, MbS could still not travel abroad because of the Kingdom's precarious domestic stability.

While Bahrain's King Hamad Bin Isa Al Khalifa had declared in October that he would not attend the summit if Qatar was invited, his son, Crown Prince Salman, was believed to be attending the summit in his father's place. During his visit to Washington on November 30, the Trump administration had asked the Bahraini Crown Prince to participate at the GCC Summit.[164] It is unclear, however, whether he had responded to the US request in the affirmative or provided an evasive answer. Ultimately, he did not attend.

Regarding the UAE, it was unclear who would eventually attend as a consensus in Washington had emerged in early September, after the Tamim–MbS call, that MbZ was the driving force behind the crisis. It was therefore unlikely that MbZ would attend, but the ruler of Dubai, Mohammed bin Rashid Al Maktoum (MbR), was expected to represent the UAE.

From Oman, Deputy Prime Minister Sayyid Fahd bin Mahmoud Al Said would represent the Sultanate at the GCC Summit in Kuwait.

Going into the summit, it was clear that its success would hinge on the Saudi King's participation as neither Bahrain nor the UAE would hesitate to snub the Summit by sending lower-ranking officials instead. During the planning stage, it was also unclear whether the foreign ministers from the six GCC countries would arrive to prepare the Summit's agenda. At the end, Bahrain, the UAE, and Saudi Arabia all snubbed the gathering by dispatching lower-ranking officials.[165]

What was not publicly understood before the Summit, however, was that the GCC crisis itself was never on the agenda. From the Quartet's perspective, Kuwait was only able to secure the Summit on the condition that the crisis was not on the agenda, which was how the Kuwaiti hosts managed to convene it in the first place.

Top-ranking officials of the blockading states decided at the very last minute not to attend the Kuwait Summit. Concern that Amir Sheikh Tamim would use a public forum, which likely would have been covered live on GCC state television during the Summit, for grandstanding purposes against his fellow monarchs spurred their decisions to not attend.

This fear seemed, at best, hypocritical given how furiously the Quartet's state-run media outlets had attacked Qatar, Amir Tamim, and other members of the Qatari royal family throughout the crisis. Additionally, the hatred witnessed on social media through Saudi and Emirati twitter surrogates in particular also underscored the amount of viciousness in the Gulf that the GCC crisis quickly fueled.

Kuwait's Amir sought nonetheless to address the concerns by assuring the monarchs of Bahrain, the UAE, and Saudi Arabia that Amir Tamim would not use the occasion for a public pronouncement on the crisis. Yet those assurances were not enough to convince the three countries to send the highest-ranking officials among their leaderships.

It is unclear whether the discussions of what Amir Tamim would say during a public forum (or whether he would issue an official apology, as had been suggested by Saudi state media) led to the collapse of the talks among GCC foreign ministers the day prior to the 2017 GCC Summit. Uncertainty over what to expect from Amir Tamim, coupled with renewed demands that Doha sever diplomatic relations with Iran in exchange for resolving the crisis, could help explain why Qatar's Foreign Minister Al Thani chose not to attend a pre-scheduled luncheon with his Saudi and Omani counterparts and instead returned to Doha to brief Amir Tamim on the talks.

Another sticking point was that the Bahrain, Saudi Arabia, and the UAE insisted at the time that Egypt belong to the reconciliation process, even if it is not a GCC member. Washington, however, swiftly rejected this proposal, urging the Gulf nations themselves to resolve the standoff.

US–QATAR STRATEGIC DIALOGUE

During the immediate aftermath of the 2017 GCC Summit, Washington and Doha began preparations for the first US–Qatar Strategic Dialogue, scheduled to take place on January 30 in Washington. The US–Qatar Strategic Dialogue, built on the US–Qatar Economic Dialogue, launched in 2016.

Prior to the crisis, Doha had sought to expand the Economic Dialogue and had requested a bilateral Strategic Dialogue months before the Gulf standoff. But in light of the crisis coupled with the Quartet's unwillingness to solve the matter, Washington sought to frame the Strategic Dialogue as part of an effort to signal its commitment to the US–Qatar strategic partnership and strengthen the bilateral relationship in the process.

US Secretaries Tillerson and Mattis co-chaired the opening session jointly with Qatari Minister of State for Defense Al Attiyah and Foreign Minister Al Thani.

During the Dialogue, the two countries signed the following four MoUs:

- To Enhance Political Cooperation
- Defense
- Counterterrorism
- Trade and Investment

While the MoU on Political Cooperation was formally meant to signal US support for Qatar's sovereignty to the blockading countries, it also demonstrated how bilateral relations had strengthened throughout the crisis. Notably, relations between Amir Tamim and President Trump strengthened too. For instance, between July 2017 and the Strategic Dialogue, President Trump and Amir Tamim held three phone calls that all focused on GCC reconciliation and appreciation for Qatar's counterterrorism policies.

On July 2, 2017, President Trump spoke separately to King Salman, MbZ, and Amir Tamim. Trump called for a resolution to the crisis.[166] On September 8, 2017, Trump spoke separately to the same three leaders again, emphasizing the need for GCC unity.[167] On January 15, 2018, President Trump called Amir Tamim and reiterated his call for unity among Washington's Arab Gulf partners. He also "thanked the Emir for Qatari action to counter terrorism and extremism in all forms."[168]

The US–Qatar Defense Cooperation MoU once again reiterated Washington's support for Doha's sovereignty, while praising Qatar for expanding the AUAB. "Qatari funding of capital expenditures and sustainment offers the possibility of an enduring presence, as with US facilities in Europe and the Pacific. The two governments acknowledged the strong and lasting bilateral security partnership, and look forward to further discussions on the possibility of permanent basing," the US State Department said.

Washington's pronounced support for the US military presence at AUAB was directly attributed to efforts by the UAE, its US surrogates and its various UAE-funded pressure groups in Washington to wrest AUAB away from Qatar during the peak of the Gulf crisis and its proxy war in Washington.

The joint MoU on Counter Terrorism announced during the Dialogue sought to reconfirm the commitments from both countries as outlined in the initial MoU on Counter Terrorism signed in July of 2017.

Finally, the MoU on Trade and Investment builds on the initial US–Qatar Economic Dialogue of 2016 but includes updates on Qatari investments in the US, including from the Qatar Investment Authority's previously committed investment of $45 billion in American firms, real estate, and jobs.

Then-US Secretary of Energy James R. Perry and US Secretary of Commerce Wilbur L. Ross Jr. co-chaired the Trade and Investment session. The sessions included Qatar's Minister of Energy and Industry Mohammed Al Sada and Qatar's Minister of Economy and Commerce Ahmed Bin Jassim Al Thani, respectively. The Dialogue's closing ceremony was co-chaired by US Secretary of Treasury Steven T. Mnuchin and Qatari Minister of Finance Ali Sharif Al Emadi.[169]

During the planning process of the Dialogue, Mnuchin and Perry traveled to Doha. Between Tillerson and Mattis's repeated engagements, including to Qatar, more US cabinet secretaries traveled to Doha during the second half of 2017 than during any six-month span of time in the past.

The Dialogue not only presented Doha with a diplomatic victory, as it effectively demonstrated that the accusations leveled against it were false and politically motivated, but more broadly signaled that Washington saw reconciliation between Qatar and the Quartet as key to stability in the Gulf, itself a key national security interest of the United States and major powers worldwide. The US–Qatar Strategic Dialogue has since become an annual event, rotating between Washington and Doha.

US–GULF DIPLOMACY

On February 28, 2018, a month after the inaugural dialogue, President Trump and Amir Tamim discussed regional developments, including how to solve the crisis and dealing with Iran.[170] At that point, the planning began for Amir Tamim's upcoming White House visit and his second meeting with Trump.

On March 20, 2018, Trump hosted MbS at the White House. During his joint press conference with Trump, MbS did not discuss reconciliation in the Gulf.

In conjunction with MbS's visit to Washington, the UAE's National Security Advisor Tahnoun Bin Mohammed Al Nahyan came to Washington too. His purpose was to establish a UAE/Saudi/US-Trilateral Summit as part of an apparent counterweight to the US–Qatar Strategic Dialogue that took place on January 30, 2018.[171] Ultimately, the Trump administration rejected the proposed trilateral strategic dialogue. Yet MbS, Tahnoun, and the White House discussed the Yemeni civil war instead.

On April 11, 2018, President Trump hosted the Amir Tamim at the White House where he praised the Qatari leader and announced that the US–Qatar relationship "works extremely well."[172]

Less than a month after the Amir's White House talks, the UAE's Tahnoon approached Bannon to convey to Kushner that MbS was willing to meet with Amir Tamim without preconditions in Riyadh. Under the proposal, Kushner would guarantee the Amir's safety, but the White House outright rejected the proposal. It is also unclear whether the White House even passed the proposal on to Qatar because officials in Doha would have likely rejected it as well. The UAE likely picked Bannon as a messenger because of his business interests, which he had developed in the UAE after leaving the White House.[173] Another factor for Bannon's selection was his initial role in encouraging Trump's tweet against Qatar in the very early stage of the blockade and for having accepted the Saudi/UAE proposal to siege Qatar. Tahnoon's proposal to Bannon was presented ahead of UAE Foreign Minister Abdullah bin Zayed Al Nahyan's (AbZ) visit to Washington on May 14, 2018.[174]

The UAE proposal, which centered on establishing a UAE/Saudi/US Trilateral Strategic Dialogue, arguably sought to disrupt the steadily improving US–Qatar relationship while Abu Dhabi's standing in Washington was slowly diminishing over its refusal to engage Doha.

The Trump administration had initially planned to host MbS, MbZ, and Amir Tamim in individual back-to-back meetings as part of an effort to settle their differences before convening a US–GCC Summit at Camp David right before the Ramadan of 2018, which was in May that year.[175]

On May 1, 2018, the UAE's Minister of State for Foreign Affairs Anwar Gargash tweeted,

> A sincere advice for Qatar to end its crisis: there will not be any non-Gulf mediation. No pressure will work. The media will not change your situation. You'd better get wise for your

crisis will continue. From now on, manage your affairs wisely and negotiate within the framework of your neighbor demands [13 principles], as they represent real grievances.[176]

MbZ never ended up visiting the White House. Instead, he paid Russian President Vladimir Putin an official visit on June 1, 2018. The Crown Prince of Abu Dhabi's visit to Putin was likely part of a geopolitical effort to balance Abu Dhabi's relationship with Washington with a strengthened partnership between the UAE and Moscow after Trump had withdrawn the Emirati leader's White House invitation. In Moscow, MbZ and Putin signed Declaration on Strategic Partnership Agreement, which stipulated that the two countries would coordinate on policy pertaining to the global aluminum market.[177] The following month, MbZ hosted Chinese President Xi Jinping, also part of Abu Dhabi's grander foreign policy objective of making the UAE more independent from its traditional Western partners, the United States and the United Kingdom.[178]

Washington's efforts to accelerate Gulf reconciliation were tied to the fact that its ambassadorships to Abu Dhabi, Doha, and Riyadh had, until recently, been empty. In August 2017, Trump nominated businessman David Urban as US ambassador to Saudi Arabia, but his nomination was dropped, and former USCENTCOM Commander General John P. Abizaid was confirmed by the US Senate to serve this role on March 6, 2019. In May 2018, Trump nominated businessman John Rakolta as his ambassador to Abu Dhabi, which was confirmed by the US Senate in September 2019,.[179] For Qatar, Trump initially nominated Molly Phee, a US career State Department official, but her nomination was withdrawn and replaced by former US Congressman Scott Taylor (Republican of Virginia). As of writing, the US Senate has not confirmed Taylor.

In November 2017, career diplomat Justin Siberell was sworn in as Washington's ambassador to Bahrain. He served previously as Acting Coordinator for Counterterrorism at the US Department of State and was in that capacity responsible for overseeing the launch of Counter Terrorism Center during the 2017 Riyadh Summit.

Career diplomat Lawrence R. Silverman has served as US ambassador to Kuwait since 2016. Leslie Tsou assumed her duties as US ambassador to Oman in January 2020, replacing fellow career diplomat Marc J. Sievers, who was Washington's ambassador to Muscat from 2016 to 2020.

Washington has also unsuccessfully attempted to mediate between Saudi Arabia and Qatar regarding the Hajj pilgrimage. The US wants to ensure that the pilgrimage to Mecca does not become a politicized issue. No Qatari citizen was granted permission to perform Hajj from 2017 through 2019, which highlighted the extent to which this pillar of the Islamic faith became an issue of contention in relations between the two Arab Gulf neighbors.

QATAR FILES COMPLAINTS AGAINST UAE AND BAHRAIN

In anticipation of the US–Qatar Strategic Dialogue, which took place in Washington on 30 January 2018, Saudi Arabia and UAE began to pressure Bahrain to reopen its territorial dispute claims with Qatar despite the manner being resolved in 2003.

With that objective in mind, on January 8, 2018, the Bahrain Center for Strategic International and Energy Studies (DERASAT) hosted an event focusing on Qatar's "subversive role" as a destabilizing actor in the Middle East.[180] On June 30, 2018, DERASAT hosted a separate event titled "Al Khalifa Rule in the Qatar Peninsula:

History and Sovereignty," which focused again on reopening Bahrain's historic territorial dispute with Qatar.[181]

Following the US invasion of Iraq in 2003 and after the regime of Saddam Hussein had collapsed, Qatar and Bahrain negotiated a settlement to the two states' longstanding territorial dispute. The diplomatic breakthrough was partially attributed to the fall of Saddam Hussein's regime as he had supported Qatar against the foreign-orchestrated coup d'état attempt against Qatar's leader in 1996. In turn, Qatar mediated between Baghdad and Kuwait after the Gulf crisis of 1990/1991, and in 1999 Doha advocated removing sanctions on Baghdad, a position which Kuwait and Saudi Arabia opposed.[182]

In conjunction with Bahrain's quest to reopen its territorial dispute with Qatar, military tensions between UAE, Bahrain, and Qatar rose on January 14, 2018.

Doha responded on March 11, 2018, by filing a complaint with the UNSC and UN Secretary-General António Guterres about Bahrain and the UAE's three alleged violations of Qatar's airspace.

The complaint stated:

A UAE military transport aircraft violated the airspace of Qatar on January 14 2018. Another UAE C-130 military transport aircraft violated Qatari airspace on February 25. On February 28, a Bahraini military aircraft flew into the exclusive economic zone of the State of Qatar.

The complaint added that the Bahraini aircraft had entered Qatar's exclusive economic zone without prior diplomatic authorization from the concerned authorities in Qatar. "An immediate flight order was issued for a warning aircraft cabin, prompting the Bahraini aircraft to leave the country's exclusive economic zone," it concluded.

Qatar also informed the UNSC and the Secretary-General that on January 19, 2018, an Emirati naval ship had kidnapped a Qatari fishing boat carrying eight people. The Emiratis purportedly forced the fishermen (all Indian nationals) at gunpoint to enter the UAE's economic zone.[183]

The UAE, however, framed the aviation incidents differently. Through "fake news," the Emiratis accused Qatar of having intercepted two of the UAE's civilian planes over Bahrain on January 15, 2018.[184] The other two military incidents, according to Emirati officials, on January 3 and 12, 2018, involved a UAE Twin Otter aircraft and a C-130 cargo plane.[185]

Qatar also filed a separate complaint with the UN's International Civil Aviation Organization (ICAO) to force Saudi Arabia, the UAE, and Bahrain to reopen their respective airspaces, but the blockading countries deemed the ICAO as too incompetent to rule on the matter.[186] The ICAO, however, rejected this allegation about lacking competency.[187]

3

UAE-Israel

DUBAI PORTS WORLD CONTROVERSY AND
UAE–ISRAEL RELATIONSHIP IN CONTEXT

Despite Dubai's remarkable success in transforming itself into a sprawling global financial hub, the UAE faced a significant diplomatic crisis in 2006.

In 2005, the UAE's state-owned DP World (formally known as Dubai Ports World) acquired the Peninsular & Oriental (P&O) Steam Navigation Company, a British company. Under the agreement, DP World acquired the right to operate in six major US ports, including terminals in the New York / New Jersey area, Philadelphia, and New Orleans.

In Washington there was fierce Congressional opposition. Several lawmakers argued that a foreign-owned company could undermine US national security. These American politicians also pointed out that 2 of the 19 hijackers on September 11, 2001, were Emirati citizens and that they had drawn funds from Dubai banks just before they committed their acts of terrorism on US soil.[188]

The opposition in the Democrat-controlled US House of Representatives was spearheaded by then-Representative Rahm Emanuel (D-Illinois). He sought to challenge the George W. Bush administration on national security grounds. The House leaders signaled that they would block the commercial agreement, citing national security concerns. Consequently, the UAE withdrew its bid.

This Congressional opposition took Abu Dhabi by surprise and led to a UAE-led public relations campaign to convince policymakers inside the Beltway that the UAE needed to be understood not only as a reliable US partner but also an Arab state that shared most of Washington's strategic interests, including those related to Israel.

The DP World controversy triggered Emirati fears of losing both access to US military hardware as well as participation in joint intelligence sharing, especially on issues pertaining to Iran. Abu Dhabi also worried that US investments could be hampered and that the scandal could impact the UAE's ties with the country that possesses the world's strongest military might and largest economy.

To protect the UAE from tumultuous partisan politics in Washington, Abu Dhabi sought to overcome the DP World controversy by strengthening its relationship with Israel and subsequently its US supporters. Thus, although official bilateral relations date back to 1971 and the United States has had a permanent ambassador in residence in Abu Dhabi since 1974, it was in the 2000s when Emirati officials began to push for a major strengthening of bilateral ties.[189] The Emirati efforts were aimed at convincing US lawmakers on both sides of the partisan divide and foreign policy elite that the UAE was a "moderate" Arab/Muslim country and an indispensable ally of Western powers with a unique role to play on the forefront of countering violent extremism in the Islamic world.

With the strategic objective of protecting itself from tumultuous US partisan politics, Abu Dhabi sought to overcome the DP World controversy by strengthening its relationship with Israel and subsequently its supporters in Washington. Indirect diplomatic relations between Israel and the UAE, however, had been established in the 1990s.

With this objective in mind, Ambassador Al Otaiba had his first meeting with an Israeli official in Washington in 2008. He met Major General Amos Gilead, then-director of the Political-Military Affairs Bureau at Israel's Ministry of Defense. Gilead had been dispatched to Washington for discussions on Iran within the framework of strategic dialogue between the UAE and Israel on a bilateral basis.

Following the initial Gilead–Otaiba meeting, the two countries established a formal diplomatic channel via Israel's Ministry of Defense and its Emirati counterpart. This channel's sole focus was for the Emiratis and Israelis to coordinate Iran policies. As part of that effort, senior officials from the UAE and Israel convened in Europe throughout 2008 and 2009 to discuss the Iranian threat.

In addition to the Defense Ministry channel, the second stage of Emirati–Israeli cooperation established commercial links, including an Israeli trade office in Dubai. While the trade office had officially been established in 2006—but after the DP World controversy—it was first inaugurated in 2008 after the Defense Ministry backchannel had been established by Gilead and Otaiba.

On the commercial side, Israeli companies have exported a host of civilian national security technologies, as well as water and irrigation technologies, to the UAE primarily through straw companies established in Europe.[190] Israelis are also involved in Dubai's diamond market, among other industries, and have invested in real estate using their second passports. Because most commerce between Israel and UAE (and between Israel and the other GCC states) goes through straw companies in third countries, no Israeli trade statistics exist on the matter.

But with the Defense Ministry channel strengthening confidence, cooperation between the UAE and Israel extended beyond coordinating Iran policy. The bilateral relationship slowly but gradually became strategic in nature.

Subsequently, the UAE and Israel established a forum for crisis communications, which included intelligence cooperation on "senior threats." Whether Israel's formal lines of crisis communications included a direct military hotline between its Defense Ministry and the UAE's military is unclear.

The bilateral relationship transcended into establishing political links.

For instance, during Israel's February 2009 election, several candidates for prime minister, including Benjamin Netanyahu of the Likud Party, Tzipi Livni of the Kadima Party, and Isaac Hertzog of the Labor Party, traveled to Europe to meet with senior Emirati officials, including Tahnoon Bin Zayed Al Nahyan, the head of UAE's intelligence.

The third stage of the Israeli–Emirati relationship entailed the Emirati and Israeli embassies in Washington beginning to coordinate on policies, including on sensitive regional issues.

Israeli and Emirati coordination in Washington first became evident after Barack Obama's inauguration in January 2009. Shortly after Netanyahu's election to Prime Minister the following month, Israel's then-ambassador to Washington, Michael Oren, found much common cause with Otaiba. In fact, the two ambassadors met at the White House where they presented a unified position on Iran.

Obama had, after all, promised throughout his campaign to engage Tehran, which had unnerved Netanyahu in particular.

After the Israeli–Emirati tracks had been firmly established, including in Washington, Abu Dhabi began its respective engagement with America's pro-Israel community to put the DP World controversy to rest before it would further impact strategic cooperation with the United States in a negative way.

86

Abu Dhabi also sought to telegraph aspects of its nascent diplomatic relationship with Israel to the broader public, and to the US foreign policy establishment in particular, by requesting US political and diplomatic support for its bid to permanently host the United Nations' International Renewable Energy Agency (IRENA). To secure approval from elites in Washington, Abu Dhabi turned to America's pro-Israel community. Partially to ensure that no Congressional opposition would take hold (as it did amid the DP World controversy), Abu Dhabi stressed that by hosting IRENA, "all" UN members (a reference to Israel) would be welcomed to fully participate.

Thus, with Israel's support, American Jewish groups vigorously supported the initiative while championing quiet diplomatic efforts to ensure Israeli business and professional organizations access to international conferences and conventions in the Emirates.

Ever since IRENA was established in Abu Dhabi in 2009, Israeli diplomatic representatives and ministers have traveled to the Emirati capital for meetings pertaining to the UN agency. Israeli officials have also used the venue to hold side meetings with their Emirati counterparts. The IRENA file is only one out of several diplomatic channels between Jerusalem and Abu Dhabi.[191]

The UAE was also able to receive nuclear know-how, materials, and equipment from the US for its own civilian nuclear program without facing any Congressional opposition. Significant is that this was only three years after the DP World controversy, underscoring how successful Abu Dhabi's public relations were proving.

Under the so-called 123 Agreement for Peaceful Civilian Nuclear Energy Cooperation in 2009, the UAE committed itself to forgoing domestic uranium enrichment and the reprocessing of spent fuel.[192]

The UAE also signed the IAEA's Additional Protocol, which institutes a more stringent inspections regime on its nuclear activities. The

UAE's agreement to forgo enrichment and reprocessing has become known as the nonproliferation "gold standard" for nuclear cooperation agreements because the signatory renounces the sensitive technology and capabilities that can be used to produce a nuclear weapon.

Prior to signing the 123 Agreement, Emirati officials also reassured the Israeli defense establishment, via its Defense Ministry channel, that their civilian nuclear program would fully comply with the IAEA and that its program would be fully transparent.

The UAE nuclear power program is a joint venture between the UAE's state-owned Emirates Nuclear Energy Corporation and Korea Electric Power Corporation.[193]

With congressional support, a 2009 US–UAE bilateral agreement for peaceful nuclear cooperation did not meet any objection from influential pro-Israel organizations, such as the American Israel Public Affairs Committee, the American Jewish Committee, and the Anti-Defamation League.

From an Emirati perspective, US diplomatic support for Abu Dhabi's quest to host IRENA along with the US-Emirati 123 Agreement suggested that the bilateral crisis triggered by the DP World controversy was over.

From a US perspective, strengthening ties with Abu Dhabi during the post-9/11 phase was a strategically important move for Washington, especially throughout the immediate aftermath of the US/UK invasion of Iraq in March 2003.

THE MAHMOUD AL MABHOUH ASSASSINATION IN DUBAI

Mahmoud Al Mabhouh had been a cofounder of the Izz ad-Din Al Qassam Brigades, the military wing of Hamas. Because of his role in the kidnapping and murdering of two Israeli soldiers in 1989, as well as his arms purchases from the Islamic Republic of Iran, Israel wanted him. Israel moved ahead with its plans to assassinate him in Dubai on January 18, 2010. Within a narrow span of several hours that day, 27 Mossad operatives arrived in Dubai. These Israeli agents arrived in the UAE on flights from various European cities. They entered the Gulf country with Australian, British, French, German, and Irish passports.[194]

At the time, the Al Mabhouh assassination received widespread international media attention. But Israel, consistent with its long-standing policy of ambiguity, declined to comment on the episode. Nonetheless, within the UAE, internal political pressure mounted, and Abu Dhabi chose to request the closure of Israel's trade office in Dubai.

The fallout over the assassination, however, was reversed by September 2012 when Netanyahu met with UAE Foreign Minister Abdullah Bin Zayed Al Nahyan (AbZ) during the sidelines of the UNGA in New York. The UAE ambassador to Washington accompanied AbZ to his meeting with Netanyahu. Then-National Security Advisor Yaakov Amidror, along with Netanyahu's military secretary, Major General Johanan Locker, accompanied the Israeli leader as well.[195]

Israel and the UAE, however, do not enjoy formal diplomatic relations as defined through the establishment of an embassy in each other's respective capitals. Neither does the UAE formally recognize Israel.

4

THE WASHINGTON INFLUENCING GAME

PROPOSED CONGRESSIONAL LEGISLATION AGAINST QATAR

On May 26, 2017, the House Foreign Affairs Committee (HFAC) Chairman Ed Royce (R-CA), HFAC Ranking Member Eliot Engel (D-NY), Rep. Josh Gottheimer (D-NJ), and Rep. Brian Mast (R-FL) introduced H.R. 2712, the Palestinian International Terrorism Support Prevention Act. However, the bill never made it to the House Floor for a vote, and no companion legislation was introduced in the Senate. The bill, if enacted, would have imposed sanctions on foreign persons, agencies, and governments that assist Hamas, the Palestinian Islamic Jihad, or its affiliates. The lawmakers cited support for Israel and Hamas acting as an Iranian proxy as rationales for introducing the legislation.

H.R. 2712 mentions Qatar several times. In the findings section, the lawmakers write:

Hamas has received significant financial and military support from Qatar. Qatar has hosted multiple senior Hamas officials, including Hamas leader Khaled Mashal since 2012, who has

91

had regular interviews carried on Al Jazeera, a news organization based in Qatar and which receives some funding from members of the country's ruling family. In March 2014, the Department of the Treasury's Under Secretary for Terrorism and Financial Intelligence confirmed that "Qatar, a longtime US ally has for many years openly financed Hamas."

Per the legislators, the bill requires the president to submit an annual report to Congress for the next three years that identifies foreign persons, agencies, or instrumentalities of a foreign state who knowingly and materially assist Hamas, the Palestinian Islamic Jihad, or an affiliate or successor of one of those organizations. The president must also include a report of any foreign government that provides support for acts of terrorism and material support to any of the aforementioned groups or any government that the President determines to have engaged in any significant transaction to knowingly and materially provide support to these groups.

Once these governments have been identified, the President must:

- suspend US assistance to that government for one year;
- instruct the executive directors of each international finance institution to vote against any loan or technical assistance to that government;
- prohibit the government's transactions in foreign exchanges that are subject to the jurisdiction of the United States; and
- prevent transfers of credits or payments between financial institutions subject to the jurisdiction of the United States.

The President will then impose two or more sanctions to any group identified, including denying:

- export-import guarantees;
- defense support;
- the export of munitions;
- the export of goods or technology controlled for national security reasons; and
- loans more than $10 million or seizure of property held within the United States.

The bill was referred to the House Foreign Affairs Committee and the House Committee on Financial Services. Original cosponsors include:

- Rep Brad Sherman (D-CA)
- Rep. Ted Poe (R-TX)
- Rep. Ileana Ros-Lehtinen (R-FL)
- Rep. Ted Lieu (D-CA)
- Rep. Theodore Deutch (D-FL)
- Rep. Thomas Suozzi (D-NY)

All sponsors include:

- Rep. Adam Kinzinger (R-IL)
- Rep. Paul Cook (R-CA)
- Rep. Matt Gaetz (R-FL)
- Rep. Brad Schneider (D-IL)
- Rep. Randy Weber (R-TX)
- Rep. Thomas Garrett (R-VA)

- Rep. Steven Chabot (R-OH)
- Rep. Debbie Wasserman Schultz (D-FL)
- Rep. Louie Gohmert (R-TX)
- Rep. Patrick Meehan (R-PA)
- Rep. Brian Fitzpatrick (R-PA)
- Rep. Kristi Noem (R-SD)
- Rep. Alcee Hastings (D-FL)
- Rep. Robert Latta (R-OH)
- Rep. Michael McCaul (R-TX)
- Rep. Ron DeSantis (R-FL)
- Rep. Mark Meadows (R-NC)

HOUSE FOREIGN AFFAIRS COMMITTEE MARKUP AND AMENDMENTS

The House Foreign Affairs Committee held a markup hearing of 2712 on November 15, 2017, at which time three amendments to the legislation were approved by a voice vote. Three separate amendments were introduced by Rep. Dan Donovan (R-NY), Rep. Brad Schneider (D-IL), and Rep. Ron DeSantis (R-FL); Reps. Schneider and DeSantis are currently cosponsors of the bill.

The amendment offered by Rep. Donovan impacts the "findings" section of the legislation. The amendment strikes the following text from the document:

(3) Hamas has received significant financial and military support from Qatar. Qatar has hosted multiple senior Hamas officials, including Hamas leader Khaled Mashal since 2012, who has had regular interviews carried on Al Jazeera, a news

organization based in Qatar and which receives some funding from members of the country's ruling family. In March 2014, the Department of the Treasury's Under Secretary for Terrorism and Financial Intelligence confirmed that "Qatar, a longtime US ally has for many years openly financed Hamas."

It inserts the following text to replace the stricken text:

(3) In March 2014, the Department of the Treasury's Under Secretary for Terrorism and Financial Intelligence stated that, "Qatar, a longtime US ally has for many years openly financed Hamas." Qatar had hosted multiple senior Hamas officials, including Hamas leader Khaled Mashal who, prior to being replaced by Gaza-based Ismail Haniyeh, had regular interviews carried on Al Jazeera. In early 2016, it was reported that senior Hamas terrorist Saleh Al Arouri, who was named Hamas' deputy leader in October 2017 and was the reported mastermind of the kidnapping and murder of three Israeli teens in June 2014, moved to Qatar after leaving Turkey. In June 2017, it was reported that the Qatari government expelled Arouri, and Hamas terrorist Musa Dudin, who was also resident in Qatar until that point.

The amendment removes the assertion that Al Jazeera receives funding from members of Qatar's ruling family from the first section and leaves the remaining information intact. The amendment further adds that Saleh Al Arouri at one time held residency in Qatar, but in June 2016 it was reported that Arouri was expelled from Doha, along with Musa Dudin.

The amendment offered by Rep. Donovan also impacts the "report" section of the legislation, where the president is to submit an annual report to Congress for the next three years that identifies foreign persons, agencies, or instrumentalities of a foreign state who knowingly and materially assist Hamas, the Palestinian Islamic Jihad, or an affiliate or successor of one of those organizations.

In addition to a list of foreign persons, agencies, and states that knowingly and materially assist Hamas, the following clause be added:

> (ii) if a member state of the Gulf Cooperation Council, including Qatar, is not on the list required by clause (i), an assessment of whether Hamas maintains significant portions of its financial networks, including financiers, in those countries;

If any member of the Gulf Cooperation Council is not on the list of foreign persons, agencies, and states in the report that the president submits to Congress, there is to be an assessment of whether Hamas maintains any financial networks or financiers within any of the GCC countries.

The report from the president to Congress must include the following:

> (F) an assessment on the status of the implementation of the US-Qatar Counterterrorism Memorandum of Understanding signed in Doha on July 11, 2017, and any other memorandum of understanding that resulted from the Riyadh Declaration agreed to by the United States and other Gulf Cooperation Council governments in May 2017, including—
>> (i) the extent to which all countries in the Gulf Cooperation Council, including Qatar, participate in initiatives of the Terrorist Financing Targeting Center; and
>> (ii) the extent to which the Terrorist Financing Targeting Center has been utilized to address financial support for

Hamas, the Palestinian Islamic Jihad, or any affiliate or successor thereof, coming from the foreign countries listed under subparagraph (A) or (C).

The amendment offered by Rep. Brad Schneider only impacts the "findings" section of the legislation. The amendment adds the following text to the findings section of the document:

(3) Hamas has created an extensive underground tunnel network, which is used not only to smuggle weapons, money, and supplies into Gaza, but also as rocket launching sites, weapons caches, bunkers, and to conduct terrorist attacks.
(11) The Palestinian Islamic Jihad, as a means to conduct terrorist attacks, has dug underground tunnels from Gaza that run near to and penetrate Israel.

The amendment offered by Rep. Ron DeSantis impacts the "imposition of sanctions" section of the legislation. However, the amendment only adds additional information to be included in the president's report to Congress. The amendment adds:

(5) Additional Determination to be Included in Report—
(A) In General—For each agency or instrumentally of a foreign state that is identified in a report under paragraph (1)—

(i) the Secretary of State shall include in the report a determination as to whether or not the government of the foreign state, on or after the date of the enactment of this Act, acting through such agency or instrumentality has repeatedly provided support for acts of international terrorism pursuant to section 6(j) of the Export Administration Act of 1979 (as continued in effect pursuant to the

International Emergency Economic Powers Act), section 40 of the Arms Export Control Act, section 620A of the Foreign Assistance Act of 1961, or any other provision of law; and

(ii) if the determination of the Secretary of State under subparagraph (A) is that the government of the foreign state has not repeatedly provided support for such acts of international terrorism, the Secretary of State shall include in the report a justification for such determination.

(B) Form—Each determination required under subparagraph (A) shall be submitted in unclassified form, but may contain a classified annex.

The Secretary of State shall include a determination of whether or not the foreign state has repeatedly provided support for acts of international terrorism in the report and provide justification for that determination.

The inclusion of Qatar in this legislation was deliberately made to misrepresent Qatar to the US Congress. At the time of its introduction, it was evident that the representatives were not fully aware of the many avenues Qatar was pursuing, many in conjunction with Israel, to eliminate terrorism financing within its borders and create a safer and more secure Middle East. In particular, as it pertains to this legislation, there was an acute lack of understanding of the role Qatar plays in monitoring Hamas, in working to moderate its policies, and in pushing for Middle East peace.

Immediately after the legislation was introduced, the bill's sponsor, Rep. Royce, repeatedly declined to meet with Qatari officials to discuss the proposed legislation. Qatari diplomats were only able to present their case to Royce and his staff after the Central

Intelligence Agency (CIA), along with the State Department, had contacted then-Speaker Paul Ryan (R-WI) to address the bill's severe implications for America's national security interests.

IMPLICATIONS

If signed into law, Qatar would be exposed to substantial risk. The bill does not explicitly define "assist," so it is possible that simply harboring Hamas figures or funding Palestinian initiatives that "knowingly" benefit the organization would be classified as support under this proposed legislation. Being found in violation of this law could have meaningful consequences, including (but not limited to) the seizure of Qatari assets in the US, the prohibition on foreign military sales to Doha, plus an overall chilling effect on bilateral relations.

The legislative process followed a similar course in the Senate, where the legislation (if it is introduced) would be referred to the Committees of Foreign Relations and Banking.

Just as many experts faulted the Justice Against Sponsors of Terrorism Act (JASTA) as bad policy but most members of Congress supported it for political purposes, the Palestinian International Terrorism Support Prevention Act had the potential to chart a similar course. Yet a swift and meaningful education campaign to highlight the bill's flaws prevented that outcome.

With the objective of passing HR 2712, UAE surrogates began to systematically reach out to various American Jewish groups, including AIPAC, to solicit their support for a lobbying campaign in favor of the bill.

Notwithstanding these dynamics, the inability of the UAE to mobilize AIPAC—along with other pro-Israel groups—to support the anti-Qatar legislation illustrates that Israel actively opposed HR 2712.

Thus, the combination of US government opposition against the measure and Israel's de facto veto, which explains AIPAC's decision not to push for HR 2712, explain how the bill was for all practical purposes withdrawn.

On November 19, 2017, then-House Democratic Leader Nancy Pelosi's (D-CA) made an appearance during Qatar's National Day celebration in Washington, illustrating strong Congressional support for Qatar. During Amir Tamim's visit to Washington in April 2018, he met with Speaker Ryan, further highlighting Qatar's overall positive reputation among lawmakers.

In July 2019, the House of Representatives passed the Palestinian International Terrorism Support Prevention Act (HR 1850). Subsequently the Senate passed a bill which was almost identical, but the issue of Qatar was stripped entirely.[196] The legislation was supported by AIPAC.[197] The two identical bills revealed once again Israel's decision to prevent the anti-Qatar legislation from moving forward.

Meanwhile, US Congressional leaders have repeatedly been briefed on the US–Qatar MoU aimed at combating the financing of terrorism. At the same time, Emirati lobbyists in Washington have repeatedly lobbied for the declassification of the MoU.

AL JAZEERA

On March 6, 2018, US Representatives Lee Zeldin (R-NY) and Josh Gottheimer (D-NJ) delivered a letter urging then-Attorney General Jeff Sessions to enforce the Foreign Agents Registration Act (FARA) with respect to Al Jazeera. After an extensive lobbying push by UAE surrogates, 19 members of Congress signed on to the latter, as has one member of the US Senate, Ted Cruz, a Republican from Texas.[198]

The letter states:

> We find it troubling that the content produced by this network often directly undermines American interests with favorable coverage of US State Department-designated Foreign Terrorist Organizations, including Hamas, Hezbollah, Palestinian Islamic Jihad, and Jabhat Al-Nusra, Al-Qaeda's branch in Syria. Furthermore, Al Jazeera's record of anti-American, anti-Semitic, and anti-Israel broadcasts warrants scrutiny from regulators to determine whether this network is in violation of US law.[199]

On the topic of Qatar and anti-Semitism, those behind the public relations effort featured older clips of Qaradawi on Al Jazeera criticizing Israel and providing negative commentary about Jews in general. The anti-Qatar material did not disclose that the 2014 GCC agreement had barred Qaradawi from the network.[200] Qaradawi has not appeared on television since 2014 and has become a largely irrelevant figure in Qatar and throughout the Arab world in general.

The topic of anti-Semitism in Qatar and the state of Qatar's alleged support for it never became an issue that Israeli officials encountered in Doha throughout the 13-year tenure in which the two countries enjoyed formal diplomatic relations (1996 to 2009). Thus, the topic was never raised by Israeli officials with their Qatari counterparts throughout this period.

Even though the UAE's surrogates had failed to secure AIPAC's support for HR 2712, they attempted to add the issue of Qatar and Al Jazeera in particular to the agenda of AIPAC's 2018 Policy Conference. The issue of Al Jazeera was informally raised during the conference, yet it failed to become an agenda item.

A year-and-a-half later, in June 2019, Kushner granted Al Jazeera Arabic an interview. The White House had brokered this interview nearly one year earlier. The Kushner interview suggested that the Trump administration recognized the network's legitimacy.[201] The network took additional steps to distance itself from past controversies, including those generated by Qaradawi, by interviewing US Special Envoy to Monitor and Combat Anti-Semitism Elan Carr on Al Jazeera Arabic's flagship program "From Washington."[202] Despite the two high-profile exclusives, the UAE continued to target Al Jazeera in Washington, illustrating the extent to which Abu Dhabi remained determined to cripple the network as opposed to seeking genuine improvement on topics sensitive to the American Jewish community.[203]

Only days before the Kushner interview, on June 18, 2019, six US senators—Charles E. Grassley (R-IA), Tom Cotton (R-AK), Jon Cornyn (R-TX), Todd Young (R-IN), Marco Rubio (R-FL), and Ted Cruz (R-TX)—along with US Representatives Mike Johnson (R-LA) and Lee Zeldin (R-NY), sent Attorney General William Barr a letter requesting that Al Jazeera register as a foreign agent.[204] This letter was initiated by UAE surrogates.

ANTI-QATAR PROPAGANDA IN WASHINGTON

On June 5, 2017, which was the day the blockade began, the Counter Extremism Project (CEP) published an online report titled "Qatar, Money and Terror: Doha's Dangerous Policies."[205] The following day, the CEP published two sequels titled "HARBORS Campaign: Qatar Hosts and Assists Radicals By Offering Refuge and Support" and "Will Qatar Ever Expel Terror Leaders?"[206] In addition to publishing anti-Qatar content on its website, on July 3, 2017, the CEP sent a letter to leading US businesses operating in Qatar, including American

Airlines, warning them against doing business with Doha.[207] After the letter's content leaked to the public, the ambassadors from the four blockading countries responded by writing their own letter to the US State Department denying that American businesses would have to choose between their respective markets and that of Qatar.

Several of the US influencers who had had initially published anti-Qatar op-eds during the lead up to the crisis continued with their allegations in a new string of op-eds.[208, 209, 210, 211, 212]

On June 9, Saudi Arabia blocked access to Al Jazeera in hotels across the country.

Throughout June and early July, CEP continued to publish negative reports about Qatar.[213, 214, 215, 216, 217]

On June 13, 2017, TQI, funded and operated by SAPRAC, launched.[218] The TQI public relations campaign, which deliberately targeted the broader Washington metropolitan area with the goal of persuading US policymakers and the general public opinion against Qatar, began the week after Washington and Doha signed the U.S.–Qatar MoU on counterterrorism.

The fact that the persistent diplomatic onslaught against Doha in Washington continued despite the MoU demonstrated that the crisis was never about terror financing.

Meanwhile, during the week of June 19, 2017, *Conservative Review* published two anti-Qatar op-eds. Also, the UAE's Minister of State Sultan Ahmed Al Jaber and a Bahraini scholar argued in separate articles that Qatar threatened regional stability and international peace.[219, 220, 221, 222, 223] That same week, TQI ran anti-Qatar commercials during MSNBC's *Morning Joe* news show. TQI also took out ads in *The Washington Post's* Daily202. On July 23, anti-Qatar commercials ran throughout Sunday talk shows with SAPRAC spending $138,000 on seven 30-second TV spots.[224]

Between September and December 2017, SAPRAC spent roughly $200,000 on anti-Qatar ads in the *Washington Post*, *New York Times*, *Politico*, and *The Hill*. The organization did so with funding from the Bahraini Embassy in Washington.[225]

Negative op-eds against Qatar abated during the last week of July but appeared to be resuming again at full speed during the second week of August before cooling down again until resuming after Memorial Day Weekend of 2017.[226, 227, 228, 229, 230, 231, 232]

On August 13, 2017, Qatar's Special Envoy for Counterterrorism and Mediation of Conflict Resolution Mutlaq Al Qahtani responded to the ever-increasing string of negative commentary with his own op-ed in *The Wall Street Journal* titled "Qatar Will Not Be Intimidated."

Al Qahtani noted,

> Leaked emails show that Emirati officials were conspiring with a variety of interest groups and lobbyists on a campaign to slander Qatar long before the blockade was imposed. Now intelligence experts and Qatar's cybersecurity services have identified the U.A.E. as the perpetrator of the hacking of Qatar News Agency, which set the entire Gulf crisis in motion. Surely this kind of publicity can't be what the Saudis and Emiratis hoped for when they instigated this crisis. Yet the longer the blockade goes on, the more damaging information the world will learn about them—and the more difficult it will be to resolve their differences with Qatar.[233]

On September 4, Qatari opposition activist Khalid Al Hail published an op-ed in *The Hill* in support of Abdullah Bin Ali Al Thani, who at the time was promoted by Saudi media as Qatar's Amir in-waiting.[234] Ten days later, Al Hail was featured as a keynote speaker at anti-Qatar event in London titled "Qatar, Global Security

& Stability Conference," which took place on September 14.[235] The US public relations firm that organized the conference had a $10,000-per-month retainer to target Qatar via center-left leaning media outlets.[236]

Okaz (a Saudi newspaper) hailed the conference in an editorial that called for toppling Qatar's government.[237] Perhaps Al Hail was the keynote speaker because at that point Abdullah was not allowed to leave Saudi Arabia. On January 14, 2018, Sheikh Abdullah released a video statement saying that he was a "prisoner" in the UAE and that if anything happened to him, "Sheikh Mohammed " (a veiled reference to MbZ) would be responsible. He was later released to Kuwait, where he received medical and mental health treatment stemming from his experiences in Saudi Arabia and the UAE.[238]

The purpose of the anti-Qatar event in London appears to have been pushback against Washington's support for Kuwaiti mediation.

Following the London conference, the Hudson Institute hosted a conference on October 23 titled "Countering Violent Extremism: Qatar, Iran, and the Muslim Brotherhood."

The following text is Hudson Institute's official mantra:

Promoting American leadership and global engagement for a secure, free, and prosperous future. Founded in 1961 by strategist Herman Kahn, Hudson Institute challenges conventional thinking and helps manage strategic transitions to the future through interdisciplinary studies in defense, international relations, economics, health care, technology, culture, and law. Hudson seeks to guide public policy makers and global leaders in government and business through a vigorous program of publications, conferences, policy briefings, and recommendations.[239]

The institute is widely considered neoconservative because of its foreign policy approach.

The Hudson conference's sole purpose—which featured prominent Congressional Republican and Democratic lawmakers alike who all castigated Qatar over Hamas—was to build momentum for the impending anti-Qatar legislation known as the Palestinian International Terrorism Support Prevention Act (HR 2712), which was introduced in Congress two days after the FDD conference in May 2017. In addition to its extensive Congressional participation, the event featured many of the same speakers who had participated in the FDD conference in May 2017 and those who penned anti-Qatar op-eds at earlier stages. Not only was the Hudson conference sponsored by the UAE, its ambassador to Washington was visibly seated in the front row.[240] The day after the conference, *The National*, an Abu Dhabi–based English-language newspaper, published another editorial castigating Qatar.[241]

Leading up the third anti-Qatar conference in Washington, which the Philadelphia-based Middle East Forum (MEF) hosted on February 6, 2019, over a dozen negative op-eds were published all repeating similar allegations as those prior to the FDD and Hudson Institute's conferences.[242, 243, 244, 245, 246, 247, 248, 249, 250, 251, 252, 253, 254, 255] The name of MEF's anti-Qatar conference was "Qatar: US Ally or Global Menace."

5

THE QATAR–ISRAEL RELATIONSHIP IN CONTEXT

The attempt by Bahrain, Saudi Arabia, the UAE, and Egypt to carry out a coup d'état against Qatar's head of state in February 1996 had a significant geopolitical consequence for Doha, including its position vis-à-vis Israel. Three months after Operation Abu Ali, Israel's then-Prime Minister Shimon Peres inaugurated an Israeli trade office in Doha at the invitation of Qatar's Amir. The diplomatic mission was open from May 1996 until January 2009.

Omani diplomacy orchestrated Peres's visit to Qatar. Oman's Foreign Minister Yusuf Bin Allawi and his deputy, Sayyid Badr Bin Hamad bin Hamood Al Busaidi, the Secretary General of Oman's Ministry of Foreign Affairs, spearheaded these efforts. Before Peres's historic visit to Doha, but on his very same trip to the Gulf, he inaugurated an Israeli trade office in April in Muscat.

To better understand this context, it is important to recognize that Sultan Qaboos Al Said of Oman sought to help the prime minister with his reelection campaign. Peres, however, suffered defeat to Benjamin Netanyahu on the election day of May 29, 1996.

Sultan Qaboos, a reformer and visionary in his own right, had recognized HBK as a fellow reformer and modernizer and thus sought to introduce him to Peres as fellow visionary committed to breaking the impasse in Arab–Israeli relations through the transformation of GCC–Israel ties.

Since assuming the throne in 1970 in a coup that ousted his father (another parallel between Sultan Qaboos and HBK), Qaboos has brought remarkable prosperity to his nation and modernized the country's infrastructure. According to a 2010 United Nations Development Program report, examining overall progress made in 135 countries over the past 40 years, Oman ranks first in health, education, and income, followed by Saudi Arabia as number five.[256]

As we will discuss later in this book, Qaboos, HBK, and Peres (and even Netanyahu) went on to shape Gulf Arab–Israeli relations for the ensuing two decades.

But pragmatism and realpolitik factors also motivated Qatar's diplomatic outreach to the Jewish state. Qatar, as a small state surrounded by large regional powers such as Saddam Hussein's Iraq, Saudi Arabia, and Iran, needed as many partnerships as possible. Within this context, Israel became one of Qatar's security rings even though the US was Doha's principal strategic partner.

Qatar's decision to establish diplomatic relations with Israel was attributed to HBK's vision, but day-to-day relations were spearheaded and executed by Foreign Minister Hamad Bin Jassim Al Thani (HBJ). Israel's Qatari interlocker was Jabor Bin Yusuf Al Thani, who, at the time, was serving as HBJ's Chef de Cabinet.

In November 1997, Qatar hosted the fourth Middle East North Africa (MENA) Economic Summit in Doha. These conferences began in Casablanca in 1994 in the aftermath of the Oslo Accords. The second and third meetings were in Amman and Cairo, respectively. The purpose of the MENA conferences was to strengthen private sector cooperation between Israel and the Arab states. Kuwait, Jordan,

Oman, Tunisia, and Yemen attended the conference in 1997. Syria and Lebanon never attended any of the previous MENA conferences, and Libya and Iraq never received invitations, while Algeria, Bahrain, Egypt, Morocco, Saudi Arabia, and the UAE boycotted the Doha Summit over the lack of progress on the Israeli–Palestinian peace process.[257] The Doha Summit nonetheless produced tangible results for Israel–Jordan business cooperation and for joint US–Qatar investment ventures.[258]

But despite the goodwill exhibited by Sultan Qaboos and HBK, including at the 1997 MENA Summit in Doha, Gulf–Israel relations were impacted by Israeli–Palestinian turmoil and by the Second Intifada (2000 to 2005) in particular.

In October 2000, the Arab League responded to the Second Intifada by calling for an Emergency Summit at the organization's headquarters in Cairo. The Arab League called for the closure of Israeli diplomatic missions in Morocco, Oman, and Tunisia. While Oman complied with the Arab League's resolution, Qatar did not but requested instead that Israel should "maintain a low profile" in Doha.

HBJ communicated this Qatari request to his then-Israeli counterpart Shlomo Ben Ami. He specifically stressed that the diplomatic mission should remain open until the dust of the Second Intifada settled, when relations could presumably return to what they were prior to the eruption of unrest in Palestine.

During the Second Intifada, the Israeli station chief in Doha would regularly brief Al Jazeera's leadership at its headquarters about Israel's positions.

Because of persistent rumors and media inquiries about the Israeli presence in Doha, in May 2003 HBK and then-Israeli Foreign Minister Silvan Shalom met in Paris to officially "re-inaugurate" the trade office even though it never closed. Their meeting was formally dedicated to advancing the "Road Map" for Arab–Israeli peace sponsored by the

Quartet (distinct from the blockading states), which consisted of the United States, United Nations, European Union, and Russia.

In 2005, Qatar's ambassador to the United Nations Nasir Al Aziz Al Nasir requested Israeli support for its candidacy for a UN Security Council seat. Israel's unprecedented decision to support the Qatari request was directly linked to Doha's decision not to force the closure of its mission during the Second Intifada.[259] During Qatar's two-year rotational term on the UNSC (from 2006 to 2008), its voting on Israel-related resolutions adhered to the general Arab positions as outlined by the Arab League.

The Israel–Hamas conflict of 2008 to 2009, which Israel refers to as Operation Cast Lead, took place right before President Obama's inauguration. In response to the war in Gaza, Qatar requested that Israel close its office in Doha. The move was mainly a response to domestic politics in Qatar, where support for the Palestinians is high.

Questions about how Arab states should respond to the war in Gaza fueled more rivalry between Riyadh and Doha while also trig-gering near-simultaneous meetings of Arab leaders. Qatar invited then-Iranian President Mahmoud Ahmadinejad, Syria's Bashar Al Assad, Iraqi Vice President Tariq Al Hashimi, and representatives for Hamas to Doha to discuss the war and the Palestinian plight in general, which exacerbated tensions between Saudi Arabia and Qatar and left Israel concluding that the Qataris shut down the office in order to advance their country's agenda of becoming a leader on Arab/Islamic issues such as the Palestinian struggle.

The Qatari-sponsored emergency summit took place as Israel had already begun its withdrawal from Gaza. At the eve of the Summit, which was on January 16, 2009, HBJ held a press conference at the Sheraton Hotel in Doha in which he presented the final communi-que during a press conference, which was livestreamed on Al Jazeera.

HBJ announced that the participants had decided to cut all relations with Israel. When pressed by a BBC journalist about such implications for Israel's mission in Doha, Qatar's top diplomat responded that Israel had a week to leave the country.

Israeli officials in Jerusalem were immediately informed but responded to their Doha mission that severing ties through a press conference did not adhere to international diplomatic standards.

Two days later, Qatar announced during a meeting with Israeli officials that it would freeze (as opposed to sever) relations and that they were given a week to close the office. Along with the written diplomatic rebuttal, an oral message was delivered that clarified that Qatar wanted to proceed with the same practice as it had done in 2000—in a response to the Second Intifada—by keeping the office open and managed by the local staff until the dust settled.

Upon instructions from Jerusalem, Israel rejected following the precedence from the Second Intifada, essentially keeping the mission open but in disguise, as the Israelis argued that Operation Cast Lead was over. Israel's diplomatic mission in Doha closed on January 22, 2009.

Only months later, negotiations over reopening the mission in Doha resumed, and the two countries sought to reestablish diplomatic relations, but this time through US mediation.

The negotiations took place in the form of a non-paper in 2009/2010—developed by Qatar and Israel—which was endorsed by the newly elected Israeli Prime Minister Benjamin Netanyahu and his foreign minister at the time, Avigdor Lieberman. The proposed agreement—which was endorsed by Washington—would ensure that Qatar could play a role in Gaza and Israel would reestablish its trade office in Doha. The agreement ultimately fell through because Doha changed its mind.

The Gulf Region and Israel

LEBANON-QATAR-ISRAEL

In 2006, Qatar's ambassador to the United Nations, Al Nasir, played an instrumental diplomatic role in helping to bring an end to the Israel–Hezbollah war. Holding the UNSC presidency in 2006, Qatar introduced UNSC resolution 1701. The UNSC unanimously approved the resolution on August 11, 2006. The following day, the Lebanese cabinet unanimously approved it. On August 13, the Israeli Cabinet voted 24 to 0 in favor of the resolution, with one abstention. The ceasefire began on Monday, August, 14, 2006, at 8:00 a.m. local time.

Before its passing, Washington had initially objected to UNSC resolution 1701 because it saw the Israel–Hezbollah war as an opportunity to destroy the pro-Iranian organization in its entirety with the strategic objective of weakening Iran's regional reach. During the lead up to the conflict, Iran and Syria had supported much of the deadly anti-American insurgency in Iraq. It was not just the Bush administration that initially objected to the Qatari-sponsored UNSC resolution. So did Saudi Arabia and Jordan, which both shared Washington's view about the necessity to fully defeat Hezbollah.

Israel, however, wanted the war to end as it had suffered 158 casualties, most of whom were soldiers killed in Lebanon. Israel lost 43 civilians due to Hezbollah's rocket attacks. An additional 1,500 people suffered injuries from rocket attacks in Israel, and 450 soldiers were wounded in the fighting. On top of that, an estimated 300,000 Israelis had fled their homes to escape rocket attacks on northern Israel and more than 700,000 took refuge in bomb shelters.[260]

Because of the United States and Israel's initial divergence on how to bring an end to the war, Al Nasir's resolution faced some diplomatic pushback from Washington, but Israel was actively supporting it. Al Nasir's diplomatic breakthrough vis-à-vis Washington came after he copied the language of UNSC resolution 425 from 1978. When the United States initially declared that it could not support the draft resolution of 1701, Al Nasir provided the text of UNSC resolution 425 and pointed out that Washington had supported it at the time.

The UNSC resolution 425 was adopted on March 19, 1978, five days after the Israeli invasion of Lebanon. The resolution called on Israel to immediately withdraw its forces from Lebanon and established the United Nations Interim Force In Lebanon (UNIFIL).

In the aftermath of the 2006 war, Lebanon's fragmented political system had sharpened the societal divisions. Qatar and Israel began cooperating on Lebanon a month after the war had ended.

The first step of that process was HBK's visit to Beirut in September 2006. At Qatar's request, Israel, which controlled Lebanon's airspace at the time, cleared the skies for the Amir's arrival.

His visit came as tensions were running high between Beirut's urban and Western-oriented elite and the impoverished Shiites of southern Lebanon, where Hezbollah enjoys a historic stronghold.

The Amir's initial visit to Beirut set the stage for an elaborate diplomatic process that would ultimately pave the way for what became known as the Doha Agreement of May 2008, under which Qatar successfully negotiated an end to Lebanon's political crisis.

The agreement arrived after multiple assassinations of prominent Lebanese leaders had eroded trust among the country's competing political factions.

The first wave of politically motivated assassinations was that of former Prime Minister Rafic Hariri in February 2005 by the Syrian government in conjunction with Hezbollah.

With Israel's diplomatic support, Qatar had thus entered Lebanon's treacherous political landscape with the aim of preventing another civil war from erupting while balancing between Israel and Iran.

Under the Doha Agreement, which the various Lebanese factions reached in the Qatari capital on 21 May 2008, a new cabinet would be established in which Hezbollah, supported by Iran and Syria, along with its allies, would enjoy the veto power it had sought in the negotiations.[261] The Doha Agreement paved the way for a prisoners exchange between Israel and Hezbollah. Under the agreement of July 2008, Hezbollah transferred the coffins of two Israeli soldiers, Ehud Goldwasser and Eldad Regev, in exchange for five Lebanese militants held by Israel.

Qatar's engagement in Lebanon continued to enjoy Israeli support even after Israel's Doha mission had been closed. For instance, in May 2010, HBK visited a Hezbollah stronghold, the southern Lebanese town of Bint Jbeil, and Israel was notified in advance.[262] During his visit, Qatar pledged $300 million to reconstruction assistance.[263]

Immediately after the war of 2006, Qatar dispatched a battalion as part of UNIFIL. Currently, there are only three Qatari officers serving under the UNIFIL mandate.

QATAR-HAMAS-ISRAEL

HBK genuinely believed that Hamas was the authentic voice of the Palestinian people as they were not corrupt, unlike the Palestinian leadership in Ramallah. Once Hamas won the 2006 Palestinian legislative election, HBK repeatedly shared this assessment with US and Israeli officials. He also repeatedly warned Washington against encouraging this election as he correctly predicted that Hamas would likely win.

Following Hamas's victory, then-US Secretary of State Condoleezza Rice requested Doha's assistance to host Hamas to help facilitate the peace processes between Hamas, the Palestinian Authority, and Israel. Based on Qatar's ties to Israel, it was not unsurprising that Washington asked Doha to play this role as a facilitator.

HBK's vision spearheaded Qatar's foray into Israel–Palestine peacemaking, but HBJ executed it in practice. As part of that vision, in October, Qatar presented its so-called Six Point Plan with the objective of facilitating dialogue between Israel and the Palestinians and a halt to internecine fighting among different Palestinian factions.[264]

Qatar's ability to enter the Israeli–Palestinian theater was directly attributed to Doha's successful contribution to efforts aimed at bringing the Israel–Hezbollah war of 2006 to an end.

The Six Point Plan stipulates:

1. To abide by the resolutions of international legitimacy.

2. To abide by the previous agreements signed by the Palestinian Liberation Organization (PLO), including agreements signed with Israel.

3. To establish a Palestinian Independent State within the borders of the occupied territories established in 1967, and to co-exist with the state of Israel.

4. To stop all types of violence in a complete and unilateral manner.

5. To reactivate the role of the Palestine Liberation Organization (PLO) in accordance with the Cairo agreement signed between the Palestinian factions.

6. The PLO, the President, and the Palestinian leadership should take charge of the government and call for peace talks with Israel.

Qatar ultimately failed to negotiate a unity government between the rival Palestinian factions, as outlined by its Six Point Plan. Nonetheless, since putting forth the plan, Doha has hosted several Hamas leaders and lent its good offices for mediation purposes, including between Hamas and Israel.

Over the ensuing decade, Washington has not once requested the expulsion of Hamas from Qatar. In fact, the United States prefers the group to be located in Doha as opposed to in Tehran, where Washington has virtually no influence. While US diplomats in Qatar have never interacted with Hamas, Qatari officials have passed on US messages to the group.

All Hamas officials residing in Doha are under constant surveillance and considered a liability to Qatar, given the potential international scrutiny if an incident occurred.

GAZA RECONSTRUCTION

In October 2012, HBK became the first foreign leader to visit Gaza since Hamas took administrative power in the enclave. While preparing for the visit, Israel had initially requested that the Amir fly from Doha to Amman and from there enter Israel through the Allenby Bridge border crossing en route to Gaza. There were two viable options for his travel to Gaza. The first was traveling by helicopter and the second by convoy. In either scenario, Israel would provide him with the necessary security arrangements as required for a head of state. At the end, a compromise was struck. The Amir would enter Gaza through its Egyptian border after landing at the Al Arish airport in eastern Egypt, and he would pay Palestinian President Mahmoud Abbas a separate visit in Ramallah during the spring of 2013.[265]

Once in Gaza, the Amir offered $400 million in reconstruction assistance. The funding was allocated for the construction of two housing complexes, the rehabilitation of three main roads, and the establishment of a prosthetic center.[266]

Until the present period, this $400 million has covered all of Qatar's assistance for Gaza reconstruction.

Yet, HBK never visited Ramallah. Meanwhile, preparations for his long-planned abdication in favor of his son, Tamim, accelerated as the Qatari Diwan instead focused heavily on its transition process and less so the situation in Gaza. Amir Tamim succeeded his father on June 25, 2013.

Despite the absence of formal diplomatic relations with Israel, Qatar's HBK visited Gaza with the Israelis being made aware in advance, following the pattern set forth in his visit to Lebanon in 2010. Nonetheless, without official diplomatic relations, Israeli–Qatari cooperation in relation to the Palestinian question has been limited to Gaza reconstruction with Doha paying government salaries, as well as the bills for fuel, energy, and cash assistance to the most impoverished and vulnerable people in the besieged enclave.

In addition to Qatar's $400 million pledge to Gaza, a separate track to deepen Doha's engagement in the enclave sought to secure Qatari funding for the construction of a desalination plant in Gaza. The United States and Israel actively backed this initiative.

Less than a month after the Amir's 2012 visit, violence between Israel and Hamas broke out again in Gaza. The fighting lasted from November 14 to 21, 2012.

Only days before these hostilities erupted, a multilateral forum convened at the French Consulate in Jerusalem to discuss Gaza reconstruction efforts from the 2008/2009 war. The project was an ambitious diplomatic initiative that would convene Israel, the

Palestinian Authority, Jordan, the Gulf states, and the European Union to jointly support the construction of a desalination plant in Gaza that would ultimately help secure clean water access for the coastal enclave.

Although the Union for the Mediterranean spearheaded the Gaza water initiative, the proposed construction project received its diplomatic backing and ultimate go-ahead from the Middle East Desalination Research Center (MEDRC), a Muscat, Oman-based organization seeking to advance quiet diplomacy between Israel, the Palestinian Authority, and Arab states, including Qatar and Oman.[267, 268]

MEDRC executives and Palestinian Water Authority (PWA) officials traveled to Doha in pursuit of Qatari funding at the United States and Israel's request. The PWA's then-Chairman Shaddad Attila, who met with HBJ in Doha, spearheaded the delegation.

Although Qatar initially expressed interest in funding the project, which was estimated to cost $450 million, donor fatigue with Gaza, including in Doha, ultimately prevented HBJ from supporting the project. Despite Israeli assurances about not targeting strategic infrastructure during a future war with Hamas, Qatar, along with much of the international community, had chosen at the time not to fund a project of this magnitude because of the largescale destruction that Israel's Operation Cast Lead unleashed across the enclave.

While the proposed desalination plant was a PWA initiative, it enjoyed Hamas's de facto endorsement. The PWA and Hamas have enjoyed pragmatic cooperation for many years on issues pertaining to water and sanitation in Gaza. The PWA and Hamas also agreed on the land where the plant would be standing, which is in the central part of the Gaza strip, south of Gaza City. In late 2012, discussions also focused on whether to build the desalination plan in the Egyptian city of Al Arish. As of writing, construction of the plant has not yet begun.

WHERE POLITICS AND DIPLOMACY INTERSECT

From the outset of Tamim's tenure, which began in June 2013, Qatar initially scaled back on its role in Palestinian affairs, but Doha's role in Gaza increased after the GCC crisis broke out in June 2017.

During the 2014 Gaza war, then-US Secretary of State John Kerry relied heavily on both Qatar and Turkey for diplomatic purposes as he sought to draw on their respective relationships with Hamas to apply pressure on the group. As part of that effort, Kerry and his Qatari counterpart met in Paris in July of that year, along with then-Turkish Foreign Minister Ahmet Davutoğlu, to help negotiate an end to the conflict.[269] While these efforts were ultimately unsuccessful, Egypt mediated a truce between Israel and Hamas, the third Egyptian-mediated truce since 2009.

Egypt, as Israel's neighbor and the Arab world's most populous country, enjoys a strategic relationship with Jerusalem. Thus, Israel's decisions to provide Egypt with the credit of mediating the respective ceasefire agreements underscore Israel's difficult balancing act vis-à-vis Cairo and Doha. Even if Qatari checkbook diplomacy and Doha's pragmatic relationship with Hamas played decisive roles in reaching the ceasefire agreements in question, the Egypt–Israel relationship is strategic in nature, which officials in Doha fully understand.

Yet until the Gulf crisis began in 2017, this arrangement between Israel, Egypt, and Qatar remained unproblematic. The blockade being imposed on Qatar, however, led to the Quartet bringing the issue of Qatar's relationship with Hamas to center stage by deploying misinformation and propaganda as part of its influencing game in Washington.

119

Israel's current Qatar policy is driven by Jerusalem's recognition that cooperating with Doha provides more benefits than drawbacks. Regarding Iran, a stronger relationship with Qatar can effectively reduce Iran's room to maneuver and influence vis-à-vis Hamas and other actors and developments in Gaza. Moreover, Qatar has a lengthy record of mediating between Hamas and Israel, including on issues such as prisoner exchanges, highlighting how the Jewish state's pragmatic ties with Doha can pay off from an Israeli perspective. The eventual construction of a seaport on the coast of Gaza is another file where Israeli–Qatari cooperation could possibly pay dividends in the future.

Qatar's diplomatic engagement with Israel, which Ambassador Muhammad Al Emadi spearheads, is limited to Gaza reconstruction. His mandate is narrow and limited to engagements with the Israeli Defense Forces' Coordinator of Government Activities in the Territories (COGAT), which is a unit in the Israeli Ministry of Defense that engages in coordinating civilian issues between the Government of Israel, the Israel Defense Forces, international organizations, diplomats, and the Palestinian Authority.

Because of the Quartet's strategic threat to Qatar and how anti-Qatar allegations centering on Doha's "support" for Hamas were playing out in Washington, Doha had little choice but to publicly announce its cooperation with Israel on Gaza reconstruction. The decision to do so was initially embarrassing for Qatar primarily because of how it could play out in Qatar's domestic political environment, where a large segment of the population does not necessarily support diplomatic engagement with Israel.

At the same time, Israeli–Qatari cooperation in Gaza also became a diplomatic lifeline for Doha as Qatar was able to turn a perceived disadvantage into a strategic advantage by framing its cooperation with the Jewish state as part of an objective to assist the Trump administration.

While Doha was slowly but gradually fending off anti-Qatar propaganda in Washington, Israeli–Qatari cooperation also crystalized the fact that Jerusalem did not support the anti-Qatar activities in the US capital.

But as Israeli–Qatar ties improved, Abu Dhabi sought to undermine Doha's influence in Gaza. By attempting to dispatch Mohammed Dahlan, a political rival of Palestinian President Mahmoud Abbas, to Gaza with aid from the UAE, Abu Dhabi's immediate objective could be interpreted as an attempt to counter Qatari clout in Gaza as part of the UAE's goals of isolating Doha from the Trump administration and hampering the steadily improving state of Israeli–Qatari relations.

Dahlan, who is originally from Gaza but resides in Abu Dhabi, also sought to establish himself in the process as a potential challenger to Abbas.[270]

But what is less understood, especially in light of the enormous anti-Qatar propaganda war in Washington, is that Gaza, Hamas, and Doha's "pro–Arab Spring" policies are not driving Israel's grievances with Qatar. Instead, Israel's real problems with Qatar have been about Al Jazeera as a Qatari state-owned, pan-Arab network that has a record of covering issues related to Israel and Palestine in ways which have infuriated Israeli officials on many occasions.

For instance, after the collapse of diplomatic relations between Qatar and Israel in January 2009, Israel concluded that Doha's decision was tied to its objective in becoming a leader on Arab issues, including the Palestinian struggle, through the combination of leveraging its financial wealth and soft-power influence via Al Jazeera. This first became apparent during HBK's respective visits to Lebanon and Gaza, which Al Jazeera framed as a victory for the "resistance" even though Qatar had coordinated these visits in advance with Israel. Furthermore, Al Jazeera is the only pan-Arab network to have continuously provided Israelis, including government officials, with a platform for expressing their views and articulating their positions.

Irrespective of differences pertaining to Al Jazeera, the Israeli view is that Qatar has, through the forces of globalization, transformed itself from a small state undergoing modernization after liberalizing at home during the tenure of the HBK's reign to evolving into a regional actor. Israel, through its active support for Qatar's UNSC seat and opening up the diplomatic spaces for Qatar to operate in Lebanon and Gaza, had helped transform Qatar into an Arab power for the world to contend with.

By the end of 2008, however, Israel's National Security Council officials had already begun internal deliberations over how to discuss the issue of Al Jazeera with their Qatari counterparts. The network's repeated demands that then-UN Secretary General Ban Ki-moon resign over his diplomatic efforts to bring the Gaza war to an end prompted Israelis to address the network with Qatari officials.

Thus, from an Israeli vantage point, even though the Israel–Qatar diplomatic relationship had transformed from overall friendly to merely productive on issues pertaining to Gaza reconstruction after formal ties ended in 2009, Jerusalem had concluded that Qatar had taken a backseat to Al Jazeera as the network had become more powerful than the state itself. Israeli criticism of Al Jazeera's back-to-back coverage of the Gaza war of 2008/2009 centered on the network had provided Hamas with more hard power than it ever could have obtained through the merits of its own limited military capabilities.

At the same time, as we have argued, Al Jazeera dismissed the two top editors from their positions as part of the Saudi–Qatari rapprochement following the GCC crisis of 2014. Although their dismissal was not tied to the Palestinian issue, Al Jazeera's coverage of that theater has, from an Israeli perspective, neutralized since 2014.

From Qatar's vantage point, despite its extensive engagements with Israel and its efforts to reconcile differences between competing Palestinian factions, the Jewish state failed to deliver on the Palestinian issue, which ultimately explains Doha's decision to close the Israeli office in Qatar in January 2009. Thus, Qatari grievances primarily rest on Israel's perceived unwillingness to accept a two-state solution. But, as we shall discuss in the next chapter, Israel's changing positions on whether to acquire Qatari gas contributed to Doha's frustrations with Jerusalem as well.

QATAR–ISRAEL GAS TALKS

The combination of HBK's ascendancy to the throne and Operation Abu Ali motivated Qatar's decision to offer Israel, among several other countries, the opportunity to acquire its natural gas before it began production in 1999. Israeli–Qatari talks, which took place at the Dorchester Hotel in London, began in 1995, and Israel's Ministry of Energy and the Enron Corporation, a US energy company, spearheaded them. Because there were no formal diplomatic relations at the time, Enron served as a proxy for Qatar because it held the initial concession to export Qatari gas. Enron reported directly to HBJ on its talks with Israel.

The parties had identified the following two options on how to export Qatari gas to Israel:

The first—and preferred—option was to transport the gas to Israel through an already existing elaborate network of pipelines

123

between the Gulf and the Levant, which included end destinations in cities such as Beirut and Haifa. Because of the existing pipeline infrastructure, the parties had identified that only several hundred kilometers of new pipelines needed to be constructed, which meant that not only would potential Israeli importation of Qatari gas be cost-effective, Doha would profit highly from such an arrangement. For Qatar, exporting gas to Israel would bring strategic benefits to Doha too because Qatar's gas wealth is tied to Iran's, and by exporting Qatari gas to Israel, Doha would possibly balance Tehran and Jerusalem off each other while enjoying protection under Washington's security umbrella.

The second option was to transport the LNG to Israel via ship, which would not be cost-effective as the projected cost was estimated to be billions more than the first option.

Enron Corporation's bankruptcy in 2001 formally brought the talks to an end. But Saudi Arabia was also a factor. Riyadh had effectively vetoed the plan as it would not allow the transshipment of Qatari gas to Israel through the Kingdom's territory. Israel was still able to acquire Qatar's gas, but it would have to be transported via tankers.

Although Israel had initially concluded that it needed Qatari gas to meet domestic energy needs for the 2000s, the country reversed this decision, only to re-express its interest in 2008.

At the latter stage, Israel's then-Foreign Minister Tzipi Livni, who had been invited by HBJ to address the 8th Doha Forum on Democracy, Development, and Free Trade in April 2008, led Israeli efforts to revitalize the gas issue.[271] Prior to her departure, Livni had received a broad mandate from then-Energy Minister Benjamin Ben-Eliezer to begin talks with Qatar's Minister of Industry and Energy, Abdullah bin Hamad Al Attiyah.

No breakthrough came in 2008. Al Attiyah told Livni that Qatar was already exporting its gas at full capacity and that ramped-up production would be of diminishing value to Doha. He also reasoned that ramped-up production could impact Qatar's security in the future—a subtle reference to its neighbors—at which point future gas revenues would be needed for national security purposes. Al Attiyah nonetheless encouraged Israel to apply for a waiver for the next concession, scheduled for 2011.

During the Livni–Attiyah meeting, Qatar's position regarding the gas talks of the 1990s was also revisited. Al Attiyah maintained that Doha had concluded at the time that Israel had not been interested in acquiring Israeli gas but that it had primarily opened negotiations with Doha as part of a tactic to negotiate a lower price for its gas imports from Egypt. He also argued that it was Israel that had missed the opportunity to acquire Qatari gas during the initial negotiations of the 1990s while playing down Saudi objections. From 2005 to 2012, Israel imported gas from Egypt via the Al Arish-Ashkelon pipeline.

With the departure of President Mubarak in March 2011, however, Egyptian supplies were repeatedly interrupted by the sabotage of sections of the pipeline in the Sinai Peninsula. In April 2012, Egypt canceled the contract, complaining of poor payments.[272]

Back in Doha, Livni denied that Israel had played Egypt and Qatar against each other in order to bring down the price of Egyptian gas. Instead, the Israeli official maintained that the assassination of then-Prime Minister Yitzhak Rabin in 1995 had upended Israel's political life. Put simply, the event paralyzed the country and its decision-making process, including on foreign policy issues such as gas from Qatar.

Israel's dependence on foreign sources for its gas has reduced since the discovery of more than 30 trillion cubic feet of gas off its Mediterranean coast over the last decade.[273] Because of newly discovered energy riches, Israel is now a gas exporter to its immediate neighbors, including to Egypt and Jordan. In light of this reality, importing Qatari gas is no longer a move the Jewish State is considering.

While in Doha, Livni also met with her Omani counterpart, Yusuf Bin Alawi. It was the first Israeli–Omani bilateral ministerial meeting since the closure of Israel's trade office in Muscat in October 2000.

6

OMAN, THE UAE, AND ISRAEL

THE OMAN–ISRAEL RELATIONSHIP

With 49 years on the throne, from 1970 to 2020, Sultan Qaboos Al Said (1940–2020) was the Arab world's longest-serving monarch. Under his leadership, Oman transformed itself on the international stage and became an important diplomatic player. Muscat has established informal relations with Israel and plays an important role in terms of helping to bring about greater Arab–Israeli dialogue.

Following the Egyptian–Israeli peace treaty of 1979, Oman, Somalia, and Sudan were the only Arab League members that did not boycott Egypt.

But Oman's support for Arab–Israeli peace-making was not limited to Egypt as Muscat adopted a proactive stance during the Madrid Conference of 1991 where five multilateral working groups were established.

The multilateral track focused on attempting to shape the future of the Middle East by addressing regional problems in a variety of areas which transcend boundaries in order to promote long-term development and security throughout the Middle East.

One of the five working groups established as part of the Madrid Conference—and the only surviving organization of the Oslo

Accords—is the Muscat-based Middle East Desalination Research Center (MEDRC). MEDRC is a research and capacity-building institution established in April 1996 to share desalination technologies and clean fresh water supply with the people of the Middle East, the most arid region in the world.

Since its inception, the Omani government classified MEDRC as a diplomatic organization.

The Madrid Conference's remaining multilateral working groups, which no longer exist, focused on[274]:

1. Environment
2. Arms control and regional security
3. Refugees
4. Water (MEDRC)
5. Economic Development

Oman, with roughly 82 percent of its land made up of sand and gravel desert, benefits from the research while playing a key diplomatic role by hosting such an international organization in its capital.

Beyond MEDRC's scientific research and capacity-building work, the institute has, since its inception, served to advance multilateral track diplomacy between Israel and Arab states. Israeli officials have visited the institute every six months for executive committee meetings. While in Muscat, Israeli officials also hold bilateral side meetings with their Omani counterparts.

As of 2019, Israel, the Palestinian Authority, Jordan, Oman, Qatar, the United States, Spain, the Netherlands, Japan, and South Korea are all MEDRC members. Sweden is an observer. The Executive Committee is composed of two officials from each member. Sayyid

Badr Bin Hamad Bin Hamood Al Busaidi, the Director General of Oman's Ministry of Foreign Affairs, remains MEDRC's Chairman.

MEDRC's inauguration took place at the same time as an Israeli trade mission was established in Muscat. Then-Prime Minister Shimon Peres inaugurated the two diplomatic missions in April 1996 during the runoff of the Israeli elections, which took place the following month.

Benjamin Netanyahu, who would visit Oman two decades later, defeated Shimon Peres in the 1996 elections and served his first term as prime minister until 1999.

In 1994, then-Prime Minister Yitzhak Rabin became the first Israeli leader to visit Oman. The following year, after Rabin's assassination in November 1995, Omani Foreign Minister Alawi paid Israel his first visit to attend Rabin's funeral.[275]

Alawi was accompanied by his deputy, Secretary General Al Busaidi.

Oman and Qatar were the only GCC members to attend Rabin's funeral.

Qatar was represented at the funeral by Information Minister Ahmed El Aziz Al Kuwari.[276]

At the request of Qaboos, Alawi instructed Israel to close its trade office, located in the Sheraton Hotel in Muscat, shortly after the Second Intifada had erupted in 2000. The request to close it came after the Arab League's Extraordinary Summit held in Cairo in October 2000, where a decision was made to close Israeli trade offices in Oman as well as Morocco and Tunisia.

The Second Intifada, nonetheless, did not result in the MEDRC closing down. In fact, the MEDRC remains open to this day and serves as a diplomatic channel for Israel–Arab peacemaking.

Fast forward to 2011. Then-President Obama called Qaboos and asked the Omani head of state to lead Arab goodwill gestures toward

Israel in exchange for a settlement freeze moratorium.[277] Qaboos agreed, but ultimately no movement took place on the Oman–Israel front because Netanyahu decided to continue Israel's settlement expansion.

The premises of Oman's diplomatic, strategic, and friendly relationship with Israel are tied to Muscat's historic support for promoting peace between Arabs and Israelis.

Thus, two days before Netanyahu's visit in October 2018, Qaboos hosted Palestinian President Mahmoud Abbas in Muscat. The back-to-back visits by the Palestinian and Israeli leaders were designed to demonstrate Muscat's support for resolving the conflict between Palestinians and Israelis while also promoting wider peacemaking efforts between Arabs at large and the Jewish state.

After Netanyahu's visit to Muscat, then-Transportation and Intelligence Minister Yisrael Katz paid Oman a follow-up visit. Katz presented his "Tracks for Regional Peace" plan, a railway that will connect the Mediterranean and the Persian Gulf through Israel and Jordan.[278]

The Mossad coordinates Israel's day-to-day relationship with Oman. The director of Israel's intelligence organization, Yossi Cohen, travels to Muscat on a regular basis. The Israelis do not publicize Cohen's visits to the Sultanate, unlike Katz's visit.

Building on Netanyahu's visit, Oman announced in June 2019 that it would open an embassy in Ramallah, Palestine.[279] The Sultanate would be the first GCC to establish an embassy in the West Bank. A month later, Cohen announced that Israel would reestablish its own diplomatic mission in Muscat, a matter Oman swiftly denied.[280]

The Oman–Israel relationship is multifaceted as it ranges from the multilateral MEDRC channel to bilateral cooperation carried out through various Israeli government ministries, including the Prime Minister's Office, the Ministry of Foreign Affairs, and the Mossad.

Israel attributes its relationship with Muscat to Qaboos's strategic vision for the country, which includes establishing lines of communications between nations across the Middle East's geopolitical fault lines in pursuit of peace and regional stability. Foreign Minister Alawi and his deputy continue guiding Muscat's foreign policy vis-à-vis Israel.

Britain initiated Oman's relationship with the Jewish state, which stretches back to the 1970s, shortly after Qaboos took power, when Mossad was carrying out the initial stages.

During the 1970s, the Omani–Israeli relations focused on assisting Qaboos in his struggle against the Dhofar rebellion (1962 to 1976). Backed by the Soviet Union, the Democratic People's Republic of Korea (DPRK), the People's Democratic Republic of Yemen (PDRY), and other leftist Arab regimes, the Marxist rebellion sought to overthrow Oman's ruling family. Sultan Qaboos is the 14th generation of the Al Busaidi dynasty ruling Oman.

While Britain and Iran provided military assistance against the rebellion, Israel provided military and political advice.[281]

Thus, Israel, along with Iran and Jordan, were the main regional countries—together with Britain—to support Qaboos during this critical stage of Oman's history.

EMIRATI SPIES AND THE OMAN–ISRAEL RELATIONSHIP

Muscat's initial isolation from the Trump administration, which became apparent during the May 2017 Riyadh Summit, resulted from the UAE's influence over a White House staffed by outsiders lacking expertise. But in addition to a murky influencing game in Washington, the Oman–UAE relationship faced another crisis following the discovery of an Emirati spy ring in the Sultanate in 2018.

Four Emiratis recruited an Omani national and served as his handlers. These four were lured to the Sultanate during the fall of 2018. The Omani authorities promptly arrested them as part of a high-stakes sting operation.

On April 10, 2019, the four Emiratis and one Omani received 10-year prison sentences after being found guilty of espionage.

Before their sentencing, however, Sayyid Assad Bin Tariq Al Said, a senior member of Oman's royal family and Qaboos's first cousin, sought to play down tensions with the UAE over the spy ring. During a meeting with tribal elders on March 26, 2019, Sayyed Assad addressed "the importance of having a good relationship with our neighbors no matter what happens."[282]

Oman's Foreign Minister Yusuf Bin Alawi similarly asserted that "we should be kind to our neighbor," another reference to the UAE and the espionage issue. [283]

Beyond the Omani government announcing the eventual sentencing and general statements calling on the need for upholding neighborliness by Sayyid Assad and Alawi, officials in Muscat have yet to release any official and conclusive statement about the spy ring case, which suggests that the investigation is ongoing.

On the evening of October 25, 2018, shortly after Omani authorities uncovered the Emirati spy ring, Netanyahu arrived in Muscat for talks with Sultan Qaboos.

While Netanyahu's surprise visit equated to Israeli support for Oman and its sovereignty, including a de facto endorsement of its independent foreign policy, Qaboos also helped boost Netanyahu's international standing while he was campaigning for reelection at home. The visit helped Netanyahu convince more Israelis that the Jewish state was strengthening diplomatic relationships with Gulf countries with him at the helm.

Sultan Qaboos Al Said to the right and Prime Minister Benjamin Netanyahu to the left. Courtesy: Oman News Agency.

Netanyahu's wife, Sara, accompanied him. So did Mossad Director Yossi Cohen, National Security Adviser Meir Ben-Shabbat, Foreign Ministry Director General Yuval Rotem, Netanyahu Chief of Staff Yoav Horowitz, and Col. Avi Blot, the prime minister's military secretary.[284]

Sultan Qaboos and Prime Minister Netanyahu point north towards the UAE. Courtesy: Oman News Agency.

133

While the Sultanate's longstanding relationship with Israel set the stage for Netanyahu's surprise visit, its timing was directly attributed to the discovery of the Emirati spy ring.

Israel, through the Herzeliya-based NSO Group, a Q Cyber Technologies company, had licensed the company to sell its Pegasus software, which can penetrate various smart phones—including Apple's iPhone and iPad's operating systems—to the UAE.

Although the NSO Group developed its technology to enable government, intelligence, and law enforcement agencies to prevent and investigate crime and terrorism, the UAE had used the software in an attempt to hack Amir Tamim's iPhone prior to the eruption of the GCC crisis.[285] The UAE also hacked the smartphones belonging to several senior Omani officials, both in Oman and abroad, again using the Pegasus software.

Through its Ministry of Defense, Israel had licensed the NSO Group to sell its technologies to the UAE. Yet Israel also maintains a backdoor capability to surveil how its foreign government clients employ NSO technologies as part of the country's quest to uphold its own military and intelligence supremacy. Hence, the combination of Abu Dhabi's attempt to isolate Oman in Washington coupled with the strategic objective of destabilizing the Sultanate through its spy ring—carried out through the NSO acquisition—may very well have been a red line for Israel, which explains Netanyahu's visit to Muscat, which was arranged at the last minute. Nonetheless, Israel's export of NSO technologies to the UAE contributed significantly to reputational damages for the Jewish state.

Netanyahu's visit to the Sultanate also coincided with FDD having published a string of negative articles about Oman, especially concerning Muscat's relationship with Iran.[286, 287, 288, 289] FDD's relationship with the UAE, Otaiba, and his American surrogates in particular, which was demonstrated through its lead role during the initial phase of the campaign against Qatar in Washington, was not lost on anyone in Jerusalem or Muscat.

The 2018 flare-up between the UAE and Oman, however, resembles a previous Emirati attempt to overthrow Qaboos in January 2011 through establishing a spy network targeting the Omani government and its military.[290]

At the time, the Omani authorities announced the arrests during a broadcast on Oman television.[291] The Oman News Agency, however, released a brief summary in English which said that the Emirati spy network had "targeted the government in Oman and the mechanism of the government and military." The statement also made clear that the UAE's objective was to overthrow Qaboos, saying, "May the Almighty protect His Majesty the Sultan and our beloved country against all harm."[292]

Muscat made this announcement in 2011 after the UAE had closed its borders with Oman, which accelerated anti-government protests. Oman's Arab Spring took place that year when hundreds of demonstrators took to the streets in the northern port city of Sohar to demand jobs and an end to corruption. The border closure, which prevented Omanis from traveling to Dubai for work, sparked mass protests in the northern part of the country. By doing so, Abu Dhabi sought to play tribal politics against Oman by playing up economic differences between wealthier tribe members residing on the Emirati side of the international border and their poorer Omani cousins.

Responding to these challenges, Qaboos swiftly responded by firing 12 cabinet ministers and raising government salaries while agreeing to boost unemployment benefits to 150 Oman rials ($380) a month.[293] He also promised to create 50,000 new jobs. After the Sultan increased minimum wages by 40 percent, the unrest subsided almost as quickly as it had erupted.

The timing of the 2011 Emirati spy network coincided with much speculation about a potential Israeli military strike against Iranian nuclear facilities. Analysts speculated at the time that the coup d'état attempt was tied to Oman's pragmatic relationship with Iran.

In March 2011, MbZ and Muhammad bin Rashid Al Maktoum (MbR) paid a visit to Muscat, which enabled the two Gulf countries to settle the spy saga from two months earlier. The Emir of Kuwait spearheaded the Emirati–Omani reconciliation process. Kuwait's leader flew from Kuwait City to Abu Dhabi, where he picked up MbZ and MbR before arriving with both Emirati leaders in Muscat for talks with Qaboos. The Obama administration actively supported the Kuwait emir's diplomatic engagement between the UAE and Oman.[294]

Subsequently, Qaboos departed for Abu Dhabi where he paid UAE President Sheikh Khalifa II Bin Zayed Bin Sultan Al Nahyan an official visit. MbZ and MbR attended that meeting as well, which signaled a resolution of the feud.[295]

That following October, then-US Secretary of State Hillary Clinton traveled to Muscat, where she demonstrated Washington's support for Oman's independence and its neutral foreign policy with much praise for Oman's leadership.[296]

OMAN-IRAN

Despite being a member state of the mostly anti-GCC block, Oman enjoys a relationship with Tehran which is extremely pragmatic. As the two countries share the strategic Strait of Hormuz, through which an estimated 35 percent of all crude oil carried by ship passes annually, Oman and Iran have interests in maintaining positive ties. Geography aside, the two countries also share a unique history as the

Shah of Iran, Mohammad Reza Pahlavi, and Jordan's King Hussein were the only two regional leaders to initially support Qaboos's palace coup against his father in 1970.

The Shah also came to Oman's rescue by dispatching 4,000 troops to help quell the Dhofar Rebellion, a communist insurgency from 1962 to 1975. Iran lost more than 700 soldiers in the conflict, a sacrifice that Qaboos never forgot. Following Iran's revolution of 1979, Qaboos maintained overall positive relations with the new Iranian government. Throughout the Iran–Iraq war (1980-1988), when most GCC member states backed Baghdad, Muscat maintained neutrality. Oman's decision to not back Iraq, a fellow Arab state, against Tehran in that conflict earned Sultan Qaboos much trust from the Islamic Republic.

US–OMAN–IRAN BACKCHANNEL

In March 2011, at the request of the National Defense University, a division of the US Department of Defense, MEDRC hosted a two-day seminar for strategic studies centers from across the broader Middle East, including from Iran and Israel. Iran's Center for Strategic Studies, which was at the time headed by Hassan Rouhani, currently the President of the Islamic Republic, sent a representative. Oded Eran, then the director of Tel Aviv University's Institute for National Security Studies, represented Israel.

In front of the entire audience, the unidentified Iranian representative provided a briefing about Iran's nuclear program. The representative's briefing provided sufficient details for the participants to obtain an understanding about Iran's technological know-how and the scope of Tehran's program. The briefing served as a platform for the launch of a backchannel between Washington and Tehran in Muscat.

Following his presentation, MEDRC hosted a reception at the Diplomatic Club in Muscat in which all seminar participants from a range of countries, including Israel and Iran—as well as the Iranian ambassador to Oman—partook.

Upon his return from Muscat, the Iranian participant was arrested and held for an unspecified amount of time in the Evin Prison in Tehran prior to being released.

The MEDRC conference of March 2011 took place around the same time the previously discussed Emirati spy ring was unveiled in Oman.

Meanwhile, but directly attributed to the MEDRC conference, Sultan Qaboos offered several of his Defense Ministry villas in Muscat in May 2011 where US and Iranian officials carried out their backchannel talks focusing on Tehran's nuclear program.

The purpose of these talks was for each party to understand each other's narrative, which in itself was a confidence-building measure. Oman provided the US and Iranian officials everything from communications to security guarantees to the last detail required for their endeavors. Jake Sullivan, then-Vice President Joe Biden's National Security Advisor, and William J. Burns, who was then Deputy Secretary of State, led the American delegation.

Oman continuously briefed Israel on the backchannel, which both Washington and Tehran clearly understood.

Once the parties achieved critical progress, Sultan Qaboos granted an interview to Judith Miller, an American journalist, in January 2012. In this interview, the Omani leader said that Tehran had turned to Oman to convey its wishes to commence nuclear talks with Washington.[297] By the time the interview took place, the backchannel had already produced its desired objectives, and Qaboos's decision to go on the record was to help build public support in the

United States, Israel, and Iran for the ensuing US–Iran diplomatic process.

Thus, the Omani backchannel set the stage for the Interim Agreement (or Geneva Interim Agreement), which the so-called P5+1 and Iran reached on November 24, 2013. The P5+1 included the five permanent members of the UNSC (the United States, United Kingdom, France, Russia, and China) plus Germany. The Interim Agreement stipulated a short-term freeze on portions of Tehran's nuclear program in exchange for lifting some economic sanctions on Iran. The Geneva Interim Agreement set the stage for the Joint Comprehensive Plan of Action (JCPOA), which the P5+1 and Iran signed on July 14, 2015, and sought to ensure that Iran's nuclear program would be exclusively peaceful.

By the time of the Geneva Interim Agreement's signing, the Omani backchannel had arrived at its logical conclusion as US and Iranian diplomats began direct talks within the framework of the multilateral framework leading to the JCPOA.

The US–Iran exchanges, through the Omani backchannel, helped build the foundation for the first direct talks between Washington and Tehran since Iran's revolution in 1979.[298]

The JCPOA's passage gave Oman a major diplomatic achievement that demonstrated to the world how Muscat was capable of playing a critical role in helping major powers and Iran avoid any military confrontation in relation to Tehran's nuclear activities. Oman's contribution to the JCPOA's success underscored how the Sultanate was a truly "neutral" Arab state that was willing to take risks in order to help the international community resolve global security challenges. Additionally, as a longstanding ally of the United States, the help that Omani officials gave Washington amid the talks that led to the JCPOA's watershed passage did much to further cement close ties between Muscat and the United States, particularly the Obama administration. That then-US Secretary of State John Kerry took the highly unusual step of attending the Omani national day celebration in Washington on November 18, 2015, was further evidence of the closeness between Obama's administration and the Sultanate.

Oman's help to the Obama administration vis-à-vis Iran began in early 2009, shortly after Obama's presidency began. At that time, the administration requested Oman's assistance in securing the release of three Americans detained by Iranian security forces while hiking in northern Iraq, close to the Iranian border. Although the release of the hikers did not involve direct US–Iranian engagement, the Omani facilitation of their release engendered an apparent optimism that this success could be built upon, and it also demonstrated Muscat's willingness to take risks and pay prices in order to show Oman's commitment to being a solid and reliable partner of the United States as well as an effective backchannel between Washington and Tehran.[299]

7

UAE–Omani Tensions

BATTLE OVER CULTURE AND NATIONAL IDENTITY

The Sultanate of Oman occupies a prominent geographical and historical position at the world's great waterways. Since the ancient Magan civilization, from the fourth millennium BCE, Omanis have sought contact with the nations of the ancient and modern world by taking advantage of Oman's unique geography, located at a junction of sea routes between Arabia, the Red Sea and East Africa.

By the eighth century, Omani merchants navigated the perils of the Indian Ocean and sailed to Canton in China, and to East Africa. In the first half of the nineteenth century, Oman's ruler, Sultan Said bin Sultan (1797–1856), sent merchant ships to London and New York and subsequently forged strong commercial and diplomatic ties with both Great Britain and the United States. During the peak of the Ottoman Empire, Sultan Said bin Sultan first established Oman's strategic alliances with the West. More than two centuries later, London and Washington remain Muscat principal strategic allies.

During Said bin Sultan's reign, the Omani Empire held vast territories along the Persian Gulf, including in present-day Iran, southern

OMAN EMPIRE AROUND 1850

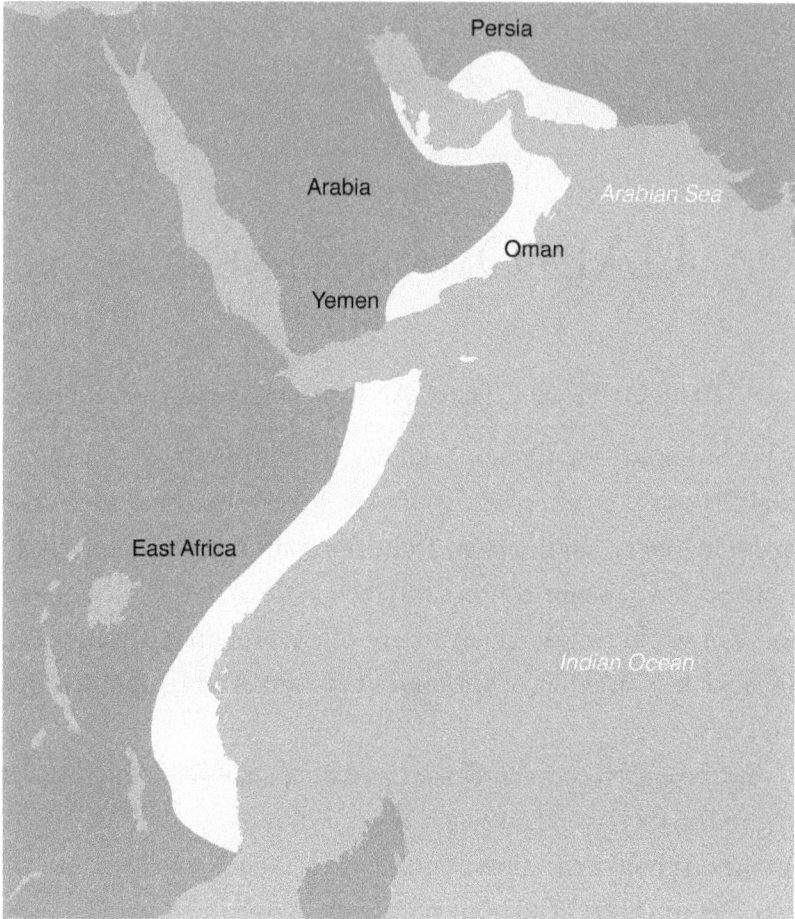

Yemen, Socotra, along with much of the East African littoral, all the way down to present-day Mozambique. According to Vincent McBrierty and Mohammad Al Zubair,

> At the height of Sayyid Said bin Sultan's rule, Oman's possessions stretched from Dhofar to Ras Musandam in Oman; in Persia, from Bostanah to Jask and Bandar Abbas, Minab and the port of Chahbahar; they included islands in the

142

Arabian-Persian Gulf, Kunk, Quesham, Laraq and Hormuz; in Asia, the coastal district of Gwadar (later transferred to Pakistan in 1958); in the Red Sea, the island of Perim, the entire east African coast from Cape Guardafui (in present-day Somalia) to Cape Delgado (in present-day Mozambique; and the inland cities of Mogadishu and Brava (in present-day Somalia), Lamu, Malindi, and Mombasa (in present-day Kenya), and Querimba and Kilwa (in present-day Tanzania).[300]

Linda Pappas Funsch similarly argues that Sultan Said bin Sultan had

elevated Oman's international stature substantially as he acquired new territories, such as Gwadar, a strategic port on the coast of Baluchistan, as well as Zanzibar, making Oman the only non-European country in the nineteenth century to hold possessions in Africa.... In time, Zanzibar became a twin capital, along with Muscat, of all territories under Oman's control, elevating Said bin Sultan to the title "First Sultan of Oman, Zanzibar and Gwadar."[301]

Meanwhile, the UAE consists of seven emirates. Sheikh Zayed bin Sultan Al Nahyan, MbZ's father, founded the country as a federation on December 2, 1971. Six of the seven emirates (Abu Dhabi, Dubai, Sharjah, Ajman, Umm Al Quwain and Fujairah) combined on that date. The seventh, Ras al Khaimah, joined the federation on February 10, 1972.

Prior to the establishment of the UAE, Sharjah, Ajman, Umm Al Quwain, and Fujairah were Omani territory, and Zayed's quest to establish the UAE was directly tied to his quest to seek independence from Oman. Under Zayed, the UAE sought to establish its own national identity, which centers on secularism, modernism, and laissez-faire capitalism.

Oman, on the contrary, has under Qaboos sought to balance its historical heritage with modernization. Until recently, however, the UAE and Oman's respective cultural outlook and national identities could not have been more different.

But since 2011, after MbZ sought to overthrow Qaboos, the issue of "cultural appropriation" has become another focal point of tensions between the two neighbors.

To that end, Oman has recently publicly accused MbZ of having expropriated its Al Azi, which is a tradition of sung poetry that for decades was integral to Omani culture and sung on all national occasions such as football matches and military parades.

Al Azi is performed in conjunction with a theatrical swordplay, known as Al Rahza, which usually relates victory in battle from the time when Oman was divided into warring tribes: the Al Azi and Rahza. The Rahza would be accompanied by horns and drums. Then the poets would begin their recitations, the Al Azi, opening with a melodious "Allahu Akhbar."

In December 2017, while the GCC crisis was at its peak in Washington, the UAE issued an application through UNESCO, the UN's world heritage body, to claim Al Azi music as its own.[302] This came after UNESCO had accepted Oman's application to register the Al Azi, which was in 2012.[303]

At the 2017 annual UNESCO meeting in South Korea, the UN decided that Al Azi "is a significant and important cultural heritage performance, reflecting UAE culture and Emirati society."[304]

Adding to the existing tensions over the UNESCO controversy to recognize Al Azi as UAE heritage, the UAE has also decided to claim the ceremonial khanjar dagger, which had been an Omani national icon for centuries, as its own.[305]

Tensions between Abu Dhabi and Muscat over the Al Rhaza dance culminated on December 2, 2017, when MbZ displayed the Al Rhaza dance in front of the Emirati National Guard during the UAE's National Day celebration.

In Oman, the perception was that MbZ's Al Azi performance constituted a veiled assault on the Sultanate's national identity and character. Qaboos's principal advisor for culture and heritage, Abdul Aziz Muhammad Al Rowas, said in an interview with Omani television on May 9, 2018, "We are gathered at this seminar to stop the aggression on the history of [our] ancestors."[306]

The conference he referred to was organized by the University of Nizwa and dedicated to the life and legacy of Al Muhallab Bin Abi Sufra Al Azdi, whom the Al Azi dance is named after. The conference's purpose was described by Mohammed bin Nasser al Mahrooqi of the University of Nizwa as organized "within the framework of the national efforts exerted by scientific research to make an effective contribution to safeguarding the legacy of our great nation in both material and non-material aspects."

Al Mahrooqi added,

> The figure of this symposium is the Omani Al Muhallab Bin Abi Sufra al Azdi, this outstanding leader, who excelled in the art of war and the making of victories, as well as in the management of the regions and the consolidation of the reign. He grew up in the house of leadership of his people, he is Abu Sufra Sariq bin Dhalim al Atki al Azdi who accepted the faith of Islam and was named by the Prophet [Muhammad] as Abu Sufra. Then, he came to the Caliph Abu Baker as

part of an Omani high-ranking official delegation headed by Abd al Julanda." He also emphasized Oman's 7,000-year-old history, including how "Oman's Empire…[had] dominated the seas of the world and extended to Asian, Indian, and African lands.[307]

In November 2017, however, Oman registered the traditional Ardha camel race as part of its "intangible cultural heritage" with UNESCO. Welcoming the development but indirectly referring to the UAE, Minister of Education Madeeha Bint Ahmed Al Shaibaniyah said, "The intangible cultural heritage has been accorded with the royal interest of His Majesty Sultan Qaboos who has been very keen on encouraging the Omani society to maintain the heritage of ancestors and not to allow modernity to take it away from its deep rooted heritage."[308]

But culture is only a proxy in the geopolitical struggle between Abu Dhabi and Muscat. Since 2011, the UAE has established a strong Emirati military presence in Somalia, Yemen, and the Bab Al Mandeb as part of a quest to gain geopolitical, economic, and military power. [309] The strength of the UAE's standing in the Horn of Africa can be directly attributed to its successful efforts in mediating an end to 20-year war between Eritrea and Ethiopia. The 2018 agreement was possible because of Emirati aid pledges, including investments in ports throughout Eritrea, which were also meant to benefit landlocked Ethiopia.

Meanwhile, in January 2018, the Louvre Abu Dhabi Museum published a new map, which omitted Qatar and showed the Omani Governorate of Musandam as part of the UAE.[310]

The omission of Musandam was an unmistakable message to Oman, which followed a pattern of tensions.

OMAN, MUSANDAM AND AL BURAIMI REGIONS

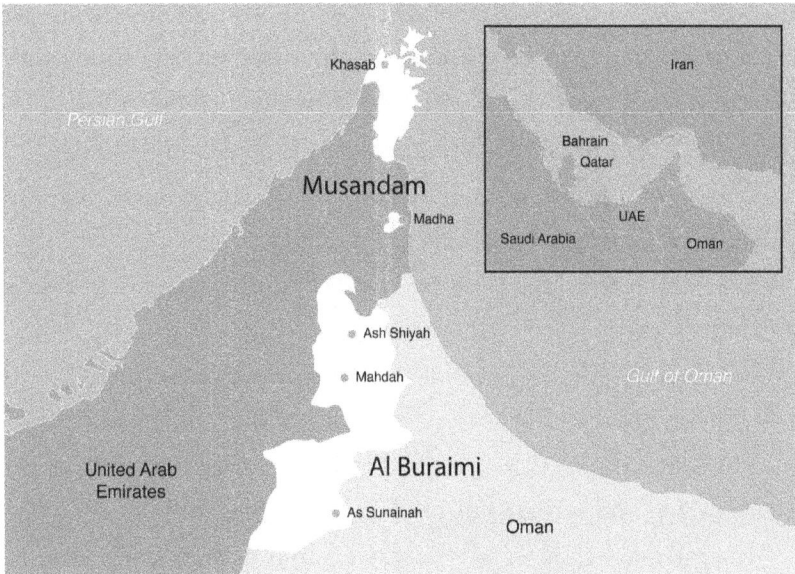

Fast forward to November 2018. A month after Netanyahu's visit, Qaboos formally responded to Emirati efforts to purchase land and property in strategic locations throughout the Sultanate and in the northern border region with the UAE in particular.

On November 11, 2018, Qaboos issued a Royal Decree that banned noncitizens from owning agricultural land and real estate in Buraimi, Musandam, Dhofar, Dhahirah, Wusta, Shinas, Liwa, Jabal Akhdhar, and Jebel Shams, along with heritage sites, agricultural lands, and sensitive locations.

Noncitizens who own land in these designated areas have to sell their properties within two years or they will be confiscated and sold by the judiciary. The properties have to be transferred to Omanis by November 11, 2020.[311] Oman's government also prohibits noncitizens from owning land on islands, sites near palaces and security and military authorities, archaeological sites, and ancient houses.[312]

The Buraimi, Musandam, and Dhahirah provinces are located in northern Oman along with the UAE border. This includes the border town of Shinas. Qaboos subsequently followed up appointing new governors for Buraimi and Musandam, both members of Oman's dominate Al Busaidi tribe, to which the royal Al Said family belongs.[313]

The Liwar province is where the city of Sohar is located and where Arab Spring protests erupted in 2011.

The Wusta province is where the strategic port city of Duqm is located.

The Jebel Akdhar is part of Al Hajar Mountains range in Ad Dakhiliyah province.

The Jebel Shams is located in northeastern Oman north of Al Hamra town and is the country's highest mountain.

Muscat fears that Abu Dhabi's regional agenda will come at Oman's expense, including that the consortium of UAE-controlled ports throughout the Horn of Africa and Yemen are meant to drive Sohar, Duqm, and Salalah into bankruptcy and strategic irrelevance.

A copy of the Royal Decree has been included in this book's reference section, in English and Arabic.

8

YEMEN

THE YEMEN WAR AND STRATEGIC
ENCIRCLEMENT OF OMAN

MbZ's previously discussed visit to Trump Tower in New York in December 2016 also proved be a watershed event for US–Gulf relations. While the high-profile visit took place when President Barack Obama was still in office, Abu Dhabi declined to notify his administration about the visit despite that being customary for foreign dignitaries to notify the US government in advance about their travels.[314] Abu Dhabi's failure to do so only underscored how eager the UAE was to influence the incoming administration on a host of issues regarding Qatar, Oman, and Yemen.

The Trump Tower meetings gave MbZ an opportunity to form his own assessments about the incoming Trump administration, including about its regional priorities. Given that the then-president-elect had initially surrounded himself with political outsiders and nonexperts, coupled with the fact that Trump had partially run on opposing the JCPOA, the Crown Prince of Abu Dhabi saw an opening to Trump's inner circle through anti-Iran rhetoric that was especially focused on Yemen.

Immediately after his Trump Tower meetings, MbZ dispatched George Nader, a controversial advisor to the UAE's de facto leader, to New York for talks with the incoming Trump administration, including then-national security advisor designee Michael Flynn and Bannon to discuss strategies for countering Tehran.[315]

MbZ came away from the Trump Tower meetings recognizing that his country had a unique opportunity to sharply increase Abu Dhabi's influence over the greater Arab region, the Gulf and Yemen in particular, by appealing to Trump's anti-Iran sentiments. But a strong relationship with the incoming Trump administration by itself would be insufficient in terms of empowering Abu Dhabi to achieve what it wanted to achieve throughout the grander Arab world. To make the UAE an increasingly influential actor in the Middle East and North Africa, MbZ recognized that strengthening his relationship with MbS was a strategic necessity. Within this context, MbZ did much to protect and advance Saudi (as well as Emirati, of course) interests when dealing with individuals from the incoming Trump administration, especially regarding the Yemeni conflict.

On behalf of the Crown Prince of Abu Dhabi, Nader brought Saudi General Ahmed Al Assiri, the spokesman of the Saudi-led coalition in Yemen, to New York for talks with Trump's inner circle. Of course, the subject was Iran. In New York, the Emirati and Saudi officials discussed efforts to promote regime change in Tehran.[316]

Immediately following Nader and Al Assiri's meetings, the UAE withdrew its Special Forces from Yemen's eastern Al Mahra Governorate, which borders Oman. But under the leadership of Al Assiri, Saudi troops swiftly replaced the Special Forces.

The UAE had maintained Special Forces in Al Mahra since 2015, but even after Saudi forces replaced their troops, the UAE kept its intelligence officers in place, who remain there until today, primarily under the Red Crescent's auspices.

The Saudi justification for entering Mahra, which is located some 1,300 kilometers from the flashpoints where the Saudi-led coalition is fighting the Houthis, was to distribute aid from the King Salman Charitable Organization to Yemenis. As part of that effort, the Saudis resumed control of Al Ghaydah Airport, which is the governorate's administrative capital and sole airport. Immediately after usurping control of the airport, the Saudis built a prison on site.

From an Omani vantage point, the Saudi presence in Mahra is destabilizing and provocative. For many decades, Oman has been the most influential non-Yemeni power in the governorate. The Omanis have been heavily involved in Mahra by providing humanitarian assistance and other forms of aid.

Most residents of Al Mahra maintain Omani, Saudi, and Emirati citizenship. In fact, because of geographical and tribal links, along with deep historical ties, Mahra has for all practical purposes served as an Omani buffer zone against the war in Yemen. Because of tribal affiliations, relations between Oman and Al Mahra are centuries old. But ever since the Dhofar rebellion, Oman has operated charitable groups in Mahra.

AL MAHRA, YEMEN

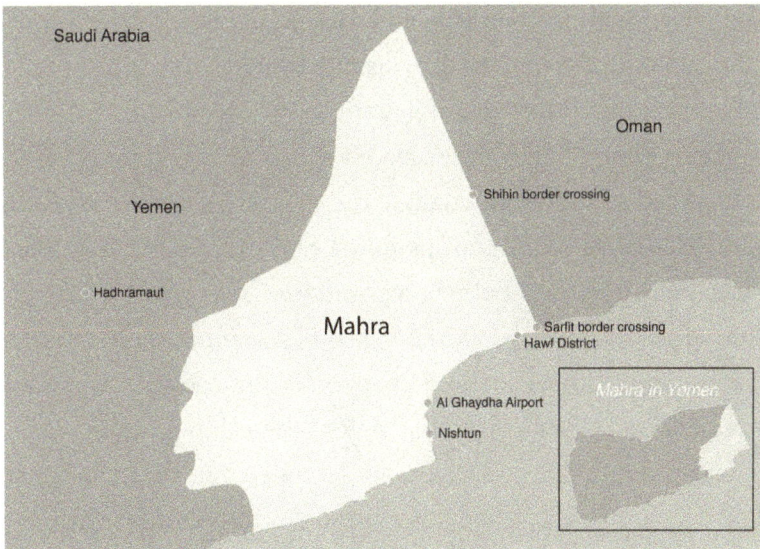

151

Mahra residents maintain close cultural and traditional links, including dress such as wearing the Khanjar—Djanbia in the Yemeni context—and the turbans in similar fashions.

A sizable part of the population in Al Mahra does not speak Arabic as a primary language. Non-Arabic speakers primarily speak Mehri or Mahri, a modern southern Arabian language. The people that speak Mahri call themselves "Mahris" and are presumed to be descendants of the ancient people of 'Ad.

Considering these longstanding ties, local tribes swiftly objected to the Coalition's decision to take over the Al Ghaydah Airport. Because of local opposition, the Coalition's commander in Mahra, Brigadier General Abdulaziz Al Sharif, and the tribes reached an agreement in March 2017 in which the airport should only be used for humanitarian efforts and not be turned into a military base.

The agreement, however, was swiftly violated by the Coalition as it turned the airport into a military base where Coalition military planes arrive on a daily basis and all civilians, including locals, are barred from entering its premises. Apache helicopters are stationed there, along with ammunition and weapon depots.

No Coalition aid has to date been delivered to Mahra.

In parallel with resuming control of the airport, Yemeni President Abdrabbuh Mansur Hadi forced the long-term governor, Mohammed Abdullah Kuddah, to resign after he spoke out against Saudi Arabia's presence and appointed its own governor, Rajeh Said Bakrit. Hadi approved Bakrit's appointment, which was instrumental in order to quell the initial opposition against the Coalition's presence in the governorate. His appointment took place as Saudi forces entered. Ever since that point, there has been a gradual yet consistent deployment of Saudi forces to Yemen, including to Mahra's coastal areas. These forces now control fisheries, which is of strategic importance as most of the local population is economically dependent on fisheries.

Since entering this part of Yemen, the Saudis have established 26 military checkpoints along the coast of Al Mahra. Saudi Arabia's coastal command is located in the center of the port city of Nishtun, Al Mahra's only seaport.

Because the Coalition Commander makes all the final decisions, the new governor has limited power. Hadi has fired all local officials who initially protested the Saudi presence in Al Mahra.

Local tribes have also protested against Saudi Arabia's presence in Nishtun. The protests started in January 2017. They are ongoing. So far, they have been peaceful but are taking place throughout Al Mahra's nine districts, three of which are coastal and six inland.

In November 2018, Saudi-backed Yemeni militias killed two protestors in the Hawf district. Subsequently, a crackdown on protestors took place. The joint Saudi/Emirati command in Hadhramaut Governorate ordered the arrest of its leaders after hacking their phones.

The tribes of Al Mahra reported that the military camps should be run by locals. Initially, the Coalition and the locals reached an agreement to do so, but the agreement was violated. Outsiders, mostly from Abyan Governorate, where they have been trained by Saudi and Emirati forces, staffed it. When they arrived in Al Mahra, they were disguised as members of Yemen's Coast Guard but were in fact militia members operating outside of the Yemeni state, which in turn concerned the local tribes. Some of these militia fighters belonged to Al Qaeda in the Arabian Peninsula (AQAP).

Saudi troops have also deployed to the Omani–Yemen border, which is roughly 300 kilometers long. Along this boundary, the Saudis have established 20 military checkpoints, as well as a large camp.

In March 2018, the Saudi commander, Brigadier General Abdulaziz Al Sharif, reached an agreement with local tribal leaders and protestors represented by Sultan Abdullah Issa Al Afror, who is the grandson of the last sultan of Mahra and Socotra.

The agreement outlined the following goals:

1. Saudi troops would leave the airport and turn the management over to civilians.

2. The airport would not serve any military purposes.

3. Saudi Arabia would withdraw from the Nishtun seaport.

4. Saudi Arabia would withdraw from the Sarfit and Shehen border crossings with Oman, the only two border crossings that are still open. Saudi Arabia has closed all of its border crossings with Yemen.

5. Local authorities would manage airport and border crossings.

The protests ended once the agreement was reached. But three months later, the Saudis violated it as Riyadh continued deploying additional troops and weapons to this part of Yemen.

Saudi Arabia's justification for establishing checkpoints along Yemen's border with Oman and along the coastlines was to crack down on weapons smuggling and drug trafficking to the Houthis. The Saudis have caught no weapons or drugs during this period, neither at land nor at sea, nor before the Saudi presence in Al Mahra.

Despite various media reports suggesting alleged weapons smuggling from Oman into Yemen, then-Secretary Mattis praised Sultan Qaboos for his commitment to regional peace and stability when pressed on the matter, underscoring Washington's apparent satisfaction with Muscat.[317] This was reconfirmed in the United

States' subsequent official statements, including following Secretary Pompeo's visit to Muscat in January 2019.[318]

The United Nations has similarly concluded in its latest report about ISIS, Al Qaeda, and other associated groups that Al Mahra does not serve as a transit point for smuggling. Instead, it notes that the financing of ISIS's local franchise(s) in Yemen

> depends on external support. Cash is reportedly smuggled via intermediaries through the Syrian Arab Republic to neighboring Gulf countries, then into Yemen. The group's finance chief, Sanad Al Jazrawi (not listed), often travels to the city of Ghaydah in [Mahra] Governorate to receive payments. Funds are sometimes brought in by new members, or are smuggled into Yemen by sea to Hudaydah and the coastal strip.

As of March 2019, Saudi Arabia dispatched two brigades, each consisting of 2,500 Saudi troops (5,000 in total), to Al Mahra, but the number of troops arriving on a daily basis is increasing. In addition to the Saudi troops stationed in Mahra, the following contingencies have been deployed as well:

- The Yemeni Coast Guard, which is made up of militia fighters operating outside of the Yemeni state, now accounts for 1,300 service members.

- Special Forces, also militia fighters operating outside of the Yemeni state, account for 1,500 service members.

- Among the various militia fighters brought into Mahra, a significant number are believed to be AQAP members. Several of the AQAP fighters arrived in Mahra following an agreement between the UAE and AQAP in Hadhramaut in 2017. Others came from Abiyan, an AQAP sanctuary.

- The UAE has also sought to bring Southern Transitional Council (STC)-linked militias to Mahra. The STC is an Abu Dhabi-sponsored group, which aims to (re)-establish an independent state in southern Yemen.

According to officials in the area, locals prefer to take security into their own hands, and they are prepared to do so.

Fears of Saudi Arabia possibly closing the only two border crossings into Oman, which currently serve as the only exit points for wounded Yemenis seeking medical treatment at the Sultan Qaboos Hospital in Salalah, are increasing tensions in Al Mahra, where no hospitals function. The fact that the Saudis have already closed the Sarfit border crossing for commerce and trade, limiting its use to movement of people, has added to such local worries, contributing to a narrative that the Saudis shut it down in order to make the economy of Al Mahra increasingly dependent on Saudi Arabia while also increasingly cut off from Oman. Furthermore, in Oman many are concerned about purported Saudi/Emirati goals of making Muscat submit to the regional agendas of its GCC neighbors, which are fueling tensions with Muscat via their actions in the part of Yemen bordering Oman.

SALAFIST EXTREMISTS

Oman is the only Arab country where a majority of its people practice Ibadi Islam, which is neither Sunni nor Shiite. Ibadism has its origin in an early Islamic movement whose principals are anchored in the belief that the leadership of the faithful, an Imam, should be elected on the basis of his scholarship and piety.[319] Out of the 4.6 million Omanis, almost 3 million practice Ibadism.[320]

Some Muslims also practice Ibadism in East Africa, especially in Zanzibar, and in parts of the Maghreb, including in Tunisia, Algeria and Libya.

Thus, Saudi Arabia's Salafist interpretation of Islam is widely considered threatening to Ibadism as Saudi clerics, even citizens, routinely denounce Ibadi Muslims as "infidels." These dynamics, along with Riyadh's longstanding support for Salafists, created significant tensions between Saudis and Omanis.

Thus, with Bakrit's appointment as Mahra governor, Saudi Arabia evacuated Salafists from Yemen's Saada Governorate, which is the heartland of the Houthis, a Shiite Zeidi sect whose historic origins are based in northern Yemen along the Saudi border, to Mahra.

The ongoing war between Yemen's Houthi rebels and Coalition can be directly attributed to Riyadh's longstanding support for Salafist educational centers in northern Yemen, including the Dammaj Institute, which has a Wahhabi ideology.

The present state of tensions between Saudi Arabia and the Houthis can be partially explained by a contentious relationship between the two neighbors that stretches back to the 1960s. At that time, Riyadh began granting generous government subsidies to various Yemeni factions, ranging from tribal sheikhs to clerics and political leaders. The tribes residing along the border benefited in particular as a result of this Saudi effort, which the Yemeni government saw as destabilizing.

Riyadh also sought to influence Yemeni affairs by supporting a number of Wahhabi educational institutions throughout the county. Over time, as Saudi influence increased and its Wahhabi institutions grew stronger, former President Ali Abdullah Saleh, the country's strongman for nearly 33 years (1978 to 2012), initially sought to counterbalance his mighty neighbor by incrementally supporting Houthi militants and providing them with cash grants.

Just as the Salafist presence in Saada was threatening to the Zeidi's interpretation of Islam—and a tool of the Saudi state exerting its influence while spreading Wahhabism by setting up a Salafist institute in the city of Dammaj—so too is it threatening to Mahra and its local population. After locals protested reestablishing the Dammaj Institute in Al Mahra, the Saudi coalition commander reached an agreement in April 2017. Under this agreement, he was to disperse the estimated 1,000 Salafists (mostly Saudi, French, and Nigerian citizens) throughout Al Mahra's nine districts and prevent them from opening up their institute. The Salafists, however, now control an estimated one-third of Al Mahra's 314 mosques, from where they propagate their interpretation of the Islamic faith, and also live.

The Salafist presence in Al Mahra also threatens Oman's Dhofar province, which is mostly Sunni. In this part of Oman, many locals fear that the Salafists in eastern Yemen could influence a younger generation.

There is, however, a precedence for Saudi Arabia's decision to dispatch Salafists to Al Mahra, as it had previously done so to Al Buraimi during the 1950s.

Buraimi is an oasis and province on the Oman–UAE border. In 1949, Saudi Arabia made a sovereign claim to the territory as Riyadh sought to expand the Kingdom's oil exploration activities, nearly triggering a war with Oman. Oman's major oil and natural gas infrastructure is located in the northeastern part of the country, along the UAE/Saudi borders but not in Buraimi itself.[321]

Britain, which acted on behalf of Oman and Abu Dhabi, expelled Saudi Arabia from the oasis in 1955, ultimately thwarting another conflict in the Middle East. But the Omani–Saudi border dispute over Al Buraimi remained unsettled until the 1990s, when the matter was resolved by Sultan Qaboos and King Fahd Bin Abdulaziz Al Saud.[322]

Back in Yemen, where Washington has fought AQAP for over a decade, the newly established Salafist presence in Al Mahra threatens to radicalize the local youth, and it could also evolve into a spiritual and ideological center for the AQAP and likeminded groups.

In 2009, AQAP demonstrated its global reach when one of its members, Umar Farouk Abdulmutallab, also known as the "Underwear Bomber," was convicted of attempting to detonate plastic explosives hidden in his underwear while on board Northwest Airlines Flight 253 en route from Amsterdam to Detroit, Michigan, on December 25, 2009. Abdulmutallab, a Nigerian national, had studied at a Salafist institution in Sanaa known as Iman University. Iman University was spearheaded by Abdul Majid Al Zindani, who remains in self-imposed exile in Saudi Arabia despite a US extradition request. Al Zindani was once a theological adviser to Osama bin Laden.[323]

After capturing Sanaa in September 2014, the Houthis closed down Iman University, which Al Zindani established. In 2004, the US Treasury Department classified Al Zindani as a Specially Designated Global Terrorist. The United Nations has also sanctioned him.

But beyond AQAP potentially establishing an intellectual center in Al Mahra through its networks of now Salafist-controlled mosques, the local al-Qaeda franchise has also obtained advanced US weapons, which Washington initially sold to Saudi Arabia and the UAE.[324] Some of the US manufactured weapons that Saudi Arabia and the UAE transferred to AQAP include guns, anti-tank missiles, armored vehicles, heat-seeking lasers, and artillery. Whether any of these weapons are currently present in Al Mahra is unclear.

Tensions in Al Mahra prompted Hadi to attend an extraordinary Parliamentary session on April 21, 2019, in the government-controlled city of Sayoun, located in eastern Yemen.

Among the items Hadi discussed was an exclusive report authored by tribal leaders, which is included in this book's reference section in Arabic and English. The report outlines the fragile security situation in Al Mahra. A copy of an agreement reached between Al Mahra tribal leaders and the commander of the Saudi Coalition in Al Mahra is also included.

SOCOTRA

In April 2018, UAE Special Forces took over control of sea and airports on Yemen's Socotra, a remote albeit strategically located archipelago made up of six islands. Without any Houthi presence on Socotra, the conflict between the Iranian-backed insurgents and the Saudi-backed, UN-recognized Yemeni government has not led to violence in the Yemeni archipelago.

Abu Dhabi's decision to exert control over Socotra was not only about facilitating the UAE's access to East Africa. The Emiratis' vision for Socotra has to do with efforts to encircle the Sultanate, at least according to many Omanis. The UAE Special Forces, however, eventually withdrew, and some 1,000 Saudi troops have replaced them. Efforts have also been made to grant Emirati nationality to the people of Socotra.[325]

The Saudi troops are stationed at the Hadebo Airport, which also serves as the local military headquarters. The Emirati presence is limited to intelligence agents who primarily serve in the disguise of the Emirati Red Crescent.

The UAE's respective decisions to dispatch Special Forces to Al Mahra and Socotra, only to eventually withdraw once Saudi troops moved in to replace them, while establishing military headquarters at the local airports follow a clear pattern. The fact that there is no Houthi presence in either Mahra or Socotra, only exacerbates Omani fears of strategic encirclement.

SOCOTRA ARCHIPELAGO

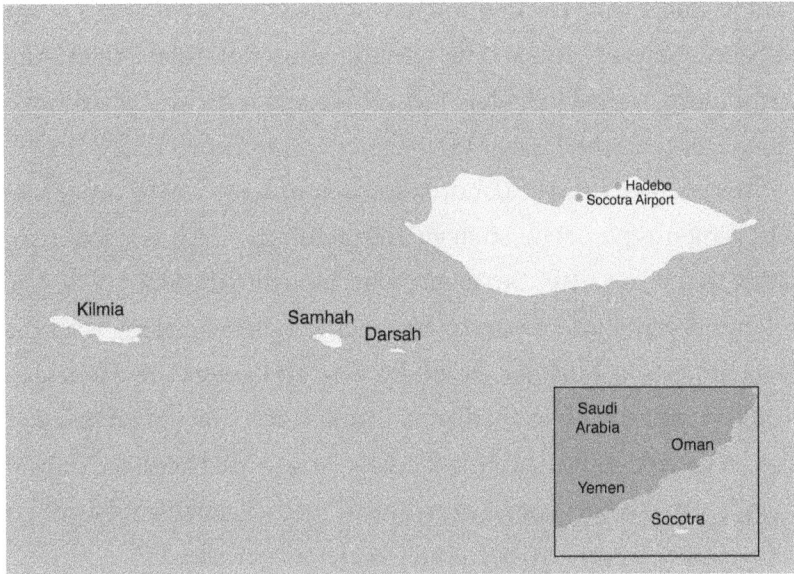

UAE-OMAN-YEMEN

In June 2019, Abu Dhabi announced its decision to withdraw some of its forces from the areas surrounding Yemen's western port city of Hodeidah amid increasing US congressional opposition to the Trump administration's involvement in the war.[326]

Controlled by the Houthis, the Hodeidah port is presently Yemen's only operational port. All humanitarian aid entering the war-torn country goes through this port.

Thus, the UAE's decision to withdraw from Hodeidah came after Washington had repeatedly denied numerous requests from Abu Dhabi to capture the city in order to prevent a countrywide famine in the event of the port's closure.[327] The humanitarian crisis in Yemen remains the worst in the world, according to the United Nations.[328]

The UAE's withdrawal from Hodeidah should thus be seen in the context of America's rancorous partisan politics. Seeking to preserve the UAE's standing in the United States, Abu Dhabi wanted to prevent its image from eroding and having the UAE be seen as too close to Saudi Arabia's MbS and his signature war. Regardless, the UAE's withdrawal from Hodeidah was consistent with the Stockholm Agreement, reached under UN auspices on December 13, 2018.[329]

Irrespective of the UAE's drawdown from Yemen, MbZ appears to see "Yemen as part of his strategy to establish the UAE as a dominant player in the larger Red Sea arena, stretching into the Horn of Africa. Emirati domination of eastern and southern Yemen, along with the Yemeni ports at Mukalla, Aden, Mocha, and potentially Hodeidah would ensure the UAE's ability to establish a command presence in crucial shipping lanes through the Arabian and Red Seas, the Bab Al Mandeb, to the Suez Canal when paired with its growing presence on Africa's Red Sea coast," according to Gerald Feierstein.[330]

The present power play against Oman, triggered by the UAE's espionage attempts and the Saudi military presence on the Yemen/Oman border, suggest that Abu Dhabi and Riyadh's strategic objectives may entail squeezing Oman as the Sultanate adjusts to the post-Qaboos era. These objectives explain the UAE's support for the STC.

In August 2019, thousands of Yemenis demonstrated in the southern city of Aden in favor of southern Yemen gaining independence from the north after STC fighters had successfully entered and occupied a presidential place in Aden, which also served as the regional headquarters for President Hadi, who nominally governs from exile in Saudi Arabia.[331] Meanwhile, in Washington, the UAE is funding the STC's lobbying agenda with the ultimate objective of securing US support for an independent southern Yemen.[332]

The STC is an umbrella under which militia groups that support southern independence, including the so-called Security Belt and

Shabwani Elites, operate in tandem. The Security Belt hails from Aden and its surrounding areas, and the Shabwani Elites are from Shabwa Governorate. The STC leadership, which has excluded the veteran leadership of the southern secessionist movement from the 1990s, is arguably a UAE proxy.[333] As of writing, the vice president of the STC, Hani Bin Buraik, has a picture of MbZ on his twitter profile.[334] Because of the STC's close affiliation with Abu Dhabi, the STC faces its share of opposition from southerners in general.[335]

PEOPLE'S DEMOCRATIC REPUBLIC OF YEMEN

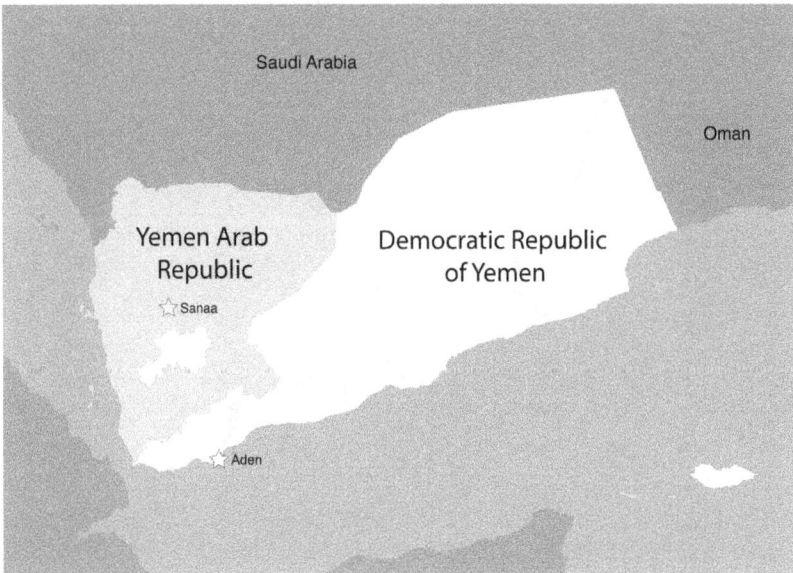

9

Conclusion

HOW DURABLE IS THE SAUDI ARABIA-UAE ALLIANCE?

The murder of Saudi journalist Jamal Khashoggi at the Kingdom's Consulate in Istanbul on October 2, 2018, was a watershed moment for the US–Saudi strategic partnership.

While Trump initially provided conflicting assessments over whether MbS had ordered the murder, the UAE, followed by Bahrain and Egypt, immediately rallied behind Saudi Arabia and the Crown Prince. They did so symbolically in a few ways, including by hosting him while he was on his way to South America in 2018 for the G-20 Summit in Buenos Aires.[336] MbS did not visit Oman even though Muscat had "welcomed" Saudi Arabia's investigation into the murder. His decision to omit Oman from his regional tour once again added some tension to Muscat–Riyadh relations.[337]

At a critical moment for MbS, when the Khashoggi affair was harming the US–Saudi relationship, the Quartet demonstrated that Riyadh's regional allies would not abandon MbS. Saudi Arabia, for its part, has denied MbS's involvement and instead pledged to bring those responsible for the murder to justice while maintaining that it had been carried out by a "rogue" entity within the Saudi state.[338]

Amid growing US and international outrage over the murder, which culminated in Congressional opposition to Trump's military support for the Saudi Arabia–led coalition fighting in Yemen, the leaders of the UAE, Bahrain, and Egypt truly stood by MbS, solidifying their close alliances with him in the process.[339]

These dynamics informed Saudi Arabia's decision to invite Amir Tamim to attend the 2018 GCC Summit in Riyadh, which was the first diplomatic olive branch extended by the Quartet to Doha since the crisis erupted.

But just prior to the Summit, Emirati and Bahraini officials escalated their anti-Qatar rhetoric, which in turn suggested that the crisis would linger on past the Summit regardless of whether the Amir of Qatar decided to attend.

For instance, in an interview with *Asharq Al-Awsat*, a Saudi-owned newspaper based in London, Bahrain's Foreign Minister Khalid Al Khalifa accused Qatar of having burned its bridges with the rest of the GCC and aligning itself with "enemies of the region like Iran." He added, "These issues do not indicate that Qatar will remain a member of the GCC, but we are dealing with this topic realistically."[340]

On December 6, 2018, the UAE's Minister of State for Foreign Affairs Anwar Gargash declared, "The [GCC] political crisis will end when the cause behind it ends and that is Qatar's support of extremism and its interference in the stability of the region."[341]

From a Qatari vantage point, such rhetoric from Quartet countries suggested that the Saudi invitation was aimed at making concessions to the Trump administration, rather than a genuine desire to resolve the GCC crisis. Because the animosity toward Qatar remained in place, Amir Tamim declined the invitation to attend.

Instead, Qatar dispatched Minister of State for Foreign Affairs Sultan bin Saad Al Muraikhi, who had the same level of representation as the officials sent by Saudi Arabia, UAE, and Bahrain to the 2017 GCC Summit in Kuwait.[342] The level of participation from both sides of the GCC schism were political messages that left no ambiguity about their entrenched positions. Predictably, Bahrain's government criticized the Amir's decision not attend the Riyadh Summit.[343]

It can be argued that Abu Dhabi is resolute in its opposition to Gulf reconciliation. The Emirati leadership appears more intent on strengthening its ties with Saudi Arabia and Bahrain along with non-GCC partners such as Egypt and Libya's Tobruk-based administration—which allies with General Khalifa Haftar—than in restoring GCC unity, which would require Emirati concessions to Qatar.

Because of Saudi Arabia's geography and large population, the Kingdom will continue to dominate the Gulf region irrespective of the GCC's status.

Qatar, of course, being the small state that it is, would benefit the most from GCC reconciliation, which in practical terms means lifting the blockade. Such a development would allow Qatar's citizens to reunite with family members or conduct commerce throughout the Gulf region uninterrupted even if the personal relationships between the ruling GCC families, particularly between Abu Dhabi and Doha's rulers, remain fraught.

Saudi Arabia's strategic alliance with Abu Dhabi has proven to be of particular value to Riyadh as the Kingdom has directly benefitted from the UAE's web of strong relationships, especially in Washington throughout the messy Khashoggi affair.

This became apparent when several Washington think tanks announced that they would no longer accept Saudi funding, which in turn strengthened Riyadh's dependency on Abu Dhabi to champion its interests in the US capital. For the Saudis, the Emiratis did so through Abu Dhabi's networks within the US foreign policy establishment.[344]

The following Washington research organizations have received funding from the UAE: Atlantic Council, Center for Strategic & International Studies, Middle East Institute, and the Arab Gulf States Institute in Washington.[345], [346], [347] The Center for a New American Security and the Center for American Progress have also received Emirati funding.[348], [349]

The Brookings Institution receives partial funding from Qatar.[350]

Qatar is also funding the Arab Center Washington DC (ACW), which is a branch of the Doha-based Arab Center for Research and Policy Studies (ACRPS), and Gulf International Forum.

The UAE's web of alliances in Washington, however, extend beyond mainstream think thanks, advocacy groups, and lobbying firms. Now they likely include the Security Studies Group (SGCC). Through its messaging and articles published by its affiliated research-ers, the SGCC actively targets Trump's Make America Great Again constituency. Since its inception, SGCC has almost exclusively been committing itself to attacking Qatar while advocating for broader US strategic cooperation with the UAE, Saudi Arabia, Bahrain, and Egypt.

The SGCC and its affiliated researchers also published sev-eral columns attacking Khashoggi, whom they have also targeted on Twitter.[351], [352] The Jerusalem Post published an article based on Khashoggi's own social media posts, including some of them which he made at least a decade ago. The piece was meant to portray Khashoggi as an "anti-Semite."[353] The UAE, through SGCC, made a strategic decision to smear the slain journalist for political gain.

Despite the UAE's strong standing in Washington, MbZ has not visited the White House since the GCC crisis broke out in mid-2017. It is unclear whether this has been his own decision to keep a distance from Trump and his unpredictable foreign policy or the Trump administration has deliberately not invited him because of the Gulf crisis.

Robert S. Mueller III's investigation into Russia's role in the 2016 election was another sensitive and controversial topic for the UAE. President Vladimir Putin of Russia and MbZ were the only two foreign heads of state named in the Mueller report.[354]

Nader, on behalf of MbZ, brokered a meeting between Trump campaign confidant Erik Prince and Kirill Dmitriev, the head of Russia's sovereign wealth fund, in the Seychelles in early January 2017. The Mueller report concluded that Dmitriev had acted as an emissary for Putin, hoping to cultivate ties with the Trump administration. [355]

While Prince, the founder of the private military firm Blackwater, enjoyed relations with Trump officials, Dmitriev had requested Nader's assistance to access Trump transition team members, according to the Mueller report.[356]

From the Emiratis, however, the Seychelles meeting was part of an effort to help establish relations between the incoming Trump administration and Moscow. Abu Dhabi most likely did not envision that its backchannel would devolve into a political football in America's hyper-partisan environment.

MbS, for his part, is no longer able to visit the United States because of the Khashoggi murder despite the Trump administration's continuous support for him.

The Qatari Amir and his Kuwaiti counterpart are the only GCC leaders to have visited the White House on an annual basis. Amir Sabah of Kuwait was set to visit Trump at the White House in September 2019, but such plans were canceled because of the ailing monarch's declining health.[357]

Irrespective of the MbZ–Trump dynamic, Abu Dhabi temporarily succeeded in influencing US policy vis-à-vis Libya after the president accepted a phone call from Libyan commander Khalifa Haftar in April 2019. Trump and Haftar discussed the UAE-backed Libyan National Army (LNA)'s advances on Tripoli. Following their conversation, the White House released a statement that said that the United States "recognized Field Marshal Haftar's significant role in fighting terrorism and securing Libya's oil resources, and the two discussed a shared vision for Libya's transition to a stable, democratic political system."[358]

A day before the Trump–Haftar phone call, Pompeo hosted his Emirati counterpart, Abdullah bin Zayed Al Nahyan (AbZ), in Washington.[359] Prior to the Pompeo–AbZ meeting, Egyptian President Abdel Fattah El Sisi hosted the Libyan strongman in Cairo in order to provide support for the LNA as it was fighting to capture Tripoli.[360] Prior to AbZ's visit to Washington, his deputy, Anwar Gargash, visited the US capital on the day after El Sisi hosted Haftar in Cairo.

At the end of 2019, Haftar had not secured a White House visit, and neither has he been able to capture Tripoli, which in turn illustrated Abu Dhabi's diminishing influence on the Trump administration in relation to Libya.

AbZ became the first and only senior-level UAE official to visit Washington in nearly a year. He last visited Washington in May 2018, a month after Amir Tamim's White House meeting.[361]

All considered, the UAE's only senior level visitors to Washington since the crisis erupted have been AbZ and National Security Advisor Tahnoun Bin Mohammed Al Nahyan, who sought to establish a US–UAE–Saudi Trilateral Summit during MbS's visit to Washington in March 2018. But that effort failed as UAE/Saudi conversations with US officials exclusively focused on the war in Yemen.

CONCLUSION

UAE AND IRAN

Tensions in the Persian Gulf have incrementally increased since May 2019 when four oil tankers were sabotaged off the UAE's coast in the Sea of Oman. Also in July, Iran seized an Emirati-based ship, which it accused of illegally smuggling Iranian fuel. The UAE, however, sought to downplay tensions by claiming that the ship was neither owned nor operated by the state.[362]

Iran subsequently seized two British-flagged oil tankers in the Persian Gulf in what Tehran described as a retaliation for British authorities seizing an Iranian tanker in Gibraltar.

At the time, Iranian officials also began to threaten the UAE directly, warning that in the event of a US–Iran war, Tehran would strike all of the UAE's territory deliberately and indiscriminately.

Tehran's decision to escalate tensions with the UAE arguably resulted from Abu Dhabi's support for anti-Iranian pressure groups in the United States, such as United Against a Nuclear Iran (UANI) and FDD.

In August 2019, well after Iran had started to threaten the UAE, Tehran also threatened FDD by accusing the organization of imposing "economic terrorism" on the Islamic Republic.[363] In September, Iran's government similarly threatened UANI ahead of its annual conference.[364]

Responding to Iranian pressure, the UAE demonstrated flexibility regarding its position vis-à-vis the Islamic Republic by dispatching a Coast Guard delegation spearheaded by Emirati Coastguard Commander Brigadier General Mohammad Ali Mosleh Al Ahbabi to Tehran in July 2019.[365] Although the talks were publicly framed as focusing "on maritime security" in the Gulf, the UAE and Iran reached an agreement under which Abu Dhabi would not be attacked by Tehran provided that it withdrew from Yemen and stopped funding anti-Iranian activity in Washington.

The Emirati–Iranian understanding was reached once it became clear that Trump would not pursue a military confrontation against Iran after the IRGC shot down a US military drone in June 2019. The agreement between Iran and the UAE was sealed during a visit to Tehran by Tahnoun Bin Zayed Al Nahyan.

Commenting on the US drone, Iranian Foreign Minister Javad Zarif tweeted: "At 00:14 US drone took off from UAE in stealth mode & violated Iranian airspace. It was targeted at 04:05 at the coordinates (25°59'43"N 57°02'25"E) near Kouh-e Mobarak."[366]

That the UAE had changed its position vis-à-vis Iran became evident during UANI's annual conference, which took place during the sidelines of the UNGA in New York on September 25, 2019. No Emirati officials were listed as speakers.[367] That was significant given that Ambassador Otaiba delivered a keynote address during the organization's annual conference in 2018.[368]

Arguably, the UAE's diplomatic flexibility vis-à-vis Iran was directly tied to Abu Dhabi's diminishing influence vis-à-vis the Trump administration coupled with Tehran's repeated threats against the Emirates.

Iran's successive warnings to the UAE set the stage for the unpresented missile and drone attacks on Saudi Arabia's Abqaiq plant and its Khurais oil field, which led to the interruption of an estimated 5.7 million barrels of the Kingdom's crude oil production per day.[369] Yemen's Houthi rebels claimed the attacks, frequently labeled as the Aramco attacks, which took place on September 14, 2019.

The United States and Saudi Arabia accused Iran of orchestrating the Aramco attacks, which Tehran denied. Riyadh has also maintained that 25 missiles and drones struck Khurais and Abqaiq.

Purportedly, 18 drones hit Abqaiq, with 3 cruise missiles failing to strike directly, and 4 missiles hit Khurais.[370]

Despite Tehran's successive threats against the UAE prior to the Aramco attacks, Iran's decision to strike the heart of the Kingdom's oil industry must be interpreted as a warning to all six GCC member states regarding the Islamic Republic's ability to capitalize on their lack of trust in the Trump administration. Furthermore, the attacks against Saudi oil infrastructure in September 2019 were partially an Iranian attempt to split the Abu Dhabi–Riyadh nexus.

In a direct response to Trump's decision not to respond militarily to the Abqaiq and Khurais attacks, Saudi Arabia tasked Pakistani Prime Minister Imran Khan to carry messages to Iran as part of an effort to reduce regional tensions.[371] Riyadh's decision to solicit Pakistani (as opposed to Omani) assistance was indicative of the tense state of Omani–Saudi relations.

Regarding Yemen, Saudi Arabia and UAE clearly have diverging interests as Riyadh supports the Islah Party, a local MB offshoot, whereas Abu Dhabi opposes the organization.

Despite Saudi Arabia and the UAE's differences over the Islah Party, their strategic alliance solidified further during the aftermath of the Khashoggi killing, including in Washington, where Riyadh continued to benefit from Abu Dhabi's relationships.

Trump's unpredictable foreign policy, especially toward Iran during the immediate post–Abqaiq and Khurais attacks, also contributed to reinforcement of the Saudi–Emirati strategic partnership.

AN ASSESSMENT OF THE GULF–ISRAEL–IRAN NEXUS

It became clear after Trump's Riyadh Summit that his Middle East strategy rested on Saudi Arabia and Israel serving as co-pillars of the

US security architecture, which would align the GCC, Egypt, and Jordan against Iran while at the same time the US administration would begin to draw up its own comprehensive plan for a peace between Israelis and Palestinians.

In Washington, a narrative emerged that an opportunity existed for Israeli–Saudi realignment in wake of mutual opposition to the Obama administration's policies in the Middle East, especially those related to Iran. A few developments led some analysts to conclude that a strategic shift was underway. First was Riyadh's decision to grant Air India permission to use Saudi airspace when flying from New Delhi to Tel Aviv.[372] Second were the agreements with Israel regarding the transfer of sovereignty over the Tiran and Sanafir Islands from Egypt to Saudi Arabia.[373] Third was a more nuanced media coverage of Israel in the Saudi media.

TIRAN & SANAFIR ISLANDS

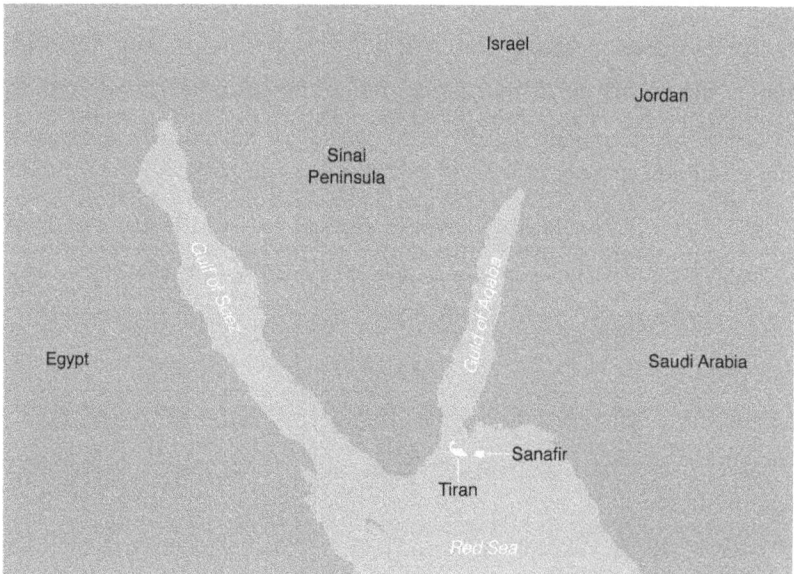

Since Trump entered the Oval Office in early 2017, the highly regulated Saudi media has interviewed senior Israeli military officials, including then-Defense Minister Avigdor Lieberman and Chief of General Staff of the Israel Defense Forces Lt. Gen. Gadi Eisenkot.[374], [375]

At the same time, MbS's de facto recognition of Israel's right to exist, which he articulated in an interview with US journalist Jeffrey Goldberg, was a further boost to his public relations campaign in America.[376]

Goldberg writes, "On Iran's supreme leader, Ayatollah [Ali] Khamenei, who is, in the prince's mind, worse than Hitler; and on Israel. He told me he recognizes the right of the Jewish people to have a nation-state of their own next to a Palestinian state; no Arab leader has ever acknowledged such a right."

Washington saw MbS's rhetoric as further evidence of Saudi Arabia's leadership trying to make the Saudi public increasingly accustomed to the possibility of further public engagement with Israel. The stark contrast between how the Saudi media covered Qatar and Israel throughout the Gulf crisis underscored how significant changes in Saudi foreign policy were becoming with MbS and his father at the helm in Riyadh.

Despite then-President Obama's best efforts to narrow Israeli–Saudi differences during the post-JCPOA environment, in parallel with his own efforts to promote Arab–Israeli peace, at the time Riyadh rejected all initiatives, including the proposal to allow overflight between Israel and Saudi Arabia, which it recently approved.

These dynamics set the stage for Netanyahu's unprecedented statement on November 2, 2018, on the Khashoggi- ontroversy. He declared that even though the murder was "horrendous," it was still necessary to preserve Saudi Arabia's stability. His statement demonstrated Israel's de facto support for MbS at a sensitive time in order to strengthen the Israel–Quartet relationship while balancing off Turkey.

Netanyahu's statement came only weeks after UANI had hosted Mossad Director Yossi Cohen, Secretary of State Mike Pompeo, US National Security Advisor John Bolton, Saudi Foreign Minister Adel Al Jubair, and the UAE's ambassador to Washington, Yusuf Al Otaiba, along with his Bahraini counterpart, Abdullah bin Rashed bin Abdullah Al Khalifa.[377]

The UANI event left little doubt about the robust relationship between Israel and the Quartet. The UAE and Israel's diplomatic activity in Washington did much to lay the ground for preparations for the event. Whether or not any additional Emirati or Saudi concessions were made to Netanyahu for his de facto support for MbS in wake of the Khashoggi affair is unclear.[378]

But the Israel-Quartet relationship is significant. For instance, in March 2018, Netanyahu met with the Emirati and Bahraini ambassadors to Washington.[379] The Israeli Prime Minister's visit at the White House was tied to Iran.[380] This visit was also connected to the Trump administration's ultimate decision to withdraw the US from the JCPOA. Jerusalem and Abu Dhabi's decision to leak the Otaiba/Khalifa meeting with Netanyahu was also meant to send an obvious message to Tehran that Israel–GCC relations had become a political reality.

The UAE and Bahrain's decision to publicly embrace Netanyahu, a well-known critic of the Iranian nuclear deal, also signaled their support for Trump's decision to pull Washington out of the JCPOA.

The Quartet's pronounced relationship with Netanyahu, as illustrated by the UANI event and the Otaiba/Khalifa meeting with the Israeli Prime Minister, combined with the constant US media chatter about the friendship between MbS and Kushner, may have emboldened Riyadh and Abu Dhabi in their respective dealings against Doha and Muscat.

These dynamics may have informed Qaboos's decision to invite the Israeli Prime Minister to visit Muscat.

Meanwhile, the UAE–Israel relationship—and how it plays out in Washington—was put on display when Israel's ambassador to the United States and his Emirati counterpart jointly attended the 2018 annual dinner of the Jewish Institute for National Security (JINSA), a neoconservative organization which received funding from Abu Dhabi.[381, 382]

The timing of the dinner coincided with heightened US media attention on the Khashoggi affair, which in turn may have been a factor for Otaiba to publicly attend the JINSA event despite the sensitive state of Emirati–Israeli relations. It was Otaiba, after all, who did so much to promote MbS in Washington as a reformer.

The Trump administration's public support for the Israel–Quartet relationship became evident once again during a Middle East Summit in Warsaw in February 2019. Poland and the United States co-hosted this event called the US-led Middle East Conference in Warsaw.

The Summit addressed terrorism, extremism, missile development and proliferation, maritime trade and security, and threats posed by proxy groups across the region. US Vice President Mike Pence spearheaded the summit, which primarily focused on Iran. Representatives of more than 60 countries attended, including Netanyahu and all of the GCC foreign ministers, including Yemen.[383] While Netanyahu's only public meeting with a GCC foreign minister was with Oman's Bin Alawi, he met privately with the remaining GCC foreign ministers, except for Qatar's.[384]

The emerging ties between Israel and the Quartet left Qatar relatively isolated.

But with the benefit of hindsight, it has become clear that the hacking of the QNA in May 2017 triggered the GCC crisis. Ironically, the QNA's hacked message vis-à-vis the Amir and Israel, which subsequently triggered the anti-Qatar campaign in Washington where the topic of Qatar–Hamas became a key line of attack, rested on the assumption that the Quartet could exploit Israeli–Qatari grievances for their own political purposes in their quest to influence Trump's against Doha.

In this regard, the crisis exposed that HBK and HBJ were the Qatari leaders who enjoyed longstanding personal relationships with their Israeli counterparts. Thus, when HBK abdicated in favor of his son, Amir Tamim had not been introduced to Israeli leaders as the Israel portfolio had been carried out solely by the Amiri Diwan under the careful supervision of his father and HBJ. The fact that the generational power transfer in Qatar did not include a transmission of institutional knowledge about the complex state of the Qatar–Israel relationship was an issue that the UAE and it's for-hire surrogates could easily exploit to advance their own anti-Qatar agenda in Washington.

Despite these dynamics, the Gulf crisis also shattered a widely held preconception, namely that Israel and the Gulf states are drawing closer because of their shared animosity toward Iran and its regional agenda. While Saudi Arabia, the UAE, and Bahrain have adopted anti-Iranian narratives, Kuwait, Oman, and Qatar, support dialogue with Iran in order to reduce regional tensions.

Notwithstanding these dynamics, what the Gulf crisis has crystalized is that despite Trump's quest to align Israel and the GCC against Iran through his Maximum Pressure campaign, Abu Dhabi's primary objective was to advance its inter-Arab agenda as opposed to collectively confronting Iran by aligning itself with the Jewish state. Instead, Abu Dhabi arguably pushed its anti-Iranian messaging in Washington, which appealed to neoconservative groups and the

Trump administration in particular, as a rhetorical asset to obtain the necessary support in the American capital for altering the Arabian Peninsula's geopolitical landscape.

Israel's own fears of Iran and all of Tehran's regional activities initially drove the Jewish state to strengthen its ties with the UAE, but Israel found itself entangled in a high-stakes, inter-Arab struggle playing out inside the Beltway.

Within this context, it is arguable that Israel, as opposed to Iran or Turkey, is the external actor to have politically benefitted the most from the Gulf crisis. Because of the schisms within the GCC— namely a common view of UAE expansionism in the MENA region and Abu Dhabi's public relations agents in Washington as major threats—Qatar and Oman have their own interests in exploring areas for greater cooperation with Israel. Put simply, Doha and Muscat see stronger relations with the Jewish state as a means of further hedging their respective foreign policies. Thus, despite conventional wisdom suggesting otherwise, a common fear of Iran is not the driving force behind Israel's gradual move toward normalization of relations with all GCC member states. Furthermore, it should be noted that Kuwait has diverged from all of its fellow Arab Gulf monarchies vis-à-vis Israel, with Kuwait City's positions being increasingly pro-Palestinian and staunchly opposed to any official peace with Israel unless and until a two-state solution, based on the 1967 borders, is implemented.

Qatar and Oman face different threats from their fellow GCC member-states, yet they frame their respective engagements with Israel as part of an effort to support Palestine. In Doha's case, the narrative is that Qatar advances the Palestinian Cause through its actions that entail engaging Israel. Oman's message to the greater Arab/Islamic world, as well as to Israel and the West, is that Muscat is working to help all parties achieve a lasting peace.

Domestic legitimacy at home is a factor for all of the Gulf monarchs when it comes to their diplomatic overtures to Israel. Omanis revered Sultan Qaboos, who was on the throne for nearly half a century, and in Qatar the ruler is extremely popular, which is largely an outcome of the Gulf crisis and Amir Tamim's handling of the dispute. As leaders who maintain strong standings with their domestic constituents, the rulers of Oman and Qatar have been in a relatively strong position to engage Israel. Moreover, given that Muscat and Doha enjoy pragmatic relations with Tehran, neither Oman nor Qatar face any true "Iranian threat," which strengthens their gradual opening of relations with Israel. However, Oman and Qatar are likely far from normalizing official ties at the highest level as both Muscat and Doha adhere to the Arab consensus on Palestine.

Sultan Qaboos hosts back-to-back visits by Palestinian President Mahmoud Abbas and Israeli Prime Minister Netanyahu (see Appendix 9). Courtesy Oman's Ministry of Foreign Affairs.

The Trump administration's "Deal of the Century," which the President unveiled in January 2020, confirmed that the White House has a vision for settling the Palestinian–Israeli conflict in a manner that completely disregards the international consensus on how to resolve the dispute. Even though no details about the peace plan had been provided in advance, the ambassadors of Oman, the UAE, and Bahrain to the United States attended the White House ceremony along with Trump and Netanyahu. The ambassadors of Egypt and Jordan, however, did not attend. The last-minute invitation to the White House event was issued to Arab ambassadors the evening before. Even though the three GCC ambassadors attended the event where the peace plan was unveiled, their governments did not publicly endorse its content. Instead, their participation was indicative of their unwillingness to upset the Trump administration by opposing one of its signature foreign policy initiatives.

Meanwhile, the UAE's relationship with Israel could also be transformed given Saudi Arabia's relative isolation in Washington over the Khashoggi affair. Although Abu Dhabi played an indispensable role in promoting MbS as a reformer in Washington, the Saudi Crown Prince's fall from grace in Washington coupled with persistent bipartisan opposition from the US Congress against the Trump administration's stances on Yemen's civil war could force the UAE to draw closer to Israel in order to shield its reputation, which in turn served as a factor for Otaiba's decision to attend the unveiling of Trump's peace plan.

Within this context, Iran would not be the primary driver of closer Emirati–Israeli ties. Instead, Abu Dhabi's relative diminished standing in Washington as a result of the UAE's regional adventurism and resistance to the Trump administration's push for Gulf reconciliation would be the main driving force pushing the Emiratis closer to Israel. Of course, with Saudi Arabia suffering from a damaged reputation in Washington against the backdrop of problems in Abu Dhabi's relationships with Oman and Qatar, it is easy to imagine MbZ concluding that strengthening ties with Israel would serve the UAE's national interests.

Thus, within a fractured Gulf, each GCC member state (save Kuwait) has different motivations for strengthening ties with Israel.

Unlike Sultan Qaboos and Amir Tamim, MbZ and MbS do not enjoy the same level of domestic support, which is arguably required to fully normalize ties with Israel, especially within the absence of tangible progress on the Israeli–Palestinian front. The Saudi and Emirati leaders have thus already fully exploited the limited influence of America's neoconservative community and its litany of lobbyists. Now, in the post-Khashoggi period, Washington has become a treacherous ground for foreign lobbying.

But beyond GCC dynamics involving Israel, Iran, and Turkey, the crisis has demonstrated the profound failure of Arab Gulf states to preserve a collective front, let alone advance a regional agenda. Within this context, both the Arab League and Gulf Cooperation Council have devolved into irrelevant organizations as they have proven unable and unwilling to establish common ground amid the Middle East's litany of intractable conflicts and political paralysis among the resource-rich Gulf monarchies. Irrespective of these dynamics, however, the rise of the Quartet as a bloc has in practical terms become the Arab world's new order. In the process, the Arab League and the GCC have been reduced to strategic irrelevance.

A PATH FORWARD:
MIDDLE EAST STRATEGIC ALLIANCE

By the end of 2019, the situation in the Gulf remained fluid. For instance, in November 2019, KBS, who is MbS's younger brother and also Saudi Arabia's deputy defense minister, paid Sultan Qaboos a surprise visit in Muscat. In the Omani capital, he and Sultan Qaboos discussed Yemen and other regional security dilemmas.[385]

The visit took place at the backdrop of the Arabian Gulf Cup soccer tournament in Qatar, where Saudi Arabia, the UAE, Bahrain, and Egypt participated despite the Gulf crisis. When Bahrain won the competition, Amir Tamim presented the team with the cup.[386] While the Gulf Cup was indicative of a thawing in relations between the Quartet and Qatar, the parties did not achieve any breakthrough on December 10, 2019, at the subsequent GCC Summit in Riyadh, where Amir Tamim dispatched Prime Minister Abdullah Bin Nasser bin Khalifa Al Thani to represent Doha.[387]

Whether reconciliation is ultimately achieved through Kuwaiti-mediated diplomacy within the framework of traditional Gulf diplomacy, Washington remains uniquely positioned to strengthen multilateral cooperation between the Arab states irrespective of the state of affairs in the GCC.

Prior to the Khashoggi affair, Washington's strategy to solve the GCC crisis was to invite the Arabian princes to a US–GCC Summit at Camp David in Maryland. The proposed US–GCC Summit was initially set to take place in January 2019. But the combination of the Khashoggi murder and Democrats retaking control of the US House of Representatives in January 2019 made such an event less feasible for political purposes, particularly given the likely outcomes of MbS stepping onto US soil after the CIA concluded that he was responsible for the Khashoggi assassination.

Despite these constraints and the relentless negative US media coverage of Saudi Arabia—and of MbS in particular—following the brutal killing of Khashoggi, Trump has sought to preserve the of US–Saudi strategic partnership. His steadfast support for Saudi Arabia has thus salvaged the tenets of the bilateral strategic partnership, even if MbS and Trump, especially their personal relationship, remain a source of controversy among Democrats and Republicans alike on the Hill.

While these political dynamics continue to play out in Washington as part of the upcoming US presidential election, an increasingly narrow path for Gulf reconciliation is still possible, namely through the establishment of the Middle East Strategic Alliance (MESA).

Formally announced in May 2017, MESA would include the six GCC countries plus Egypt and Jordan.[388] Because of Israel's extensive role in Gulf affairs, which we have carefully documented throughout this book, the Jewish state could be granted observer status.

But Israel's participation in MESA would also be a subject of potential controversy for the Arab states in light of their own long-standing support for the Palestinian Cause, which requires the state of Palestine to be granted observer status as well.

While Israeli–Palestinian security cooperation throughout the occupied West Bank has had a stabilizing impact for Israel and Palestine, Israeli–Palestinian military cooperation through the framework of MESA—along with all GCC members, Egypt and Jordan—would enhance regional security.

Yemen could later be included in MESA as well, at least if the country's civil war resolves and Yemen is no longer a failed state. Nonetheless, in light of the geopolitical dynamics tied to Yemen's conflict, which directly impacts Oman's security more than any other conflict in the Middle East, Yemen's internationally recognized government could also be granted MESA observer status.

While it is unclear when MESA will be formally launched, it could be inaugurated at AUAB in Qatar, which could also serve as its headquarters.

By selecting AUAB for the MESA headquarters, Washington would effectively provide Qatar with the necessary security guarantees to prevent any repeats of the crises against Doha of 2014 and 2017. By selecting AUAB, which hosts the largest US military presence in the Middle East, Washington would follow the "NATO precedence" based on the selection of Brussels as NATO headquarters. Brussels (as opposed to Berlin, London, or Paris) was selected in 1949 as alliance headquarters, as Washington chose to eliminate rivalry and competition for power and prestige among the larger European powers. If Qatar is selected, Washington would be adhering to such precedent.

Given that the GCC headquarters is already based in Riyadh, establishing the MESA counterpart at AUAB would not only strengthen the balance of power within the Gulf but ensure that not all of the Gulf region's multilateral organizations are concentrated in one country. Once MESA is formally launched, its agenda could be a follow-on to the US–Arab Summit held in Riyadh in 2017.

But because of the extreme distrust among Washington's GCC partners, MESA's strategic objective would for all practical purposes be to preserve the peace on the Arabian Peninsula as opposed to establishing an anti-Iran alliance.

Ahead of the MESA launch and irrespective of if and when it ultimately takes place, US-backed Kuwaiti shuttle diplomacy can be expected to continue as part of an effort to ultimately resolve the Qatar–Quartet standoff. As part of the Kuwaiti mediating efforts, the parties could also hammer out mechanisms so that a similar conflict does not occur again. Such a mechanism is expected to be based on the various principles encompassing the 2014 agreement (including this book's reference section), which led to the resolution of the first Gulf crisis.

The 2014 agreement lays out commitments to avoid interference in the internal affairs of other Gulf nations, which includes barring financial or political support to "deviant" groups, meaning anti-government activist groups. The agreement, referred to as the

Riyadh Agreement, specifically mentions not supporting the Muslim Brotherhood, which the Quartet has repeatedly alleged Qatar supports, as well as not backing Yemeni groups that could threaten neighboring countries.

A second agreement headlined "top secret" and dated November 16, 2014, specifically mentions the signatories' commitment to support Egypt's stability, including preventing Al Jazeera from being used as a platform for groups or figures challenging the government in Cairo. The second agreement specifically targets Al Jazeera but does not mention other media outlets such as the Saudi-owned Al Arabiya.

After the agreement was signed, Al Jazeera closed down Al Jazeera Mubashir Misr, a channel dedicated to covering Egypt. A supplemental document to the 2014 agreement signed by the countries' foreign ministers discusses implementation of the agreement. This document includes provisions barring support for the Muslim Brotherhood and groups seen as a threat to GCC member states' interests.[389]

In July 2017, in the peak of the GCC crisis, the agreement was leaked to CNN when the blockading states were accusing Doha of violating the 2014 agreement and supporting terrorism.

Irrespective of where, if, or when MESA will be launched, the Gulf crisis will continue impacting regional dynamics for decades to come, even if the crisis is eventually resolved. MbZ, MbS, and Amir Tamim are all young and are expected to maintain their power well into the future. Unless the core issues of this crisis in the GCC are addressed, tensions between Qatar and its immediate Arabian neighbors, namely Abu Dhabi, could trigger into a disastrous conflict in the Gulf.

EPILOGUE

Leading up to the crisis, and to a certain extent during the initial phase of the blockade, many analysts quickly assumed that the Quartet's grievances were tied to Qatar's independent foreign policy during the post–Arab Spring period.

According to this narrative, the crisis was about philosophical differences between the UAE's model of "secularism" versus Qatar's support for political Islam and that there were two sides to the Gulf standoff. But as the crisis deepened in Washington and repeated US efforts to resolve the crisis were rebuffed, it quickly become clear that Riyadh and Abu Dhabi saw an opportunity in Trump's presidency to bring down the government in Doha and to turn Qatar into a vassal state based on the "Bahrain model."

With Trump in the White House and his family members serving his administration in their senior advisory positions, MbZ and MbS may have miscalculated by ignoring how much institutions other than the White House shape Washington's policies. With an entrenched bureaucracy, a military industrial complex, and numerous forms of checks and balances on the executive branch, the American president's powers were never as absolute as those of the rulers of some Arabian monarchies.

While the Emirati and Saudi princes sought to bring the government of Qatar to its knees, they miscalculated the extent to which the Pentagon, as a powerful institution in the United States, would use its powers to preserve the status quo, meaning a continuation of close military coordination between Washington and Doha. Furthermore, the State Department, which worked with Qatar on many past issues concerning Hamas and the Taliban, did not approve of the Quartet's efforts to bring an end to the US–Qatar partnership.

Furthermore, even though Trump had rejected Saudi Arabia's request for a green light from the White House for a military invasion of Qatar during the Trump–King Salman phone call of June 6, 2017, Riyadh and Abu Dhabi undermined all subsequent US diplomatic initiatives aimed at ending the crisis. Instead, they appeared to have concluded that Trump's free-wheeling, chaotic decision-making and ideological commitment to an "America First" foreign policy approach ultimately made him susceptible to changing his mind about Qatar.

Thus, Trump's transactional foreign policy under the "America First" agenda effectively centers on investing billions of dollars into US industries, such as defense. In order to curry favors from Trump, MbZ, MbS, and Amir Tamim sought more influence vis-à-vis US foreign policy in exchange for their states' investments in the American economy. From an Emirati point of view, that bargain meant taking on Qatar and sidelining Oman diplomatically while encroaching on its territory in tandem with Saudi Arabia.

Trump's initial foreign policy team, with the exception of Tillerson and Mattis, included political outsiders and nonexperts. The circle around the president was exceptionally close-knit and tight, which explains why Riyadh and Abu Dhabi played their cards to see to it that Trump would push out Tillerson, while at the same time engaging in vitriolic smear campaigns against influencers close to Trump who were defending Qatar or calling for Gulf reconciliation.[390] Officials in Riyadh and Abu Dhabi were against Tillerson remaining in the US administration because of his efforts to resolve the GCC crisis. Thus, when Tillerson was fired in March 2018, Saudi and Emirati newspapers and social media surrogates slammed Tillerson for his "incompetence" while gloating about the dismissal.[391, 392, 393]

Tillerson gave an interview in which the 69th Secretary of State provided his own assessment of the Gulf crisis. He said:

> And they go all the way back to the time when the Emir of Qatar abdicated [Khalifa bin Hamad Al Thani, who was Amir from 1972 to 1995] and left the country and was succeeded by his son, who is now the Father Emir [Hamad bin Khalifa Al Thani, who was Amir from 1995 to 2013], and the then beginnings of Qatar becoming economically independent because of the development of their natural gas reserves and their development as the world's largest LNG exporter, which made them very independent, and it gave them resources to have greater influence in the region than they had previously had.
>
> And I don't want to get into some specifics because it's—some of it is sensitive, but there have been some longstanding issues between the Kingdom of Saudi Arabia and the leadership in Qatar since over that period of time that have bubbled up from time to time. There have been issues between the leadership of the UAE and Qatar from time to time that bubble up.
>
> And some of them are directly—are direct issues around country-to-country relationships, between them, and some of them are issues related to regional issues and the Qataris

beginning to take a more active role in foreign affairs in the region than they had taken previously. Because with this newfound wealth they had, they had the ability now to do things—in lots of ways a very positive way—to play a role that they had not previously played. And I think so sometimes that could lead to a conflict of views among the parties.

So it really, I think, was a culmination of just a lot of things that were building up over a period of time, you know, the Qataris creating Al Jazeera network. They had the wealth to do that, so they did.[394]

OMAN–ISRAEL

A prevailing narrative in Washington is that Gulf–Israel ties have strengthened during the Trump presidency because of mutual animus towards Iran. Yet this is not fully accurate.

Although Netanyahu's positions and rhetoric on Iran are well-known, his decision to frame cooperation with Gulf states as part of a unified front against Iran should instead be understood as aspirational. His added objective is to mobilize Arab support and international public opinion against Tehran and its regional aspirations.

What Netanyahu's visit to Muscat illustrated was Israel's support for Oman's sovereignty and territorial integrity as well as a tacit endorsement of its relationship with Iran.

But beyond the Sturm und Drang of his high-profile visit, often framed by analysts as Oman's support for easing Iran–Israel tensions or its support to accelerate the Israel–Palestine peace process, the geopolitical reality was quite different. The Saudi and Emirati military and intelligence presence in Yemen's Al Mahra province had ignited an old conflict reminiscent of the Dhofar Rebellion.

The PDRY (1967–1990) supported the Marxist insurgency against Oman's government. South Yemen also joined Saudi Arabia in voting against Oman's entrance into the Arab League in 1971. It was amid these developments that the Oman–Israel relationship began. The Israelis, along with Iran and Britain, worked to help the government in Muscat quell the insurgency and preserve Oman's territorial integrity.

Thus, just like how the Mossad assisted Qaboos during his government's struggle against the Marxist rebels amid the 1970s, Netanyahu came to his side at a time when Emirati lobbying efforts in Washington were pushing the United States to support the STC in its quest for an independent state in southern Yemen while also trying to isolate Muscat from the Trump administration.

It is, of course, ironic that Israel, along with the Islamic Republic of Iran, remained unified in favor of defending Omani interests in Yemen's complicated and multisided developments. As we have seen, it was Iran that forced the UAE's military out of Yemen as part of the compromise reached during the maritime talks of August 2019.

It was perhaps because of the tacit Israel–Iran alignment on the need to support Qaboos that Iran did not criticize Mossad Director Cohen's publicly announced visit to Oman following Netanyahu's. Following Netanyahu's visit to Muscat, Iran's criticism was restrained and limited to midranking officials.[395]

QATAR AND ISRAEL

Like much of the anti-Qatar rhetoric in Washington, the UAE-sponsored policy proposal for the Trump administration was simple but apocalyptic. Trump had to choose between supporting "moderate" states such as the UAE, Saudi Arabia, Bahrain, and Egypt against a nexus of "radicalism" represented and financed by Qatar, Turkey, and Iran.[396, 397, 398]

This weaponized narrative became particularly apparent during Bannon's speech at the Hudson conference in October 2017. [399]At the event, he stated, "The single most important thing that's happening in the world is the situation in Qatar. Qatar finally had to be called to account for the continual funding for the Muslim Brotherhood, continual funding for Hamas."[400] This narrative, heavily promoted by various neoconservative groups and influencers, suggested that the new alliance between the Quartet and Israel was about confronting Iran in a collective manner, and because Qatar was small, vulnerable, and "too close to Iran," it was only a matter of time before Doha would succumb to the Quartet's maximalist demands. In order to force that change, the UAE sponsored the various anti-Qatar conferences in Washington—such as those hosted by FDD, Hudson Institute, and MEF—to drive that message home.

The anti-Qatar activity in Washington—which bore the hallmark of a foreign government operation—combined the Qatar News Agency (QNA) hack with the Foundation of Defense of Democracies (FDD) conference and legislation (HR 2712), introduced by then-Chairman Ed Royce of the US House of Representatives, which had all been tied to Trump's Riyadh Summit. The steadily building pressure on Qatar—through the combination of negative op-eds,[401] the FDD conference, the QNA hack, and what can be assumed to be behind-the-scenes diplomatic maneuvering to isolate Doha from the Trump administration—set the stage for Trump's initial tweets against Qatar, which took place the day after the blockade of Qatar was imposed.

Although the "moderate" versus "extremism" narrative may have been appealing to nonexperts and various neoconservative foreign policy circles in Washington, the geopolitical reality of the Qatar crisis was an old Arabian conflict between Qatar and its neighbors had been ignited. The crisis was an inter-Arab struggle, which did not have anything to do with Israel.

Instead, as we have seen, Israel played a key role in preventing any encroachments on the US–Qatar strategic partnership by blocking the previously discussed HR 2712.

Because of Israel's role in helping Qatar preserve its image in Washington, Qatar–Israel relations are improving. At the same time, the dynamics guiding Qatar–Israel relations are reminiscent of the Gulf dynamics of the 1990s, when Oman facilitated the diplomatic breakthrough between Qatar and Israel.

Within this context, the Gulf crisis was, for all practical purposes, a repeat of Operation Abu Ali. Just as Israel came to the support of Qatar during 1996, it did so again by extending Doha a diplomatic lifeline through publicly cooperating on Gaza reconstruction.

Israel has proven to be a stabilizing force within the Gulf region as the GCC remains divided over the Qatar rift while the Trump administration's unpredictability drives numerous layers of instability in the Arabian Peninsula. It is clear that the neoconservative groups in Washington targeting Qatar since June 2017 have provided nothing but a sideshow as the Jewish state was never going to support the Quartet against Doha.

PHOTO GALLERY

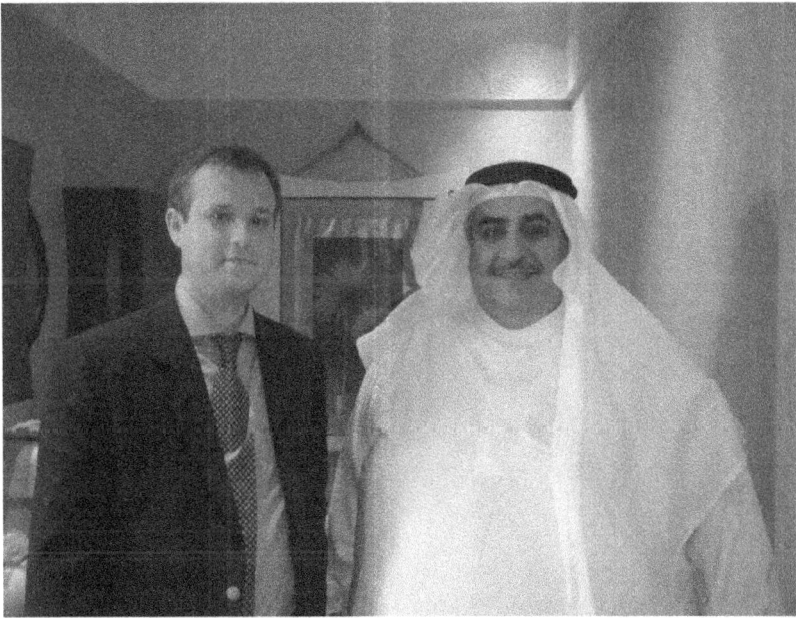

The author interviewed then Bahraini Foreign Minister Khalid Bin Ahmad Al Khalifa for his Huffington Post column about Gulf-Israel relations.[402] Manama, Bahrain, December 2010.

Author delivered his first lecture on Gulf-Israel relations at the University of Denver's Josef Korbel School of International Studies, January 2012.

Reference Section

Appendix 1

PRESIDENT TRUMP'S SPEECH TO THE ARAB ISLAMIC AMERICAN SUMMIT

21 May 2017

Remarks as prepared for delivery

Thank You.

I want to thank King Salman for his extraordinary words, and the magnificent Kingdom of Saudi Arabia for hosting today's summit. I am honored to be received by such gracious hosts. I have always heard about the splendor of your country and the kindness of your citizens, but words do not do justice to the grandeur of this remarkable place and the incredible hospitality you have shown us from the moment we arrived.

You also hosted me in the treasured home of King Abdulaziz, the founder of the Kingdom who united your great people. Working alongside another beloved leader—American President Franklin Roosevelt—King Abdulaziz began the enduring partnership between our two countries. King Salman: your father would be so proud to see that you are continuing his legacy—and just as he opened the first chapter in our partnership, today we begin a new chapter that will bring lasting benefits to our citizens.

Let me now also extend my deep and heartfelt gratitude to each and every one of the distinguished heads of state who made this journey here today. You greatly honor us with your presence, and I send the warmest regards from my country to yours. I know that our time together will bring many blessings to both your people and mine.

I stand before you as a representative of the American People, to deliver a message of friendship and hope. That is why I chose to make my first foreign visit a trip to the heart of the Muslim world, to the nation that serves as custodian of the two holiest sites in the Islamic Faith.

In my inaugural address to the American People, I pledged to strengthen America's oldest friendships, and to build new partnerships in pursuit of peace. I also promised that America will not seek to impose our way of life on others, but to outstretch our hands in the spirit of cooperation and trust.

Our vision is one of peace, security, and prosperity—in this region, and in the world.

Our goal is a coalition of nations who share the aim of stamping out extremism and providing our children a hopeful future that does honor to God.

And so this historic and unprecedented gathering of leaders— unique in the history of nations—is a symbol to the world of our shared resolve and our mutual respect. To the leaders and citizens of every country assembled here today, I want you to know that the United States is eager to form closer bonds of friendship, security, culture and commerce.

For Americans, this is an exciting time. A new spirit of optimism is sweeping our country: in just a few months, we have created almost a million new jobs, added over 3 trillion dollars of new value, lifted the burdens on American industry, and made record investments in our military that will protect the safety of our people and enhance the security of our wonderful friends and allies – many of whom are here today.

Now, there is even more blessed news I am pleased to share with you. My meetings with King Salman, the Crown Prince, and the Deputy Crown Prince have been filled with great warmth, good will, and tremendous cooperation.

Yesterday, we signed historic agreements with the Kingdom that will invest almost $400 billion in our two countries and create many thousands of jobs in America and Saudi Arabia.

This landmark agreement includes the announcement of a $110 billion Saudi-funded defense purchase—and we will be sure to help our Saudi friends to get a good deal from our great American defense companies. This agreement will help the Saudi military to take a greater role in security operations.

We have also started discussions with many of the countries present today on strengthening partnerships, and forming new ones, to advance security and stability across the Middle East and beyond.

Later today, we will make history again with the opening of a new Global Center for Combating Extremist Ideology—located right here, in this central part of the Islamic World. This groundbreaking new center represents a clear declaration that Muslim-majority countries must take the lead in combatting radicalization, and I want to express our gratitude to King Salman for this strong demonstration of leadership.

I have had the pleasure of welcoming several of the leaders present today to the White House, and I look forward to working with all of you.

America is a sovereign nation and our first priority is always the safety and security of our citizens. We are not here to lecture—we are not here to tell other people how to live, what to do, who to be, or how to worship. Instead, we are here to offer partnership—based on shared interests and values—to pursue a better future for us all.

Here at this summit we will discuss many interests we share together. But above all we must be united in pursuing the one goal that transcends every other consideration. That goal is to meet history's great test—to conquer extremism and vanquish the forces of terrorism.

Young Muslim boys and girls should be able to grow up free from fear, safe from violence, and innocent of hatred.

And young Muslim men and women should have the chance to build a new era of prosperity for themselves and their peoples.

God's help, this summit will mark the beginning of the end for those who practice terror and spread its vile creed. At the same time, we pray this special gathering may someday be remembered as the beginning of peace in the Middle East—and maybe, even all over the world.

But this future can only be achieved through defeating terrorism and the ideology that drives it.

Few nations have been spared its violent reach.

America has suffered repeated barbaric attacks—from the atrocities of September 11th to the devastation of the Boston Bombing, to the horrible killings in San Bernardino and Orlando.

The nations of Europe have also endured unspeakable horror. So too have the nations of Africa and even South America. India, Russia, China and Australia have been victims.

But, in sheer numbers, the deadliest toll has been exacted on the innocent people of Arab, Muslim and Middle Eastern nations. They have borne the brunt of the killings and the worst of the destruction in this wave of fanatical violence.

Some estimates hold that more than 95 percent of the victims of terrorism are themselves Muslim.

We now face a humanitarian and security disaster in this region that is spreading across the planet. It is a tragedy of epic proportions. No description of the suffering and depravity can begin to capture its full measure.

The true toll of ISIS, Al Qaeda, Hezbollah, Hamas, and so many others, must be counted not only in the number of dead. It must also be counted in generations of vanished dreams.

The Middle East is rich with natural beauty, vibrant cultures, and massive amounts of historic treasures. It should increasingly become one of the great global centers of commerce and opportunity.

This region should not be a place from which refugees flee, but to which newcomers flock.

Saudi Arabia is home to the holiest sites in one of the world's great faiths. Each year millions of Muslims come from around the world to Saudi Arabia to take part in the Hajj. In addition to ancient wonders, this country is also home to modern ones—including soaring achievements in architecture.

Egypt was a thriving center of learning and achievement thousands of years before other parts of the world. The wonders of Giza, Luxor and Alexandria are proud monuments to that ancient heritage.

All over the world, people dream of walking through the ruins of Petra in Jordan. Iraq was the cradle of civilization and is a land of natural beauty. And the United Arab Emirates has reached incredible heights with glass and steel, and turned earth and water into spectacular works of art.

The entire region is at the center of the key shipping lanes of the Suez Canal, the Red Sea, and the Straits of Hormuz.

The potential of this region has never been greater. 65 percent of its population is under the age of 30. Like all young men and women, they seek great futures to build, great national projects to join, and a place for their families to call home.

But this untapped potential, this tremendous cause for optimism, is held at bay by bloodshed and terror. There can be no coexistence with this violence.

There can be no tolerating it, no accepting it, no excusing it, and no ignoring it.

Every time a terrorist murders an innocent person, and falsely invokes the name of God, it should be an insult to every person of faith.

Terrorists do not worship God, they worship death.

If we do not act against this organized terror, then we know what will happen. Terrorism's devastation of life will continue to spread. Peaceful societies will become engulfed by violence. And the futures of many generations will be sadly squandered.

If we do not stand in uniform condemnation of this killing—then not only will we be judged by our people, not only will we be judged by history, but we will be judged by God.

This is not a battle between different faiths, different sects, or different civilizations.

This is a battle between barbaric criminals who seek to obliterate human life, and decent people of all religions who seek to protect it.

This is a battle between Good and Evil.

When we see the scenes of destruction in the wake of terror, we see no signs that those murdered were Jewish or Christian, Shia or Sunni. When we look upon the streams of innocent blood soaked into the ancient ground, we cannot see the faith or sect or tribe of the victims—we see only that they were Children of God whose deaths are an insult to all that is holy.

But we can only overcome this evil if the forces of good are united and strong—and if everyone in this room does their fair share and fulfills their part of the burden.

Terrorism has spread across the world. But the path to peace begins right here, on this ancient soil, in this sacred land.

America is prepared to stand with you—in pursuit of shared interests and common security.

But the nations of the Middle East cannot wait for American power to crush this enemy for them. The nations of the Middle East will have to decide what kind of future they want for themselves, for their countries, and for their children.

It is a choice between two futures—and it is a choice America CANNOT make for you.

A better future is only possible if your nations drive out the terrorists and extremists. Drive. Them. Out. DRIVE THEM OUT of your places of worship. DRIVE THEM OUT of your communities. DRIVE THEM OUT of your holy land, and DRIVE THEM OUT OF THIS EARTH.

For our part, America is committed to adjusting our strategies to meet evolving threats and new facts. We will discard those strategies that have not worked—and will apply new approaches informed by experience and judgment. We are adopting a Principled Realism, rooted in common values and shared interests.

Our friends will never question our support, and our enemies will never doubt our determination. Our partnerships will advance security through stability, not through radical disruption. We will make decisions based on real-world outcomes – not inflexible ideology. We will be guided by the lessons of experience, not the confines of rigid thinking. And, wherever possible, we will seek gradual reforms – not sudden intervention.

We must seek partners, not perfection—and to make allies of all who share our goals.

Above all, America seeks peace—not war.

Muslim nations must be willing to take on the burden, if we are going to defeat terrorism and send its wicked ideology into oblivion.

The first task in this joint effort is for your nations to deny all territory to the foot soldiers of evil. Every country in the region has an absolute duty to ensure that terrorists find no sanctuary on their soil.

Many are already making significant contributions to regional security: Jordanian pilots are crucial partners against ISIS in Syria and Iraq. Saudi Arabia and a regional coalition have taken strong action against Houthi militants in Yemen. The Lebanese Army is hunting ISIS operatives who try to infiltrate their territory. Emirati troops are supporting our Afghan partners. In Mosul, American troops are supporting Kurds, Sunnis and Shias fighting together for their homeland. Qatar, which hosts the US Central Command, is a crucial strategic partner. Our longstanding partnership with Kuwait and Bahrain continue to enhance security in the region. And courageous Afghan soldiers are making tremendous sacrifices in the fight against the Taliban, and others, in the fight for their country.

As we deny terrorist organizations control of territory and populations, we must also strip them of their access to funds. We must cut off the financial channels that let ISIS sell oil, let extremists pay their fighters, and help terrorists smuggle their reinforcements.

I am proud to announce that the nations here today will be signing an agreement to prevent the financing of terrorism, called the

Terrorist Financing Targeting Center—co-chaired by the United States and Saudi Arabia, and joined by every member of the Gulf Cooperation Council. It is another historic step in a day that will be long remembered.

I also applaud the Gulf Cooperation Council for blocking funders from using their countries as a financial base for terror, and designating Hezbollah as a terrorist organization last year. Saudi Arabia also joined us this week in placing sanctions on one of the most senior leaders of Hezbollah.

Of course, there is still much work to do.

That means honestly confronting the crisis of Islamist extremism and the Islamist terror groups it inspires. And it means standing together against the murder of innocent Muslims, the oppression of women, the persecution of Jews, and the slaughter of Christians.

Religious leaders must make this absolutely clear: Barbarism will deliver you no glory—piety to evil will bring you no dignity. If you choose the path of terror, your life will be empty, your life will be brief, and YOUR SOUL WILL BE CONDEMNED.

And political leaders must speak out to affirm the same idea: heroes don't kill innocents; they save them. Many nations here today have taken important steps to raise up that message. Saudi Arabia's Vision for 2030 is an important and encouraging statement of tolerance, respect, empowering women, and economic development.

The United Arab Emirates has also engaged in the battle for hearts and souls—and with the US, launched a center to counter the online spread of hate. Bahrain too is working to undermine recruitment and radicalism.

I also applaud Jordan, Turkey and Lebanon for their role in hosting refugees. The surge of migrants and refugees leaving the Middle East depletes the human capital needed to build stable societies and economies. Instead of depriving this region of so much human potential, Middle Eastern countries can give young people hope for a brighter future in their home nations and regions.

That means promoting the aspirations and dreams of all citizens who seek a better life—including women, children, and followers of all faiths. Numerous Arab and Islamic scholars have eloquently argued that protecting equality strengthens Arab and Muslim communities.

For many centuries the Middle East has been home to Christians, Muslims and Jews living side-by-side. We must practice tolerance and respect for each other once again—and make this region a place where every man and woman, no matter their faith or ethnicity, can enjoy a life of dignity and hope.

In that spirit, after concluding my visit in Riyadh, I will travel to Jerusalem and Bethlehem, and then to the Vatican—visiting many of the holiest places in the three Abrahamic Faiths. If these three faiths can join together in cooperation, then peace in this world is possible—including peace between Israelis and Palestinians. I will be meeting with both Israeli Prime Minister Benjamin Netanyahu and Palestinian President Mahmoud Abbas.

Starving terrorists of their territory, their funding, and the false allure of their craven ideology, will be the basis for defeating them.

But no discussion of stamping out this threat would be complete without mentioning the government that gives terrorists all three—safe harbor, financial backing, and the social standing needed for recruitment. It is a regime that is responsible for so much instability in the region. I am speaking of course of Iran.

From Lebanon to Iraq to Yemen, Iran funds, arms, and trains terrorists, militias, and other extremist groups that spread destruction and chaos across the region. For decades, Iran has fueled the fires of sectarian conflict and terror.

It is a government that speaks openly of mass murder, vowing the destruction of Israel, death to America, and ruin for many leaders and nations in this room.

Among Iran's most tragic and destabilizing interventions have been in Syria. Bolstered by Iran, Assad has committed unspeakable crimes, and the United States has taken firm action in response to the use of banned chemical weapons by the Assad Regime—launching 59 tomahawk missiles at the Syrian air base from where that murderous attack originated.

Responsible nations must work together to end the humanitarian crisis in Syria, eradicate ISIS, and restore stability to the region.

The Iranian regime's longest-suffering victims are its own people. Iran has a rich history and culture, but the people of Iran have endured hardship and despair under their leaders' reckless pursuit of conflict and terror.

Until the Iranian regime is willing to be a partner for peace, all nations of conscience must work together to isolate Iran, deny it funding for terrorism, and pray for the day when the Iranian people have the just and righteous government they deserve.

The decisions we make will affect countless lives.

King Salman, I thank you for the creation of this great moment in history, and for your massive investment in America, its industry and its jobs. I also thank you for investing in the future of this part of the world.

This fertile region has all the ingredients for extraordinary success—a rich history and culture, a young and vibrant people, a thriving spirit of enterprise. But you can only unlock this future if the citizens of the Middle East are freed from extremism, terror and violence.

We in this room are the leaders of our peoples. They look to us for answers, and for action. And when we look back at their faces, behind every pair of eyes is a soul that yearns for justice.

Today, billions of faces are now looking at us, waiting for us to act on the great question of our time.

Will we be indifferent in the presence of evil? Will we protect our citizens from its violent ideology? Will we let its venom spread through our societies? Will we let it destroy the most holy sites on earth?

If we do not confront this deadly terror, we know what the future will bring—more suffering and despair.

But if we act—if we leave this magnificent room unified and determined to do what it takes to destroy the terror that threatens the world—then there is no limit to the great future our citizens will have.

The birthplace of civilization is waiting to begin a new renaissance. Just imagine what tomorrow could bring.

Glorious wonders of science, art, medicine and commerce to inspire humankind. Great cities built on the ruins of shattered towns. New jobs and industries that will lift up millions of people. Parents who no longer worry for their children, families who no longer mourn for their loved ones, and the faithful who finally worship without fear.

These are the blessings of prosperity and peace. These are the desires that burn with a righteous flame in every human heart. And these are the just demands of our beloved peoples.

I ask you to join me, to join together, to work together, and to FIGHT together—BECAUSE UNITED, WE WILL NOT FAIL.

Thank you. God Bless You. God Bless Your Countries. And God Bless the United States of America.[403]

APPENDIX 2

AMIR TAMIM'S 2017 ADDRESS BEFORE THE NATION:
QATAR READY FOR DIALOGUE BUT WON'T
COMPROMISE ON SOVEREIGNTY

Amir Tamim addressed his nation on 21 July 2017.

In the name of Allah the Most Merciful, The Most Compassionate.
Distinguished citizens, and all those who live on the good land of
Qatar, brothers and sisters,

In these circumstances that our country is passing through, I wish
to address your conscience in the language of reason.

We speak in rational terms in assessing the phase we are going
through, to plan the promising future that our people have proved
aptly worthy of, and touched by the spirit of solidarity, harmony
and defiance that prevailed and frustrated the hopes of those who
banked on the opposite side because of their ignorance of the nature
of our society and our people.

As you know and since the onset of the blockade, day to day life
in Qatar has continued as normal. The Qatari people instinctively
and naturally stood up to defend the sovereignty and independence
of their homeland.

All those who live in this country have become spokespersons
for Qatar. Here I would like to recognize, with great pride, the high
moral standard exercised by this people despite the campaign of
incitement as well as the siege. They combined the solidity of stance
and magnanimity of behavior that has always characterized the
Qatari people. They have amazed the world by maintaining a high
level of tenacity in tackling the situation, despite the unprecedented

incitement in tone and language, the honor-related prejudices, and the unparalleled blockade in the relations between our countries.

This was tantamount to a true moral test where our society has achieved great success, as we have proved that there are basic principles and norms that we observe even in times of conflict and dispute, because we respect ourselves first and foremost. I call upon all to continue this approach, and not slip into what is inappropriate for us, nor for our principles and our values. The sons and daughters of this country have realized, with common sense and political awareness, the seriousness of this campaign against their homeland, and the goals of the siege imposed on it.

They have seen through the heavy curtain of fabrications and incitement, without blurring or distorting their vision, and were able to understand the implications of the attempt to impose pressure on this country, and the gravity of the subservience to language of incitement, threats and diktats.

It has become evident to those near and far that this campaign and the steps that followed it had been planned well in advance, and that its plotters and implementers carried out an attack on the sovereignty of the state of Qatar by planting statements that had not been spoken, in order to mislead public opinion and the world and achieve predetermined goals.

Those who took these steps did not realize that the people of the world do not accept injustice so simply, and people do not believe the forgeries of those who do not respect their minds. After all, there are limits to the efficacy of orchestrated propaganda that is not believed even by the very people who forged them.

Therefore, Arab and non-Arab countries that have a respected public opinion stood with us, or at least did not stand with the siege despite the extortion they were subjected to.

The States that have taken these steps have banked on the effect that terror-supporting charges would have in the West, while appealing to the sentiments and preconceived notions of some marginal discriminative forces in Western societies.

It soon became apparent to them that Western societies are like us, in that they do not accept leveling the accusation of terrorism purely due to political dissension, or for purposes such as suppressing pluralism at home, or distorting the image of other countries and isolating them at the international level. This behavior itself, although far from being just, ultimately inflicts damage on the war on terror.

Moreover, in a similar political stance, Western political, civil and media institutions reject diktats and impositions.

This is evident from the international reaction to the conditions that some have tried to impose on us, especially controlling our external relations, infringing on the independence of our policy, shutting down media outlets and controlling the freedom of expression in our country.

We know that there have been differences with some GCC countries over Qatar's independent foreign policy. We too do not agree with the foreign policy of some member states of the GCC, especially over the attitude towards the aspirations of the Arab peoples, supporting just causes, and distinguishing between legitimate resistance to occupation and terrorism, in addition to other issues.

However, we do not try to impose our opinion on anyone. We have never thought that these differences would spoil the sense of amity. There are many commonalities for which the GCC as a regional organization has been established.

Some brothers thought they were living alone in this world, and that money can buy everything.

They have committed yet another mistake, as many States and institutions have reminded them that this world is not for them alone, and that many countries do not favor immediate interests over principles and long-term interests, and they have come to know that even underprivileged countries have dignity and will, and that they cannot impose things that history has long left behind.

They have tried to undermine two principles that humanity has made sacrifices for. First, the principle of sovereignty and the independent will of States; secondly, freedom of expression and the right to information. Freedom of expression is meaningless if the citizen does not have the right to access information. Qatar has quashed the monopoly on information through the media revolution it started, and it is no longer possible to go back. This revolution has become an achievement for all the Arab peoples.

We have been very saddened to see how some countries have used defamation and fictions against Qatar to stir political malice against us in the West. This is a disgrace under all norms: first because the allegations are baseless, and secondly because they have wrongfully prejudiced a sister country. Do we not teach our children at a young age that lying and malicious snitching are two of the worst vices? Is slander and tarnishing a reputation not a crime punishable by law in all civilized countries?

The Emir said that Qatar is fighting terrorism, relentlessly and without compromises, and there is international recognition of Qatar's role in this regard. It does this not because we want to appease anyone in the East or the West, but because we consider terrorism, in the sense of it being an act of aggression against innocent civilians for political ends, a heinous crime against humanity; and because Qatar believes that the just Arab causes are impeded by terrorism, which affects Arabs, Islam and Muslims.

We disagree with some on the sources of terrorism. For example, we say that religion is a moral motive, and not a source of terrorism that could lie in radical ideologies whether religious or secular. Even these extreme ideologies become a source of terrorism only in socio-political environments that create frustration and desperation.

While the disease of terrorism must not be underestimated, we cannot ignore other issues in our world. We believe that the whole world, including our region, also suffers from problems such as poverty, tyranny, occupation and others. This suffering needs to be addressed, as it is also a significant root cause of violent extremism and terrorism.

I do not want to underestimate the scale of suffering and pain caused by the siege, and I hope that this malevolent approach in dealing among brothers will come to an end, and that differences may be resolved through dialogue and negotiation, for this approach has tarnished the image of all GCC countries in the eyes of the world.

It is high time to stop making the citizens of our countries pay the price of political differences among governments. Our Arab region has known the method of revenge and collective punishment of citizens of the other country in case of disagreement with its government, and we have so far succeeded in avoiding this here in the Gulf. But the countries that asked the Qataris to leave, separated members of the same family, and asked their citizens to give up their jobs, their families and leave the State of Qatar, have decided to use this method.

This behavior on their part is not only against international law, but it also affects their own citizens, the values and the norms of dealing between people.

As you know, we did not retaliate, and we have let the citizens of the other countries make their own decisions to stay in Qatar or depart, each according to their own circumstances and will.

213

Any solution to this crisis in the future must include arrangements to ensure that this retaliatory approach in dealing with innocent citizens will not be repeated when there is a political dispute between governments.

Despite the bitterness caused by these steps, the most prevalent proverbial wisdom in the Qatari society these days is: "Every cloud has a silver lining," which corresponds with the Quranic verse: "And perhaps you may hate something which is good for you."

This crisis has driven Qatari society not only to explore its human values as I have indicated, but also to draw on its sources of strength that lie in its unity, will and determination. Further, the efficiency with which the government, with its various ministries and other state institutions, dealt with the crisis to cater for all the needs of the population, has ensured that the people did not feel any difference in their daily lives.

The same qualified persons in technical, administrative, political and media fields who dealt with the situation rationally, calmly and with resolve, are capable of building our economic independence, protecting our national security and strengthening our bilateral relations with States in this world.

We are called upon to open our economy to investments and initiatives so that we produce our own food and medicine, diversify our sources of income, achieve our economic independence through bilateral relations of cooperation with other countries, in our geographical environment and worldwide, and on the basis of mutual interests and mutual respect. We also call upon ourselves to develop our educational, research and media institutions, as well as our sources of soft power at the international level and with the interaction of the best national, Arab and foreign expertise. All of this of course will be in cooperation with the residents in our country who work, contribute and live with us, and who stood with us throughout this crisis.

On numerous occasions I have directed our institutions to pursue the pursuit a policy of economic openness and diversification. At this stage, this is no longer a matter of luxury for us, but a binding and inevitable course of action, leaving no room for complacency. This is the responsibility of all of us, government and business community alike.

This crisis has helped us identify the shortcomings and obstacles in determining Qatar's national, political, economic and independent identity and in deciding to overcome and surpass these obstacles.

As we pass through this test with honor and dignity, I am addressing you to emphasize that Qatar needs every one of you to build its economy and protect its security.

We require diligence, creativity, independent thinking, constructive initiatives and interest in academic achievement in all disciplines, self-reliance and fighting indolence and dependency. This is not just wishful thinking, and these are not mere dreams. Our goals are realistic and practical, based on the continued determination that Qataris have shown during this crisis. This is not just a passing wave of enthusiasm, but rather the basis for further awareness in building the homeland.

Qatar is going through an important phase that has provided opportunities, not only to build upon, but also to bridge the gaps and address shortcomings, if any. We are not afraid of identifying errors and correcting them.

Under my direction, the government will do whatever it takes to achieve this vision, including the required economic openness, the removal of obstacles to investment, and the prevention of monopolies in the context of building the national economy and investing

215

in human development. I have also directed the government to allocate newly discovered gas revenues that God has blessed us with to investment for our future generations. Qatar has lived well so far without it.

We will also continue to work on the international arena to deepen bilateral cooperation and conclude bilateral agreements between Qatar and other countries.

We highly value the mediation efforts undertaken by my brother, His Highness Sheikh Sabah Al Ahmad Al Jaber Al Sabah, Emir of the sisterly State of Kuwait, which Qatar has supported from the outset. This is an opportunity to express my thanks once again for what he did and continues to do. We hope that his sincere efforts will be culminated in success. We also appreciate the American support for this mediation, as well as the constructive positions of Germany, France, Britain, Europe in general and Russia. I would like to commend the important role that Turkey has played in the rapid adoption and direct implementation of our Strategic Cooperation Agreement that had been previously signed, and to thank it for its immediate response to meet the needs of the Qatari market.

I also thank all those who opened their airspace and territorial waters when our brothers closed theirs.

We are open to dialogue to find solutions to lingering problems, not only for the interest of our States and peoples, but also to spare the efforts that are being wasted in vain by countries moved by malicious scheming against their brothers in the international arena, so that these efforts may be invested in serving the causes of the Ummah.

Any solution to the crisis must be based on two principles: first, the solution should be within the framework of respect for the sovereignty and will of each State. Secondly, it should not be in a form of orders by one party against another, but rather as mutual undertakings and joint commitments binding to all.

We are ready for dialogue and for reaching settlements on all contentious issues in this context.

I cannot end this speech without expressing solidarity with the brotherly Palestinian people, especially our people in Al Quds (Jerusalem), and denouncing the closure of the Al-Aqsa Mosque, the first of the two Qiblas and the third of the two Holy Shrines, hoping that what is happening in Al Quds be an incentive for unity and solidarity instead of division.

In conclusion, I would like to thank you for your solidarity, cohesion, determination, resolve and civilized behavior, and to congratulate you on the spirit of nobility, love, and amity prevailing in our land nowadays. These are our assets, our provision and energy to counter the great challenges in the way ahead.

May Allah's Peace, Mercy, and Blessings be upon you all.[404]

Appendix 3

AMIR TAMIM'S 2017 UNGA ADDRESS

Amir Tamim participated in the opening session of the 72nd Session of the United Nations General Assembly in New York on September 19, 2017.

In the Name of God the Most Merciful, the Most Compassionate. Honorable Audience.

It pleases me to congratulate His Excellency Mr. Miroslav Lajcak on assuming the tasks of President of the 72nd Session of the General Assembly, wishing him every success.

I wish also to express my appreciation to His Excellency Mr. Peter Thomson for his valuable efforts in managing the affairs of the 71st Session of the General Assembly, and I take this opportunity to commend the efforts of His Excellency the Secretary-General, Mr. Antonio Guterres, to strengthen the role of the United Nations.

Mr. President,

Maintaining the regional and international peace and security is a priority in the State of Qatar's foreign policy, whose principles and objectives are based on the United Nations' charter and the rules of international legality which calls for constructive cooperation among States, mutual respect and non-interference in the internal affairs, good neighborliness, as well as promoting peaceful coexistence and pursuing peaceful means to settle disputes.

The issue of settling of disputes by peaceful means is still being addressed as an episodic and non-binding proposal. Perhaps the time has come to impose dialogue and negotiation as a basis for resolving disputes through concluding an international convention on settling disputes between States by peaceful means.

In this context, and after major events such as the Second World War, Rwanda and Burundi and the Balkans in the last century, the danger of the impunity of perpetrators of crimes against humanity and crimes of genocide has come back again to threaten humanity to become the rule rather than the exception, because the international legitimacy is subjected to political pressures, interests of the axes and dictations of force on the ground, in a warning that the law of force may supersede the force of law.

In our view, the position of the major powers should not range between two extremes: the direct occupation to impose the will and policy on other countries, or standing idly in a spectator's position who refrain from doing anything vis-à-vis wars of genocide and crimes against humanity perpetrated by a fascist despotic regime, or a continuous repression by an occupying country of people under occupation.

Lately a feeling is spreading that peoples who are exposed to repression face their fate alone, as if the international arena is governed by the law of the jungle, and the countries under threat have to stand on their own through their alliances and relations, in the absence of a system to implement the provisions of international law, and the binding conventions and charters.

Mr. President,

We commend opting for the theme of this session: "Focusing on People: Striving for Peace and a Decent Life for All on a Sustainable Planet."

In this context, I call upon the Government of the Republic of the Union of Myanmar and the international community to assume their legal and moral responsibility to take the necessary measures to stop the violence against Rohingya minority, provide them with protection, repatriate the displaced to their homeland, prevent sectarian or ethnic discrimination against them, and ensure that they have their full legitimate rights as full-fledged citizens, and we in this regard urge all States to provide humanitarian assistance to them.

Mr. President,

Every time I stand here I speak in favor of the constructive international cooperation, just peace, the rights of peoples under occupation, as well as those who are subjected to crimes against humanity and those who are under siege.

This time I stand here, while my country and my people are subjected to a continuing and unjust blockade imposed since June 5th by neighboring countries. The blockade involves all aspects of life, including the intervention by these countries to rip off family ties. Qatar is currently managing successively its living, economy, development plans and its outreach to the outside world, with the availability of sea and air routes which these countries have no control over.

The blockade was imposed abruptly and without warning, prompting the Qataris to consider it as a kind of treachery.

It seems that those who planned and implemented it had envisaged that their move would cause a shocking and direct impact that will bring the State of Qatar to its knees and to capitulate to a total tutelage to be imposed on it.

And what is worse, the blockade planners found it necessary to rely on fabricated quotes attributed to me and posted on the website of Qatar News Agency after hacking it. The mobilized and guided media of these countries was ready to launch an all-out campaign of incitement prepared in advance in which all values, morals and norms were breached, and the truth was infringed by a torrent of lies.

Funds are still being spent unsparingly on the machine of faking and disseminating fabrications in the hope of fooling people by distorting the truth with lies.

Despite the disclosure of the hacking and falsification of quotes of the Emir of a sovereign State, the blockading countries did not back down or apologize for lying, but rather intensified their campaign, in the hope that the blockade would cause a cumulative effect on the economy and the society of my country, after it failed to bring about any direct impact.

The perpetrators of the hacking and the falsification of the quotes have committed an assault against a sovereign State. The crime was deliberately committed for political aims, and was followed by a list of political dictations which contravene sovereignty, and caused worldwide astonishment.

This disgraceful act has once again raised international queries about digital security and the unruliness in cybercrime and electronic piracy.

It also revealed the anxiety of a lot of public and official circles in the world over the absence of clear-cut international legislations and institutions to organize this dangerous and vital field and punish the perpetrators of transcontinental crimes.

It is time now to take steps in this regard, and we are ready to put our potentials to serve a joint effort in this connection.

The countries who imposed the unjust blockade on Qatar have intervened in the internal affairs of the State by putting pressure on its citizens through foodstuffs, medicine and ripping off consanguineous relations to force them to change their political affiliation to destabilize a sovereign country. Isn't this one of the definitions of terrorism?

This illegal blockade was not confined to the economic aspect and the breach of the WTO Agreement, but it exceeded that to violate the human rights conventions by the arbitrary measures that have caused social, economic and religious harm to thousands of citizens and residents of the GCC countries, due to the violation of the basic human rights to work, education, freedom of movement and the right to dispose of private property.

However, things did not stop at this point, but the blockading countries went beyond that to chase their own citizens and residents of their territory by imposing penalties of imprisonment and fines on them for the mere expression of their sympathy with Qatar, even if that was on the social media, in a precedent never seen before in the world, in violation of the human rights conventions and agreements that guarantee the right of everyone to freedom of opinion and expression of ideas.

There are countries that permit themselves not only to attack a neighboring country to dictate its foreign and media policy, but also believe that their possession of funds qualify them to put pressure and blackmail other countries to participate in their aggression, while they are supposed to be held accountable internationally for what they have done.

The countries who imposed the blockade on the State of Qatar interfere in the internal affairs of many countries, and accuse all those who oppose them domestically and abroad with terrorism. By doing so, they are inflicting damage on the war on terror, while at the same time opposing reform and supporting the tyrannical regimes in our region, where terrorists are initiated in their prisons.

We were not alone to be taken by surprise by the imposition of the blockade, as many countries whose leaders have questioned its motives and reasons were also taken by surprise. The blockading countries have promised all those who asked them about the reasons of the blockade to provide them with evidence of their anti-Qatar absurd allegations and fabrications, which kept changing according to the identity of the addressee. Everyone is still waiting for evidence that did not and will not arrive, because it does not exist. In contrast, these allegations contradict a lot of evidence about Qatar's contribution to the fight against terrorism, which is recognized by the entire international community.

The State of Qatar has fought terrorism - the whole international community bears witness to that - and it is still fighting it and will continue to do that. It stands in the camp of those who are fighting by security forces, and believes that it is necessary to fight it ideologically as well. It goes beyond that to participate in draining its sources through teaching seven million children around the world, so that they do not fall prey to ignorance and radical ideas.

We have refused to yield to dictations by pressure and siege, and our people was not satisfied by less than that. At the same time we have taken an open attitude towards dialogue without dictation, and have expressed our readiness to resolve differences through compromises based on common undertakings. Resolving conflicts by peaceful means is actually one of the priorities of our foreign policy. From here, I renew the call for an unconditional dialogue based on mutual respect for sovereignty and I highly value the sincere and appreciated mediation that the State of Qatar has supported since the outbreak of the crisis, and which was initiated by my brother, His Highness Sheikh Sabah Al-Ahmad Al-Jaber Al-Sabah, the Emir of the sisterly State of Kuwait. I also thank all the countries that have supported this mediation.

Allow me, on this occasion and from this podium, to express my pride in my Qatari people, along with the multinational and multicultural residents in Qatar.

The people have withstood the conditions of siege, and rejected the dictations with resolve and pride, and insisted on the independence of Qatar's sovereign decision, and strengthened its unity and solidarity, and maintained their refined manners and their progress despite the fierceness of the campaign against them and their country.

I reiterate my thanks to the sisterly and friendly countries which recognize the significance of respecting the sovereignty of States and the rules of international law, for their appreciated stances which were, and still are, supportive of the Qatari people during this crisis.

Mr. President,

Terrorism and extremism are among the most serious challenges facing the world. Countering them require us all to carry out a concerted action against terrorist organizations and their extremist ideology in order to maintain security for humanity and stability for the world.

The governments of the world have no choice but to cooperate in the security confrontation with terrorism, but halting the initiation of terrorism and extremism could be achieved by addressing its social, political and cultural root causes.

We must also be careful not to make the fighting against terrorism an umbrella for reprisals or shelling of civilians.

The fight against terrorism and extremism was and will continue to be our highest priority. This is affirmed by the effective participation of the State of Qatar in the regional and international efforts through the implementation of the measures included in the United Nations strategy adopted in 2006, and the implementation of all the Security Council resolutions and measures related to the fight against terrorism and its financing and through the participation in the International Alliance, regional organizations and bilateral relations with the United States and many countries of the world. The State of Qatar will continue its regional and international efforts in this regard and will develop them.

While reaffirming our condemnation of all forms of extremism and terrorism, we reject tackling this phenomenon with double standards according to the identity of the perpetrators, or by linking it with any particular religion, race, civilization, culture or society.

Mr. President,

The issues of the Middle East continue to pose the greatest threat to international peace and security, due to the vital importance of this region to the world.

Israel still stands in the way of achieving a lasting, just and comprehensive peace and rejects the Arab Peace initiative. The Israeli government continues its intransigent approach and strategy to create facts on the ground through expanding settlement construction in the occupied territories, Judaizing Jerusalem and restricting the performance of religious rituals in Al-Aqsa Mosque, which is a serious provocative act, and continuing its blockade of the Gaza Strip.

The international community must give high priority to the resumption of peace negotiations on the basis of ending the Israeli occupation of the Arab territories within a specified time frame and reaching a just, comprehensive and final settlement in accordance with the two-state solution agreed upon by the international community, based on the resolutions of international legitimacy and the Arab Peace initiative. This will only be achieved through the establishment of an independent Palestinian State on the basis of 1967 borders, with Jerusalem as its capital.

I renew my appeal to the Palestinian brothers to complete national reconciliation and unify positions and word in confronting the dangers and challenges facing the Palestinian cause and the future of the Palestinian people.

Mr. President,

The international community remains unable to find a solution to the Syrian crisis despite its consequences and serious repercussions on the region and the world. Political efforts continue to falter due to the conflicting international and regional interests, this confliction is conducive to protect those against whom we are supposed to stand united.

The international community relinquishes its legal and moral responsibilities, including the implementation of its decisions, in submission to the logic of force. What is required is to work seriously to reach a political solution to the Syrian crisis in a way that meets the aspirations of the Syrian people for justice, dignity and freedom, and maintains the unity and sovereignty of Syria, in accordance with the Geneva (1) decisions.

Qatar will spare no effort in providing support and assistance to alleviate the humanitarian suffering of our Syrian brothers and to implement our humanitarian pledges within the framework of the United Nations.

The international community has given up the task of protecting the civilians. Would it also hesitate to hold war criminals accountable? Their impunity would have dire consequences on the situation in Syria and the region, which would affect the behavior of future dictatorships towards their peoples in the absence of any deterrent.

On the Libyan issue, Libya's national consensus—which would preserve Libya's unity, sovereignty and social fabric, and restore its stability—could be achieved by means of combining domestic and international efforts. We must all intensify efforts and support the Government of national accord, which has been established with the support of United Nations, in its efforts to restore stability, counter terrorism and its grave consequences. The State of Qatar has supported international mediation efforts and will support them in the future to achieve the aspirations of the Libyan people.

Concerning the brotherly Iraq, we do support the efforts of the Iraqi government in its endeavor to achieve security, stability and unity of the territory and people of Iraq. We commend its achievements in its fight against terrorism, and affirm the necessary support to it by the State of Qatar to complement these victories by realizing the Iraqi peoples aspirations to equality among its citizens and restore its role at the regional and international levels.

Concerning Yemen, we affirm the importance of maintaining Yemen's unity, security and stability, and ending the state of infighting and war and adopting dialogue, political solution and national reconciliation as a basis for ending this crisis and implementing the Security Council resolution 2216.

We call upon the international community to facilitate the access of humanitarian assistance to various Yemeni regions. The State of Qatar supports the efforts of the UN envoy to end this crisis and realize the aspirations of the brotherly Yemeni people in unity, security and stability.

In order to achieve security and stability in the Gulf region, we renew the call that we have already launched from this podium, for conducting a constructive dialogue between the GCC countries and Iran on the basis of common interests, the principle of good neighborliness, respect for the sovereignty of States and non-interference in their internal affairs.

Mr. President,

Within the framework of the international efforts to tackle the humanitarian crises, the State of Qatar has continued to contribute to the growing humanitarian needs in the world. We have increased our financial contributions to the United Nations Office for the Coordination of Humanitarian Affairs (OCHA) to enable the United Nations to implement UN programs and provide humanitarian relief to those in need worldwide. Today the State of Qatar ranks third on the list of major donors in 2017 to the United Nations Office for the Coordination of Humanitarian Affairs.

We have continued to provide support to countries facing challenges to help them implement their development plans. It is worth mentioning here that the State of Qatar ranked first in the Arab world and 33rd in the world in the field of human development. This proves the effectiveness of our humanitarian and development policy. We look forward to achieving the goals of the United Nations Plan for Sustainable Development, which we have all committed to realize.

In conclusion, we reiterate that the State of Qatar will spare no effort in working to strengthen the role and efforts of the United Nations to achieve what the international community seeks in regard to peace and security, and to promote Human rights and advance development. Qatar will remain as is always the case a safe haven for the oppressed, and will continue its mediation efforts to find just solutions in conflict zones.

Thank you, May Allah's Peace, Mercy, and Blessings be upon you. [405]

APPENDIX 4

THE 2014 SUPPLEMENTARY RIYADH AGREEMENT

اتفاق الرياض التكميلي لعام 2014م

بناءً على دعوة كريمة من خادم الحرمين الشريفين الملك عبد الله بن عبد العزيز آل سعود ملك المملكة العربية السعودية فقد اجتمع هذا اليوم الأحد 1436/1/23هـ الموافق 2014/11/16م في مدينة الرياض لدى خادم الحرمين الشريفين- حفظه الله- صاحب السمو الشيخ صباح الأحمد الجابر الصباح أمير دولة الكويت، وصاحب الجلالة الملك حمد بن عيسى آل خليفة ملك مملكة البحرين، وصاحب السمو الشيخ تميم بن حمد بن خليفة آل ثاني أمير دولة قطر، وصاحب السمو الشيخ محمد بن راشد آل مكتوم نائب رئيس دولة الإمارات العربية المتحدة ورئيس مجلس الوزراء حاكم دبي، وصاحب السمو الشيخ محمد بن زايد آل نهيان ولي عهد أبوظبي نائب القائد الأعلى للقوات المسلحة بدولة الإمارات العربية المتحدة، وذلك لترسيخ روح التعاون الصادق والتأكيد على المصير المشترك وما يتطلع إليه أبناء دول مجلس التعاون لدول الخليج العربية من لُحمةٍ متينة وتقارب وثيق.

وبعد مناقشة الالتزامات المنبثقة عن اتفاق الرياض الموقع بتاريخ 1435/1/19هـ الموافق 2013/11/23م، وآليته التنفيذية، والاطلاع على تقارير لجنة متابعة تنفيذ الآلية ونتائج غرفة المتابعة المشتركة واستعراض ما خرج به محضر نتائج غرفة المتابعة الموقع بتاريخ 1436/1/10هـ الموافق 2014/11/3م من قبل رؤساء الأجهزة الاستخبارية في كل من (المملكة العربية السعودية، ودولة الإمارات العربية المتحدة، ومملكة البحرين، ودولة قطر).

فقد تم التوصل إلى الآتي:

أولاً: التأكيد على أن عدم الالتزام بأي بند من بنود اتفاق الرياض وآليته التنفيذية يعد إخلالاً بكامل ما ورد فيهما.

ثانياً: أن ما توصل إليه رؤساء الأجهزة الاستخباراتية في محضرهم المشار إليه أعلاه يعد تقدماً لإنفاذ اتفاق الرياض وآليته التنفيذية، مع ضرورة الالتزام الكامل بتنفيذ جميع ما ورد فيهما في مدة لا تتجاوز شهر من تاريخ هذا الاتفاق.

ثالثاً: عدم إيواء أو توظيف أو دعم -بشكل مباشر أو غير مباشر- في الداخل أو الخارج أي شخص أو أي وسيلة إعلامية ممن له توجهات تسيء إلى أي دولة من دول مجلس التعاون، وتلتزم كل دولة باتخاذ كافة الإجراءات النظامية والقانونية والقضائية بحق من يصدر عن هؤلاء أي تجاوز ضد أي دولة أخرى من دول مجلس التعاون لدول الخليج العربية، بما في ذلك محاكمته، وأن يتم الإعلان عن ذلك في وسائل الإعلام.

رابعاً: التزام كافة الدول بنهج سياسة مجلس التعاون لدول الخليج العربية لدعم جمهورية مصر العربية والإسهام في أمنها واستقرارها والمساهمة في دعمها اقتصادياً، وإيقاف كافة النشاطات الإعلامية الموجهة ضد جمهورية مصر العربية في جميع وسائل الإعلام بصفة مباشرة أو غير مباشرة بما في ذلك ما يبث من إساءات على قنوات الجزيرة وقناة مصر مباشر، والسعي لإيقاف ما ينشر من إساءات في الإعلام المصري.

وبناء على ما سبق، فقد تقرر أن مقتضى اتفاق الرياض، وآليته التنفيذية، وما ورد في هذا الاتفاق التكميلي، يتطلب الالتزام الكامل بتنفيذها. وقد كلف القادة رؤساء الأجهزة الاستخبارية بمتابعة إنفاذ ما

تم التوصل إليه في هذا الاتفاق التكميلي، وأن يتم الرفع عن ذلك بشكل دوري للقادة لاتخاذ ما يرونه من التدابير والإجراءات المناسبة لحماية أمن دولهم واستقرارها.

كما تم الاتفاق على أن تنفيذ ما ذكر أعلاه من التزامات يصب في وحدة دول المجلس ومصالحها ومستقبل شعوبها، ويعد إيذاناً بفتح صفحة جديدة ستكون بإذن الله مرتكزاً قوياً لدفع مسيرة العمل المشترك والانطلاق بها نحو كيان خليجي قوي ومتماسك.

والله ولي التوفيق.

The 2014 Supplementary Riyadh Agreement [*]

On a kind invitation by the Custodian of the Two Holy Mosques King Abdullah Bin Abdel-Aziz Al Saud, the King of Saudi Arabia, Sheikh Sabah Al Ahmad Al Jaber Al Sabbah, the Prince of Kuwait; King Hamad Bin Eissa Al Khalifa, King of Bahrain; Sheikh Tamim Bin Hamad Bin Khalifa Al Thani, Prince of Qatar; Sheikh Mohammad Bin Rashed Al Maktom, the Vice President and Prime Minister of United Arab Emirates and Rule of Dubai; and Muhammad Bin Zayed Al Nahyan, the Crown Prince of Abu Dhabi, and Deputy Commander of the Armed Forces of the UAE, met today Sunday 23/1/1436H correspondent to November 16, 2014 in Riyadh to consolidate the spirit of honest cooperation and emphasize the common destiny and the aspirations of durable cohesion and close cooperation by the peoples of the states of the Gulf Cooperation Council.

Upon discussion of the commitments contained in Riyadh Agreement signed on 19/1/1435H correspondent to November 23, 2013 and its Executive Mechanism, and upon viewing the reports of the committee tasked with following up the implementation of the mechanism and results of the joint follow-up room, and reviewing the minute of the results of the joint follow-up room signed on 10/1/1436H correspondent to November 3, 2014 by the heads of the intelligence services of the Kingdom of Saudi Arabia, the United Arab Emirates, the Kingdom of Bahrain and the State of Qatar;

The following has been reached:

First: Stressing that non-committing to any of the articles of the Riyadh Agreement and its Executive Mechanism amounts to a violation of the entirety of the agreement.

Second: The conclusions reached by the intelligence heads in the aforementioned minute is considered a step forward to implement the Riyadh Agreement and its Executive Mechanism, with the necessity of the full commitment to implementing everything stated in them [Riyadh Agreement and its Executive Agreement] within the period of one month from the date of this Agreement.

Third: Not to give refuge, employ, or support whether directly or indirectly, whether domestically or abroad, to any person or a media apparatus that harbors inclinations harmful to any Gulf Cooperation Council state. Each state is committed to taking all the regulatory, legal and judicial measures against anyone who [commits] any encroachment against any of the Gulf Cooperation Council states, including putting him on trial and announcing that in the media outlets.

Fourth: All countries are committed to the Gulf Cooperation Council discourse to support the Arab Republic of Egypt, and contribute to its security and stability, contribute in financial support to Egypt; cease all media activity directed against the Arab Republic of

---

[*] Translated by Nabeel Al Nowairah, June 11, 2020.

Egypt in all media platforms, whether directly or indirectly, including all the offenses broadcasted on Al Jazeera, Al Jazeera Mubashir Masr, and to work to stop all offenses in Egyptian media.

Based on the above, it has been decided that the Riyadh Agreement, and its Executive Mechanism, and the provisions of this supplementary agreement, require the full commitment to their implementation. The leaders have tasked the heads of intelligence agencies to follow up on the implementation of this supplementary agreement and to report regularly to the leaders, in order to take the measures they deem necessary to protect the security and stability of their countries.

It was also agreed that the implementation of the above commitments is in the interest of the unity of the GCC state and the future of their peoples. This marks the opening of a new chapter that will hopefully be a strong basis for pushing forward the course of joint work and moving towards a strong and coherent GCC entity.

Allah Grants Success.

APPENDIX 5

الجمهورية اليمنية

محافظة المهـرة

اللجنة المنظمة للاعتصام

التاريخ / ٢٠١٩م

الرقم :

الأخ/رئيس وأعضاء اللجنة الرئاسية   المحترمون

تحية تقدير واحترام وبعد

ترحب بكم اللجنة المنظمة لاعتصام أبناء المهرة السلمي أجمل ترحيب في زيارتكم للمحافظة للاطلاع على مجمل الاوضاع فيها .

وتشكركم ومن خلالكم نرفع أسمى آيات الشكر لفخامة الأخ المشير/ عبدربه منصور هادي رئيس الجمهورية الذي يولي هذه المحافظة اهتماماً كبيراً.

ونجدد تأييدنا ووقوفنا خلف قيادته الحكيمة.

وبأسم المعتصمين سلميا وفقا لما كفله الدستور والقانون ومواثيق حقوق الإنسان الدولية نؤكد دونما أدنى شك أن مطالبنا عادلة ونابعة من صدق انتمائنا وضميرنا الوطني ومن حرصنا الشديد على الامتثال الكامل لمعنى الشرعية الدستورية في الحفاظ على سيادة الدولة بكامل سلطاتها التشريعية والتنفيذية والقضائية انطلاقا من روح المسؤولية التي نتحلى بها ومن اعتبار أن الدولة وحدها وليس غيرها مطلقا هي من تنشئ القوات المسلحة والأمن للحفاظ على أمن وسيادة وسلامة أراضي الجمهورية اليمنية وفقا للنص الدستوري الواضح والذي جاء في المادة (٣٦) :{ الدولة هي التي تنشئ القوات المسلحة والأمن وأية قوة أخرى وهي ملك الشعب ومهمتها حماية الجمهورية وسلامة أراضيها وأمنها ولا يجوز لأي هيئة أو فرد او جماعة أو تنظيم أو حزب سياسي انشاء قوات أو تشكيلات عسكرية لأي غرض كان}

وهذا نص صريح وواضح لا يقبل المغالطة أو التأويلات والتفسيرات الأخرى والذي حدث للأسف الشديد ان السلطة المحلية ممثلة في المحافظ راجح باكريت قد اشتغلت بما يخالف الدستور نصا وروحا وعمدت إلى إنشاء ميليشيات خارج مؤسسات الدولة بما يفقد الوطن سيادته واستقلاله كون هذه الميليشيات المستحدثة تتبع المملكة العربية السعودية تمويلاً وتدريبا وتسليحا وتنفذ أجندة تتنافى مع سيادة الجمهورية اليمنية من خلال توجيهات المحافظ راجح باكريت الذراع في تنفيذ مخطط الرياض على الأرض المهرية.

إن هذه الميليشيات تعمل على تقويض مؤسسات الدولة الأمنية والعسكرية وتزعزع الأمن والاستقرار لكونها تعمل خارج ما كفله الدستور والقوانين النافذة في تنظيم مهام كلا المؤسستين بالاستناد إلى روح الدستور ومضامينه وهو أمر نؤكد نحن المعتصمين السلميين على أهميته ونراه مطلبا عادلا وقانونيا ويعبر عن حرص المهري على سلامة أراضي الوطن من إي نفوذ أو وصاية أو تدخلات خارجية هي رأي العين فالقوات السعودية التي يشرعن لاحتلالها مهرتنا الغالية المحافظ باكريت قد انتشرت في الموانئ البرية والبحرية والجوية منذ أن وصلت

١

بسم الله الرحمن الرحيم

الجمهورية اليمنية

محافظة المهـرة

اللجنة المنظمة للاعتصام

التاريخ / ٢٠١٩م

الرقم :

أواخر عام ٢٠١٧م وباعداد كبيرة بذريعة واهية وهي حماية الحدود اليمنية العمانية من التهريب. في حين لم يعط أحدا للسعودية الحق في هذا التدخل السافر سوى باكريت الذي ينفذ كامل المخطط الخارجي بتفاني وإخلاص عجيب.

كما أنه لم تعقد أي اتفاقيات دولية بين البلدين اليمن والسعودية بما يؤكد أن باكريت قد انتهك سيادة الدولة ممثلة في الشرعية الدستورية وتجاوز صلاحياته القانونية ومارس خيانة القيم والمبادئ والمثل العليا وكذا اليمين الدستورية التي تؤكد على الحفاظ على الأراضي اليمنية وسيادة الدولة وهو أمر يحاسب عليه القانون ونطالب نحن كمعتصمين سلميين بإحالته إلى العدالة كونه قبل بان يكون على رأس المخطط الرامي لاحتلال المهرة أولا ومن ثم اقتطاع جزء من أراضيها لمرور أنبوب النفط السعودي إلى البحر العربي دونما أي اتفاق قائم بين الدولتين ينظم العلاقة ويؤكد على سيادة اليمن على أراضيها وهو أمر بالغ الخطورة لا يمكن لأي منتم إلى هذه الأرض أن يقبل به أو يهادن فيه.

الأخوة /رئيس وأعضاء اللجنة الرئاسية

شتان بين من يدعو للفوضى وخيانة الدستور والقفز على القوانين المرعية الجانب ومن يدعو ويؤمن بالسيادة الوطنية واحترام الدستور والمواثيق والمعاهدات الدولية ويرفض تكوين وأنشأ ميليشيات خارج مؤسسات الدولة الهدف منها خلق مناخات فوضى واضطرابات واقلاق أمن واستقرار المجتمع المهري ونهب موارد الدولة. والحق بين وصريح وواضح نخاطب من خلاله ضميركم الوطني وانتمائكم إلى هذه الأرض إلى تنفيذ واحترام الدستور والقانون ونحن في هذا نثق كل الثقة في أنكم ستقفون إلى جانب الشرعية الدستورية في احترام وتنفيذ مطالبنا العادلة.

وقد أكدت السلطة المحلية بالمحافظة أن وصول الفريق السعودي كان بدون التنسيق معها في بداية التدخل السعودي في المحافظة نهاية العام ٢٠١٧م. وبعد مفاوضات ونقاشات وتعليل السعوديين بأن قدومهم إلى المحافظة يأتي ضمن المساعدة للمحافظة لإعادة تشغيل مطار الغيضة وتأهيله.

وحينها عقدت السلطة المحلية واللجنة الامنية مع المكونات السياسية وشيوخ وأعيان المحافظة اجتماعاً مشتركاً واعلنت أنه بعد اتضاح الصورة عن

٢

بسم الله الرحمن الرحيم

التاريخ / ٢٠١٩م	الجمهورية اليمنية
الرقم :	محافظة المهرة
	اللجنة المنظمة للاعتصام

طبيعة عمل الفريق ومهامه قامت السلطة المحلية بالمحافظة بتأمين الفريق السعودي في معسكر الغيضة.

ثم التقت السلطة المحلية بالمحافظة بحضور عدد من المشائخ والشخصيات الاجتماعية بالفريق السعودي واستمعت عن طبيعة الزيارة والمهام الموكلة للفريق ووضعت السلطة المحلية سته شروط لإعادة تشغيل وتأهيل مطار الغيضة وتم الاتفاق والتوقيع على ذلك.

وأهم تلك الشروط التي وضعتها السلطة المحلية للوفد العسكري السعودي هي:-

- عدم استخدام مطار الغيضة كقاعدة عسكرية
- بقاء الطاقم الاداري والأمني والعسكري للمطار على ما هو عليه
- التنسيق الدائم مع السلطة المحلية وعدم تجاوزها
- استخدام المطار للأغراض المدنية والمساعدات الانسانية فقط
- اعادة تشغيل للطيران المدني

وبهذه الشروط دخل الفريق السعودي مطار الغيضة وقد مثل هذا التدخل مخالفة صريحة وواضحة لأهداف التحالف العربي المعلنة لدعم الشرعية اليمنية، كما مثل انتهاكاً سافراً لكل الاعراف والمواثيق الدولية وميثاق جامعة الدول العربية.

وفي حقيقة الأمر أن دخول الفريق السعودي إلى المطار كان نقطة البداية لاجتياح القوات السعودية لمحافظة المهرة بشكل ممنهج لاحتلال الموانئ البحرية ، والمنافذ البرية ،والجوية ، والمنشآت الحيوية ،والسيطرة على الموقع الجغرافي المتميز وأهمية المحافظة الاستراتيجية.

وأتضح ذلك جلياً سواءً لأبناء المحافظة أو أبناء الوطن والمجتمع الدولي من خلال الآتي:-

٣

235

بسم الله الرحمن الرحيم

التاريخ / ٢٠١٩/م		الجمهورية اليمنية
الرقم :		محافظة المهرة
		اللجنة المنظمة للاعتصام

❖ عدم التزام الفريق العسكري السعودي بتنفيذ الإتفاق المشار إليه مع السلطة المحلية بالمحافظة بإعادة تشغيل مطار الغيضة وتأهيله للأغراض المدنية والمساعدات الإنسانية ورحلات الطيران المدني من وإلى المطار فقط وهذ ما لم يتم فعلاً .

وقد ادرك السعوديون أنهم لم يستطيعوا تمرير أجندتهم وتنفيذ مخططاتهم وتحقيق أهدافهم وأطماعهم إلا بوجود شخصاً راضخاً وطائعاً لتنفيذ كل ما يملى عليه على رأس هرم السلطة بالمحافظة فتم إقالة محافظ المحافظة السابق الشيخ/ محمد عبدالله كده وتعيين راجح سعيد باكريت محافظاً للمحافظة في الثلاثين من نوفمبر ٢٠١٧م.

❖ في مخالفة الإتفاق المشار إليه تم تشغيل المطار للطيران العسكري السعودي لنقل المعدات ، والآليات العسكرية ، والأسلحة ، والجنود من السعودية إلى مطار الغيضة بصورة جنونية وهستيرية .

ومن تلك الفترة حتى اليوم لم تنقطع الطائرات العسكرية السعودية فهي تصل يومياً سواءً الطيران الحربي أو طيران النقل العسكري ، إضافة الى الطيران المروحي .

كما لم تتوقف الاستعراضات للطيران الحربي في أجواء مدينة الغيضة والمديريات الخرى بشكل شبه يومي فتسبب هلعاً وخوفاً لدى السكان ورعباً للنساء والاطفال .

وجعلت السعودية المطار ثكنه وقاعدة عسكرية لقواتها يمنع الدخول اليها أو حتى الاقتراب منها ووضعت فيه أحدث وسائل المراقبة .

❖ ثم استمر تمدد السعودية لتحقيق أطماعها وامتد نفوذها بعد ذلك للسيطرة على المنفذين البريين في شحن وصرفيت مع سلطنة عمان الشقيقة ،وميناء نشطون البحري وسط استغراب واندهاش وذهول أبناء المحافظة بمخالفة هذه القوات السعودية لأهداف التحالف العربي المعلنة التي التزمت بها أمام المجتمع الدولي لمساعدة

بسم الله الرحمن الرحيم

	الجمهورية اليمنية
التاريخ / /٢٠١٩م	محافظة المهرة
الرقم :	اللجنة المنظمة للاعتصام

اليمنيين وقيادتهم الشرعية برئاسة الأخ/عبد ربه منصور هادي رئيس الجمهورية .

فاتضح للقاصي والداني أن للسعودية أطماعاً كبيرة بعيدة كل البعد عن أهداف التحالف العربي في محافظة المهرة.

خصوصاً وأن المهرة بعيدة من الناحية الجغرافية والفكرية والسياسية عن مناطق الحوثيين الانقلابيين ولا تربطهم أي علاقة بهم.

وأن قميص يعقوب الذي يعلقون عليه الأكاذيب ، والمغالطات ، والمزايدات لمكافحة تهريب الأسلحة والمخدرات وغيرها من الادعاءات العارية عن الصحة لخداع الرأي العام العربي والدولي، فمن الوهلة الاولى لتواجدهم أنكشف زيف ما يدعون من تلك الأكاذيب والمغلطات والحجج الواهية وعرف الجميع خداعهم وتضليلهم الإعلامي فلم يستطيعوا إثبات ما أدعوا به سواءً بالقبض على مهربي أي قطعة سلاح أو حتى مهربي المخدرات وغيرها .

وأمام كل ذلك لم يكن أمام أبناء المهرة خياراً سوى الاعتصام السلمي الذي بدأ في التاسع من مايو٢٠١٨م وحدد الأهداف والمطالب لأبناء المحافظة بست نقاط هي :

١-إعادة العمل في منفذ شحن وصرفيت وميناء نشطون إلى وضعهم الطبيعي ، وتسليمهم الى قوات الأمن المحلية والجيش بحسب توجيهات فخامة الأخ رئيس الجمهورية ونائبة بالبرقية رقم (٤١ لعام ٢٠١٧م) وعدم السماح لأي قوات غير رسمية بالقيام بالمهام الأمنية في محافظة المهرة بشكل عام والمنافذ الحدودية بشكل خاص والعمل على تسهيل معاملات وإجراءات المواطنين فيها .

٢-العمل على إعادة مطار الغيضة الدولي إلى وضعه السابق كمطار مدني تحت اشراف السلطة المحلية بالمحافظة وتسليمه لقوات الأمن التابعة لها .

٥

237

بسم الله الرحمن الرحيم

الجمهورية اليمنية

محافظة المهرة

اللجنة المنظمة للاعتصام

التاريخ / /٢٠١٩م

الرقم :

٣ـ رفع القيود الاستثنائية المفروضة على حركة التجارة والاستيراد والتصدير في منفذي شحن وصرفيت وميناء نشطون التي تؤثر بشكل سلبي على الإيرادات التي تحتاجها المحافظة لتوفير الخدمات الأساسية وتسيير حياة المواطنين .

٤ـ مراعاة العمل حيثما أمكن لتحقيق التكامل بين قيادة المحافظة ومدراء الأجهزة ألتنفيذية وفق قانون السلطة المحلية بحيث تصب جميع الجهود لصالح خدمة المحافظة وأبناءها .

٥ـ إعطاء الأولوية لتحسين وضع الخدمات العامة مثل الكهرباء والمياه والصحة والتعليم والطرقات وغيرها من الخدمات المرتبطة بحياة الناس .

٦ـ إعطاء إهتمام خاص لبناء مؤسسة الشرطة المحلية بناءً وطنياً تمهيد واستعداداً لقيامها بمهامها لاحقاً في إطار مشروع الأقاليم ومن ضمنها إقليم المهرة وسقطرى.

وباعتبار المجلس العام هو الكيان الجامع والحامل والممثل لكل أبناء المحافظة وقضاياهم.

خاطب الشيخ/ عبدالله بن عيسى آل عفرار رئيس المجلس العام لأبناء المهرة وسقطرى مشكوراً قيادة السلطة المحلية بالمحافظة برسالة بتاريخ ١٢مايو ٢٠١٨م تضمنت المطالبة بتنفيذ النقاط الست.

(مرفق نسخة من هذه الرسالة- مرفق رقم ١)

وتماطلت السلطة المحلية بالمحافظة بتنفيذ هذه المطالب ولم تعيرها أي اهتمام يذكر ضاربة بعرض الحائط مصالح أبناء المحافظة وسيادتهم وهويتهم الوطنية.

وكان الاعتصام الأول هذا قد علق في الثالث عشر من مايو ٢٠١٨م استجابةً لطلب رئيس المجلس العام لأبناء المهرة وسقطرى ، والمشائخ والشخصيات الاجتماعية ، وتكريماً لشهر رمضان المبارك .

٦

238

بسم الله الرحمن الرحيم

الجمهورية اليمنية
محافظة المهرة
اللجنة المنظمة للاعتصام

التاريخ   / ٢٠١٩م
الرقم :

لمنح مهلة لمحافظ المحافظة لتنفيذ ما ورد في المطالب السته حتى العاشر من شوال ١٤٣٩هـ ولم يستجب لذلك .

ونتيجة لذلك تم استئناف الاعتصام بمشاركة جماهيرية ولأول مرة في المحافظة من الشباب والشخصيات الاجتماعية ، والمثقفين، وقطاع المرأة من كل أطياف المجتمع المهري على اختلاف مناطقهم وشرائحهم الاجتماعية وانتماءاتهم السياسية يمثلون(٦٨) مكون قبلي واجتماعي.

فاستمر الاعتصام المفتوح حتى الثالث عشر من شهر يوليو ٢٠١٨م ، بناءً على ما ورد في محضر الاجتماع المشترك بين السلطة المحلية بالمحافظة وقيادة التحالف ممثلة بالجانب السعودي المنعقد صباح يوم الثلاثاء الموافق ٢٠١٨/٧/١٠م

ومحضر الاجتماع المشترك للسلطة المحلية بالمحافظة واللجنة المنظمة للاعتصام والشخصيات الاجتماعية المنعقد يوم الأربعاء الموافق الحادي عشر من يوليو ٢٠١٨م.(مرفق نسخه من المحضرين- مرفق رقم ١و٢).

وما خرجت به تلك الاجتماعات التي اعتبرتها اللجنة المنظمة للاعتصام نتائج طيبه وإيجابية ،وأكدت ترحيبه وتقديرها العالي باهتمام ومتابعة فخامة الأخ /عبد ربه منصور هادي رئيس الجمهورية لما أولاه من اهتمام لقضايا ومطالب المعتصمين وتكليف اللواء/أحمد محمد قحطان مدير الشرطة بالمحافظة بالاستماع والنظر لمطالب المعتصمين والعمل على حلها.

والحقيقة إن لدينا مخاوف لا حصر لها من ان ثمة مؤامرة كبيرة على محافظتنا تستهدف النسيج الاجتماعي واللحمة المهرية وتخلق مناخات خصومة وعنف وارهاب لا يمكننا الصمت حيال كل ذلك ونحن نرى احتلالاً يعمل على انتهاك الحقوق المدنية والشرعية الدستورية ويتنصل عما تم الاتفاق عليه.

وإن التحالف ومعه المحافظ يتنكر للقيم المتعارف عليها والأعراف الدبلوماسية والقوانين المنظمة للعلاقات بين الدول ويضرب بذلك عرض الحائط متماديا في القمع والعنف والإرهاب ولعل جريمة نفق فرتك ليست ببعيد عندما ارادت السعودية

٧

239

بسم الله الرحمن الرحيم

الجمهورية اليمنية

محافظة المهـرة

اللجنة المنظمة للاعتصام

التاريخ / ٢٠١٩م

الرقم :

ومليشياتها إنشاء استحداث نقطة عسكرية في هذا الموقع الحيوي الهام للسيطرة على المحافظة وتقسيمها إلى قسمين لوضع الحواجز بين أبناء المهرة في المناطق الشرقية والمناطق الجنوبية وغيرها .

الأخوة /رئيس وأعضاء اللجنة الرئاسية

إننا نضع بين ايديكم ملخص بأهم الانتهاكات والممارسات التي قامت بها السعودية في المحافظة كالآتي :

أ- الجرائم والاعتقالات التعسفية والاجراءات الغير قانونية

● **جريمة الأنفاق**

في الثالث عشر من نوفمبر٢٠١٨م في هذا اليوم الاسود أقدمت القوات السعودية ومليشياتها على إرتكاب جريمة إنسانية مروعة ، فقد أقدمت القوات السعودية وميليشياتها بالاعتداء على المتظاهرين السلميين الذين احتجوا رفضاً لاستحداث النقطة السعودية غرب منطقة الانفاق فباشرتهم تلك القوات بالرصاص الحي والمباشر فارتقت إلى بارئها الارواح البريئة دون أدنى وازع أو ضمير إنساني فنتج عن تلك الجريمة سقوط شهيدين هما:-

١- علي احمد عرعره الجدحي

٢- ناصر سعيد أحمد نشوان

كما اصيب بجروح بالغة المواطن/ ١- سالم سمحان غفيل الجدحي.

● **الاعتقالات والانتهاكات**

هناك الكثير من الجرائم التي تم ارتكابها من قبل القوات السعودية بحق المواطنين الذين تم اعتقالهم والتحقيق معهم خارج إطار القانون والمعاملات الغير إنسانية سواءً بالضرب والتعذيب أو التهديد والابتزاز وغيرها من المعاملات التعسفية فمنهم من تم اعتقاله لفترات طويله والبعض فترات متوسطة ومنهم أيضاً من اعتقل وسجن في سجن القوات السعودية في مطار الغيضة ومنهم من تم نقله إلى السجن في السعودية وبعد فترات تتراوح بين المتوسطة والطويلة تم اطلاق سراح البعض والبعض منهم لازالوا في

٨

240

بسم الله الرحمن الرحيم

الجمهورية اليمنية

محافظة المهرة

اللجنة المنظمة للاعتصام

التاريخ / /٢٠١٩م

الرقم :

غياهيب المعتقلات ونورد هنا بعض المعتقلين وليس جميعهم نظراً لعدم وجود معلومات عن المخفيين قسراً ولا يعلم أحد عن مصيرهم .

١- احمد بن بريك التميمي :تم اعتقاله ولم يعرف مصيره حتى اليوم .

٢- ياسين الصومالي: اعتقل لفترة ثم أطلق صراحه

٣- محمد هاشم اعتقل وتم نقله إلى السعودية وسجن لمدة شهرين ثم أطلق صراحه وطرده من عمله كونه يعمل في المطار .

٤- يونس القروي تم اعتقاله ثم اطلق صراحه بعد فترة

٥- قيام المليشيات الخارجة على القانون التابعة للقوات السعودية بارتكاب جرائم اعتداء ونهب لبعض ممتلكات المواطنين ومن ذلك على سبيل المثال نهب المحل التجاري (جولد فرتك) لصاحبه/ محمد خميس مغفيق.

٦- اعتقال المواطن/ علي سعد كده والافراج عنه بعد فترة.

٧- اعتقال المواطن/حازم محمد مخبال بحجة أن أخته مشاركه في الاعتصامات والاحتجاجات المناهضة للتواجد السعودي في المحافظة وتم التحقيق معه وتهديده ثم تم الافراج عنه بعد وساطات وتدخلات من شيوخ القبائل الذين أرادو إخماد نار الفتنة بين قبيلته والقوات السعودية.

٨- مداهمة مخازن الصيادين في منطقة الفيدمي بمديرية الغيضة في الرابع من يناير الجاري ٢٠١٩م حيث قامت القوات السعودية على تمزيق شباك الصيادين واتلاف ممتلكاتهم الخاصة.

٩- تسريح وطرد أحدى عشر ضابطاً وثلاثين جندياً من القوات الجوية بمطار الغيضة بشكل تعسفي رغم خدمتهم في المطار لسنين طويله .

١٠- اعتقال شاب من قبيلة بيت رعفيت أثناء وقوعه بعفوية عند سور المطار وتم إطلاق سراحه فيما بعد.

٩

بسم الله الرحمن الرحيم

| الجمهورية اليمنية |
| محافظة المهرة |
| اللجنة المنظمة للاعتصام |

التاريخ / /٢٠١٩م

الرقم :

١١- ضرب الرصاص الحي على احد المواطنين عندما تعطلت دراجته النارية في الطريق العام بشارع الجامعة وقد اطلقت عليه النار القوات السعودية المتواجدة في برج المطار.

١٢- اعتقال مواطنين أثنين من آل الجابر مع القاطرات التابعة لهم التي كانت تحمل السماد الزراعي واطلق سراحهم فيما بعد ومصادرة السماد.

١٣- المضايقات والانتهاكات اليومية للتجار في منفذ شحن والتعسف بتأخير معاملاتهم وخروج بضائعهم من المنفذ وهذه المعاناة تتسبب في خسائر كبيرة للتجار وتلف بعض البضائع المحدودة الصلاحية وقد رفعت عدد من الشكاوي من قبل التجار الا أنه لم ينصفهم أحد والمأساة لا زالت مستمرة.

١٤- أقدم نجل أحد الموالين للسعودية وبالطقم العسكري على ارتكاب جريمة شنعاء بقتل جنديين من قوات الأمن المركزي في مدينة الغيضة بتاريخ ٢٠١٩/١/٣م والشهيدين هما:-
- زيد محمد القميحة
- عمار محمد مرشد مفرح

١٥- اعتقال مواطنين أثنين من قبيلة بيت صموده والتحقيق معهم واطلاقهم بعد فترة.

١٦- قامت القوات السعودية باستقدام أعداد كبيرة من المتشددين السلفيين إلى مديريات قشن وحصوين والغيضة مطلع العام الماضي٢٠١٨م بهدف تغيير في البنية السكانية للمحافظة وزرع الفتنة الطائفية والدينية وإدخال المحافظة في دوامة الإرهاب وتأسيس بؤر إرهابية لاستخدامها متى شأت وقد دعمت السعودية هذه الجماعات بالأسلحة والأموال الطائلة لشراء المساكن واراضي ومحاولة بناء مركز ديني متطرف لبث سموم الإرهاب وقد وأجه المواطنين رجالاً ونساءً في

١٠

بسم الله الرحمن الرحيم

الجمهورية اليمنية

محافظة المهرة

اللجنة المنظمة للاعتصام

التاريخ / ٢٠١٩م

الرقم :

هذه المديريات بشكل خاص وفي المحافظة بشكل عام هذا المخطط بالرفض الشديد والوقفات الاحتجاجية السلمية.

١٧- استقدمت السعودية قوات عسكرية كبيرة من جنسيات غير يمنية تحت مبررات كاذبة .

١٨- توزيع الأسلحة المختلفة والاموال على بعض الاشخاص والجماعات المشبوهة لشراء الولاءات بما يخدم تعزيز تواجد القوات السعودية في المحافظة.

١٩- تحويل بعض المرافق والمواقع المدنية إلى ثكنات عسكرية.

٢٠- اعتقال المواطنين محمد عبدالله مسلم مدهوف رعفيت وعلي سعد ظليل كده ، من قرية يروب ليلاً واقتيادهم إلى مطار الغيضة الخاضع للقوات السعودية دون أي مسوغ قانوني ولم يعرف مصيرهم حتى الآن.

٢١- الحقائق والانتهاكات الواردة في التقريرين الحكوميين الصادران عن مكتب حقوق الانسان في محافظة المهرة في الـ٢٠١٨/٥/٣م وفي الـ٢٠١٨/١٣/١٠م.(مرفق نسخة من كل منهما- مرفق رقم ٤و٥)

٢٢- ما حدث في حات مؤخراً بعد رفض القبائل مرور القاطرات والمدرعات السعودية إلى شحن لاستحداث موقع عسكري حيث كان قد تم الاتفاق بين الشخصيات والقيادات بوقف التوتر وخروج الشاحنات بمرافقة الأمن والجيش التابعة للمؤسسات الشرعية إلى خارج المحافظة وقامت المليشيات بإطلاق النار على أبناء القبائل وردت القبائل على إطلاق النار دفاعاً عن النفس مما أدى إلى اصابة البعض من المليشيات وهو أمر مؤسف لا نريده لأي يمني أو أياً كان ولكن ما حدث هو نتيجة تصرفات السعودية ومليشياتها التي نحملها المسئولية بذلك.

١١

243

بسم الله الرحمن الرحيم

الجمهورية اليمنية

محافظة المهرة

اللجنة المنظمة للاعتصام

التاريخ / /٢٠١٩م

الرقم :

ب- المناطق التي تتواجد فيها المواقع والمعسكرات السعودية:

١- مطار الغيضة

٢- ميناء نشطون

٣- معسكر بالقرب من مديرية حات

٤- معسكر في منطقة درفات بمديرية سيحوت على الساحل

٥- معسكر في منطقة جدوه بمديرية حصوين

٦- موقع عسكري بالقرب من منطقة هروت بمديرية الغيضة

٧- معسكرين أثنين متقاربين في منطقة لوسيك بمركز الفيدمي بمديرية الغيضة

٨- بالنسبة للمنفذين البريين الحدوديين مع سلطنة عمان وهما منفذ صرفيت بمديرية حوف ومنفذ شحن بمديرية شحن فإنه يتم التفتيش في هاذين المنفذين من قبل الضباط والافراد السعوديين حيث يتم التفتيش للمغادرين والواصلين وكذلك البضائع وغيرها بتعسف وتعالي.

٩- نقطة عسكرية في مديرية سيحوت بمنطقة موقض.

١٠- نقطة عسكرية في مديرية سيحوت بمنطقة رخوت الشرقية.

١١- نقطة عسكرية في مديرية سيحوت بمنطقة خطر.

١٢- نقطة عسكرية في مديرية الغيضة في وادي مثول

١٣- نقطة عسكرية في مديرية العيص بمنطقة ديمون.

١٤- نقطة عسكرية في مديرية الغيضة بمنطقة أروت.

١٥- نقطة عسكرية في مديرية المسيلة بمنطقة شرخات.

١٦- نقطة عسكرية في مديرية المسيلة بمنطقة صمورح.

١٧- نقطة عسكرية في مديرية المسيلة بمنطقة ثمنون.

١٨- نقطة عسكرية في مديرية المسيلة بمنطقة حساي.

١٢

بسم الله الرحمن الرحيم

الجمهورية اليمنية
محافظة المهـرة
اللجنة المنظمة للاعتصام

التاريخ   /٢٠١٩م
الرقم :

١٩- تكوين مليشيات تابعة للمحافظ خارجة عن المؤسسات العسكرية والامنية الرسمية ومقرها دار الضيافة أثار الرعب لدى المواطنين ويقومون بنصب نقاط في مداخل مدينة الغيضة في بعض الأوقات وهم ملثمين ومعهم السيارات السوداء وقد جلبهم المحافظ من أبناء المحافظات الأخرى.

٢٠- الإعداد والتجهيز من قبل المحافظ لإنشاء مليشيا جديدة تحت مسمى حماية المنشآت والشخصيات وتم الاعلان أنه سيتم تجنيد ٧٠٠ شخص من هذه المليشيا.

٢١- ما أعلن عنه المجلس الانتقالي الجنوبي بالمحافظة من تجنيد(٤٥٠٠)جندي وهذه مليشيا جديدة فخلط الأوراق في المحافظة وتبع الامارات وبقصد منه زعزعت الأمن والاستقرار في المحافظة.

٢٢- المخالفات والتجاوزات المالية والادارية حيث يتم صرف مبالغ طائلة من قبل المحافظ الغرض منها شراء الولاءات وبصورة مخالفة للقانون.

إن ما تقوم به السعودية من إدخال أسلحة ثقيلة ومتوسطة وتوزيعها على المتطرفين وإنشاء السجون خارج سلطات الدولة الأمنية والقضائية وبناء معسكرات سعودية على الشواطئ والانتشار في المرافئ البرية والبحرية والجوية كل ذلك يتنافى مع أبسط القيم المتعارف عليها ويؤكد أن السلطة المحلية قد ارتضت ان تكون أداة تنفيذية لمخطط المحتل وتمارس هذا الإرهاب الذي وصل إلى حد القتل ولعل جريمة نفق (فرتك) التي راح ضحيتها اثنين من أبناء المحافظة شاهد حي والتستر على القتلة وحمايتهم من ان تطالهم يد العدالة.

وإنه لأمر مخيف حقا ان نرى أرضنا محتلة وسيادة الوطن مفقودة والشرعية الدستورية التي نطالب بها مغيبة تماما وهو ما يتنافى جملةً وتفصيلا مع الدستور فما بالنا وقد أعطى باكريت كل صلاحيات الدولة للاحتلال السعودي وتم تطويق المحافظة بالنقاط والمواقع والمعسكرات السعودية.

١٣

245

بسم الله الرحمن الرحيم

الجمهورية اليمنية

محافظة المهـرة

اللجنة المنظمة للاعتصام

التاريخ   / ٢٠١٩م

الرقم :

فهل نحن على خطأ حين نطالب بمؤسسات الدولة العسكرية والأمنية ومنحها كامل الصلاحيات ورفض التدخلات الخارجية والاستحداثات السعودية؟ والمطالبة بأهمية ان يحترم التحالف تعهداته في الوقوف مع الشرعية الدستورية التي نراه قد قفز عليها إلى أجندة احتلال الأرض المهرية والانحراف بما قام من أجله التحالف إلى مخطط آخر يستهدف أمن وسلامة أراضي الوطن وإنشاء ميليشيات لم تكن إلا للسحل والقتل والتعذيب والتشريد والمطاردة وإقامة السجون السرية وانتهاك حقوق وحريات الإنسان والتجربة في عدن خير مثال يدعونا إلى الاحتراز والرفض القاطع لميليشيا أجندتها خارجية وأهدافها لا وطنية وغايتها تدمير مؤسسات الدولة وإحلال الفوضى.

الأخوة /رئيس وأعضاء اللجنة الرئاسية

اننا كمواطنين مهريين لن نرضى بأن نجد من يخون الدستور وينتهك السيادة ويعمل بشكل ممنهج على تدمير مؤسسات الدولة كما هو الحال في عدن .

ان المهرة لم تكن في يوم من الأيام إلا أرض حب وسلام ووئام وأمن واستقرار وهي المحافظة الوحيدة التي نأت بنفسها عن أي صراعات وليس هناك مبرر واحد لقدوم قوات أجنبية وإنشاء ميليشيات تتعارض مع الدستور والقوانين وتزعزع الأمن والاستقرار في المحافظة .

إن من حق المواطنين ان يدافعوا عن مؤسسات الدولة وسيادة الشرعية الدستورية ونحن من هذا المنطلق نأمل منكم أن تنحازوا إلى قيم الحق وهو ابلج وأن تعاد الأمور إلى نصابها وأن تكون مؤسسات الدولة بمختلف تكويناتها هي صاحبة القرار السيادي وليس غيرها .

إن ما يحدث من تجاوزات يومية وأحداث وتداعيات مؤلمة لم تعد تحتمل في حين اننا طالما سعينا إلى أن نضع حدا لأي اختلاف مع الطرف الآخر بما لا يخل بالسيادة الوطنية ويؤكد على الامتثال المسئول للشرعية الدستورية .

إن ما يروج له أعلام السلطة المحلية من أكاذيب وتضليل للرأي العام وتشويه مواقف القبائل المنتمية إلى روح الأرض والرافضة للاحتلال العسكري السعودي إيمانا منها بالعمل الوطني الشريف ، وما يحاول من تزييف الوقائع والحقائق فإن كل ذلك إنما هو مثل زبد الريح فالقبائل تقوم بواجبها وهي شديدة الحرص على مؤسسات الدولة والنظام والقانون وفقا لما يمليه عليها ضميرها أمام الله وهي حريصة على المال العام

١٤

246

بسم الله الرحمن الرحيم

الجمهورية اليمنية	
محافظة المهرة	**التاريخ / /٢٠١٩م**
اللجنة المنظمة للاعتصام	**الرقم :**

الذي يبعثر وينزف لشراء الذمم والولاءات الضيقة وخلق مناخات الخصومة بين أبناء القبائل وتسخيره خارج ما هو مخطط له في مجالات التنمية وبناء مشاريع من خزينة الدولة من ميزانية المحافظة لتنسب إلى السعودية كتبرعات إنسانية بأسم البرنامج السعودي للإعمار وهو أمر غير صحيح في معظمه .

وانه لأمر محزن أن يتم العبث بموارد ومقدرات المحافظة وعدم استغلالها في المشاريع التي تتطلبها المحافظة لخدمة المواطنين .

إن هذا الفساد والعبث وتجاوز القوانين واللوائح قد وصل إلى حدٍ لم يشهده التاريخ في أي بلد دون حسيب أو رقيب من صرف السيارات الفارهة بأعداد كبيرة للمقربين ومن يراد شراء ولاءاتهم وكذلك المخالفات التي لم يسبق لها مثيل في التعيينات في الجهاز الاداري للدولة حيث تم تعيين مدراء عموم ونواب مدراء عموم ومدراء ادارات في عدد من المديريات والمرافق والاجهزة الحكومية من خارج موظفي الجهاز الاداري للدولة وغير مؤهلين لذلك .

الأخوة /رئيس وأعضاء اللجنة الرئاسية

إن أبناء المهرة يؤكدون في كل اعتصاماتهم على احترام الشرعية الدستورية وحق الجوار واحترام خصوصية المهرة وعدم التدخل في الشأن الداخلي .وهي مطالب دستورية وقانونية وهي تعبر بصدق وقوة انتماء وتجسيد الهوية المهرية .

الأخوة /رئيس وأعضاء اللجنة الرئاسية .

إننا نثق في انحيازكم المشرف للوطن وللقيم والمبادئ والمثل العليا وللشرعية الدستورية وأنكم ستنتظرون بأن ما نعمل من أجله ونقوم به هو واجب يمليه ضميرنا و نابع من الحرص الشديد على الأمن والاستقرار والتنمية والسيادة الوطنية وأن رفض القبائل لتواجد الميليشيات أو أي معدات عسكرية سعودية على أرضهم هو أمر يستحق المساندة من الجميع.

الأخوة /رئيس وأعضاء اللجنة الرئاسية.

إننا في لجنة الاعتصام السلمي لأبناء المهرة نجدد مطالبتنا ومناشدتنا من خلالكم لقيادتنا السياسية ممثلةً بفخامة الأخ الرئيس/ عبدربه منصور هادي رئيس الجمهورية بالآتي:

١٥

247

<table>
<tr><td>بسم الله الرحمن الرحيم</td></tr>
</table>

الجمهورية اليمنية
محافظة المهرة
اللجنة المنظمة للاعتصام

التاريخ / /٢٠١٩م
الرقم :

١- تنفيذ مطالب أبناء المهرة المتمثلة بالنقاط الست.
٢- انسحاب القوات السعودية من كل أراضي المهرة.
٣- تمسكنا بخيار أقاليم المهرة وسقطرى اقليماً مستقلاً على حدود (٦٧).
٤- الحفاظ على مؤسسات الدولة الشرعية في المحافظة ووقف العبث والفساد بالمال العام .
٥- الحفاظ على مؤسستي الجيش والأمن لتقوم بواجبها الدستوري والقانوني في الحفاظ على الأمن والاستقرار ، وعدم القبول باي مليشيات خارج هاتين المؤسستين الشرعيتين مهما كانت المبررات.
٦- إقالة راجح باكريت من منصبه كمحافظ للمحافظة واحالته للتحقيق .

سدد الله خطاكم لما فيه خير الوطن
ومحافظتنا الغالية المهرة
والحق أحق أن يتبع.
والسلام عليكم ورحمة الله وبركاته،،،

اخوانكم/ رئيس واعضاء لجنة الاعتصام السلمي
لأبناء المهرة
الغيضة-المهرة ٢٠١٩/٣/١٨م

١٦

248

THE YEMENI REPUBLIC AL MAHRAH PROVINCE COMMITTEE ORGANIZING THE PROTEST*

Date/ 2019

Brother/ the President and members of the Presidential Committee

Appreciation greetings and respect,

The organizing committee for the peaceful protest of Al Mahrah, welcomes your visit to the province on an exploring mission to fact-find the general situation.

We extend our utmost gratitude to his highness, Brother President Abdrabbuh Mansour Hadi, for his attention and concern.

We renew our support for his wise command.

On behalf of the peaceful protestors, according to the constitution and the international human rights laws and regulations, we strongly confirm that our demands are based on our national conscience and our complete adherence to the constitution's legality, preserving the full state sovereignty, as the state is the only founder of the armed forces, security and any force that preserves the safety, security and sovereignty of the Yemen territories, according to article 36 of the constitution, which states that the armed and security forces are tasked with protecting the republic, and territorial safety and integrity, thus, no other group, individual, organization or political party have the right to form any military gatherings under any pretext or circumstances.

The text is straightforward and clear. It does not need interpretation, or explanations. However, unfortunately, what had happened with the local authority represented by the governor, Rajeh Bakrit, who had worked in contradiction to the constitution by forming militias, which are out of the state control, violating the country's

---

*   Translated by Suzan Haidamous.

independence and sovereignty, as those new militias are affiliated, funded and trained by Saudi Arabia, and implement agendas that harm the sovereignty of the Yemen republic. All these actions have been into effect through Governor Rajeh Bakrit, who is in charge of implementing the project of Riyadh in Al Mahrah territories.

Those militias are seeking to undermine the state security and military institutions, and destabilizing the situation trough functioning against the spirit of the constitution. This is what we, the peaceful protesters are representing, it is a fair and legal demand to preserve the country's territorial integrity away from any hegemony, guardianship or external interferences, something we are eye witnessing, as the Saudi forces have legalized their occupation through Bakrit, over our precious province, and on the land, sea and air crossings.

Page 2

By the end of 2017, with huge numbers, and under the false pretext of protecting the Yemeni–Omani boarders from smuggling, and without any permission except from Bakirt- who was keen to implement this plan- The Saudi forces were deployed in huge numbers.

There had been no international agreements concluded between Yemen and Saudi Arabia, which means that the sovereignty of Al Mahrah was violated, and Bakrit had overpassed his legal prerogatives, thus committed treason, and breached the values and principles of his oath, that affirms on the protection of the Yemen territorial integrity.

We as peaceful protesters demand that he is brought to justice for accepting to allow the occupation of AL Mahrah, and the annexation of a part of its land to be used by the Saudis for passing the gas pipeline to the Arab sea, without any agreement between the two countries to organize the relations, something which is extremely dangerous and cannot be accepted.

My Brother the president/ the presidential committee members,

There is a huge difference between those calling for chaos, and betrayal of the constitution and overpassing the laws, and those who believe in national sovereignty and the respect of the constitution and international agreements, while also reject the formation of militias who create chaos, disturbances and anarchy, and looting the state resources.

We have full confidence that you will take the side of the constitutional legality, and answer our just demands.

The local authorities in the province have affirmed that the Saudi team did not coordinate with them when they first arrived in 2017, however, following talks and negotiation with the Saudis, who claim that their presence would rehabilitate and reactivate Al Ghaydah airport, the local authority and the security committee met with the heads of families and tribes in the province, and announced that after clarifying the nature of the team's mission, the local authority granted the Saudi team the location for Al Ghaydah camp.

Page 3

The local authority, the governor and prominent personalities later met with the Saudi team. The local authority presented six conditions to rehabilitate the airport and put it into function.

The conditions included:

- Never to use Al Ghaydah airport as a military base.
- Keep the current administrative, security and military staff of the airport in their jobs.
- Complete coordination with the local authority.
- Use the airport for strictly civilian purposes and humanitarian aid.

251

- Reactivate civil aviation.

Despite these conditions, the Saudi team controlled the airport, in clear violation of the Arab coalition goals, which aim at supporting Yemen legitimacy, and a transgression to all international rules and the Arab league pact.

In fact, the presence of the Saudi team in the airport was the starting point for the Saudi forces to invade Al Mahrah province systematically and take over its sea ports, land crossings and airport, which are importance and strategic geographical position of the province.

Page 4

It was clear to the people of the province, the Yemenis and the international community that the Saudi team entry to the airport was the starting point for the occupation of Al Mahrah province through the following:

- The Saudi military team did not adhere to implementing the agreement concluded with the local authority, mainly concerning the activation of the airport and upgrading it to be used for transportation of humanitarian aid and civilian flights.

- The Saudis were aware that they cannot implement their agenda except through a submissive official. In this regard they removed Governor Shiekh Mohammad Abdullah Kaddah, and replaced him by Rajeh Said Bakrit on Nov. 30, 2017.

- The other violation was the use of the airport for military purposes, transfer of military equipment, arms and soldiers from Saudi Arabia to Al Ghaydah airport intensively. Since that day until now, the Saudi military jets and helicopters land and take off on daily bases with military transitions.

- The daily flights of warplanes in the skies of the area had left the people of the province in panic, especially women and children. The Saudis transferred the airport into a barrack and a military base, prohibiting any entry, and have placed highly advanced surveillance systems in and around.

- The Saudi expansion reached its highest with their control over the two land crossings with Oman, and Nishtun port, as the people of the province were stunned by the Saudi violations in Yemen, and the Saudi deviation from the announced goals of the Arab coalition presented to the international community, and that is to help support the people of Yemen and their legal command headed by Brother/ Abdrubbuh Mansour Hadi.

Pages 5–6

It was crystal clear that Saudi Arabia had greedy intentions in Al Mahrah province, which are far from the goals of the Arab coalition.

Al Mahrah is geographically, politically and ideologically very far away from the Houthis, and have no connection with them.

The lies and fabrications of fighting arms and drugs smuggling and other claims are aimed at bluffing the international and local public opinion as false excuses, because they cannot proof their claims unless they catch an arms dealer or drugs smuggler.

The people of Al Mahrah had no choice but to stage peaceful protests that started on May 9, 2018.

The demands were presented as follows:

1. To run again Shahen, Sarfet, and Nishtun port and go back to normal function under the local security forces

and the Yemeni army according to the instructions of the president (telegram No. 41/2017) which, ban any unoffical forces from carrying any security mission in Al Mahrah province and mainly along the boarder areas.

2. The return of Al Ghaydah airport to its previous situation as a civilian airport under the control of the local authority and its security forces in the province.

3. Cancelation of all previous extra-ordinary restrictions on the commercial movements of import and export in Shahen, Sarfet, and Nishtunn port.

4. Seek to achieve integration between the command of the province and the executive directors for the interest and service of the people.

5. Give priority to improve the public services, such as electricity, water, health service, education, roads and other livelihood needs.

6. Focus on building up the local police, based on national values to be later involved in the provinces' projects. The general council is the gathering entity that represents all the people of the provinces and their causes.

Sheikh Abdullah Ben Essa Al Afran, the head of the general council for Al Mahrah and Sakarta, had sent to the command of the local authority the six points letter on May 12, 2018.

The local authority had been procrastinating and did not initiate any attempt to implement these demands or act for the interest of the people of the province and their sovereignty or national identity.

The first protest was suspended on May 13, 2018 in respond to the request by the general council and the prominent figures of Al Mahrah and Saktara, it was also in respect to the holy month of Ramadan, and to give a chance for the governor to adopt the demands, but there was no respond.

Page 7

Consequently, the protest resumed with huge participation, the first of such numbers, including the youth, prominent social and educated personalities and women, people from all political affiliations representing 68 tribes and social groups joined.

On Wednesday, May 11, 2018, a meeting grouped the local authority and representatives of the protesters at the province headquarters. The outcomes were reported to be positive by the protester's representatives, with appreciation to the follow up by President Abdrabbuh Mansour Hadi, who assigned Brig. Ahmad Mohammad Kahtan, the head of police in the province, to listen to the demands of the protesters and work on settling their requests.

We have high concerns that a big conspiracy is underway in the province, targeting the social fabric and creating a hostile and terrorizing atmosphere by the occupation, which is violating our civil rights and the legitimacy of the constitution.

The coalition and the governor are rebuffing the values, diplomatic regulations and rules that circulate among countries; thus, they are expanding their violence and terrorism. The crime of the Fartak tunnel is a proof, when Saudi Arabia and its militias tried to establish a military base along this vital position to control the province and divide it to separate the people of Al Mahrah from the eastern and southern areas.

Page 8

To the head and members of the presidential committee, we here presenting to you a sum[a]ry of the main Saudi violations and practices in the province:

1. **Crimes, arrests and illegal measures:**
   - **The tunnels crime**

     On Nov. 13, 2018, was a black day, the Saudi forces and their militias committed a horrible crime by attacking the peaceful protesters who opposed the establishment of a Saudi base, east of the tunnels area. They used live and direct ammunition killing two innocent people:
     - Ali Ahmad Arara Al Jadhi
     - Naser Said Ahmad Nashwan, while Salim Samhan Ghfel Al Jadhi was severely wounded.

   - **Arrests and violations**

     The Saudi forces committed several crimes against detainees and tortured them, in addition to threats and blackmails. Some were detained at Al Ghaydah Saudi jails, and others were transferred to other Saudi Arabia jails for a long period of time, some were released and others are still in prisons.

Page 9

We will name some detainees, but not all because some have vanished and no one knows their destiny.

1. Ahmad Ben Bariekm Al Tamimi, arrested, until now, his whereabouts, not known.
2. Yassin Al Soumali was arrested, but was later released.

3. Mohamad Hashem was arrested and transferred to Saudi jail, imprisoned for 2 months, then released and kicked out of his job at the airport.

4. Younis Al Karawie was arrested and released after a while.

5. The unlawful militias affiliated to the Saudi forces have ransacked and looted people's properties and shops, one of them belonged to Mohammad Khamis Maghfek.

6. Ali Saad Kadah was arrested then released

7. Hazem Mohammad Mekbal was arrested because his sister joined the protests against Saudis in the province; he was released after the tribe leaders interfered to prevent strive between his tribe and the Saudi forces.

8. The Saudi forces destroyed the fishermen's warehouse in Fedmi area on May 4, 2019 and destroyed their property.

9. 11 officers and 30 soldiers were expelled from their jobs at the air force in Al Ghaydah airport, after long years of service.

10. A young man from Beit Rafiet tribe was arrested when he fell near the wall of the airport, and was released later.

Page 10

11. A civilian was shot at from the Saudi tower at the airport when his motorcycle broke dawn in of Al Jamea Street.

12. Two civilians from Jaber family were arrested, and their vehicles confiscated when they were driving with agriculture materials loads.

13. Daily harassment of businessmen on crossings, inflicting huge loses and damages to the products, the tragedy is still going on.

14. The son of a Yemeni pro-Saudi ally killed two soldiers from the central security forces in Al Ghaydah city on March. 1, 2019, the martyrs were Ziad MohamadAl Kmayha and Ammar MohamdMorshid Mofreh.

15. Two civilians from Somouda tribe were arrested and released later after interrogation.

16. The Saudi forces brought in Extremist Salafies from Medieriat, Kashan, Hasween and Al Ghaydah, during the beginning of 2018 to change the demographic structure and plant sectarian tensions leading to terrorism.

    Saudi Arabia supplied those groups with weapons and money to buy apartments and land. They even tried to build a religious center to spread the lethal teachings of terrorism. The people confronted them with peaceful protests.

17. Saudi Arabia brought in huge numbers of military forces from several nationalities.

18. They have distributed weapons and money to some people and groups to buy their loyalty and support the Saudi presence.

19. Several civilian positions and headquarters were transferred to military barracks.

20. They abducted Mohamed Abdullah, Muslim Madhouf Rayet and Ali Saad Dalil Kadah from Yaroub village at night and brought them to Al Ghaydah airport with no legal reasons, their whereabouts are not known till now.

21. The violations are documented in two government reports from the human rights office in Al Mahrah, on 3/5/2018 and 13/10 2018 (attached are copies 4&5)

22. What happened recently in Haat, after the tribes refused to allow Saudi armored vehicles to stage a military point, led to an agreement to cease the tension and allow the vehicles out, escorted by the security and the army, the militias started to fire at the people and the people returned the fire in self defense leaving several militiamen wounded, unfortunately it was something that no one wanted, but it was all because of the behavior of Saudi Arabia and its militias.

Page 12

The areas where Saudi Arabian military positions are located:

1. Al Gahyda airport.
2. Nishtun port.
3. A camp near Haad center.
4. A camp in Darfat area, at Syhout center near the coast.
5. A military post near Harout area in Al Ghaydah.
6. Two close camps in Lousek area in Al Fedmi center at al Ghaydah headquarter.
7. Two camps near Lousik area.
8. The crossings along the Omani boarders are Sarfit crossing in Houf and Shahan crossing. Saudi officers and soldiers search the passengers and the luggage in a cruel manner.
9. A military post in Syhout in Moukadarea.
10. A military post of Syhout center East Rakout area are.
11. A military post of Syhout center in Khatar area.
12. A military post of Al Ghayta center in Wadi Mouthoul.

13. A military post of Akays center in Daymoun area.

14. A military post of Alghayta center in Arout area.

15. A military post of Al Maysala center in Sharkhat area.

16. A military post of Al Maysala canter in Samrouh area.

17. A military post of Al Maysala in Amthoun area.

18. A military post of Al Matsala center inHasay area.

Page 13

19. Militia Headquarters that are not a part of the military or security institution in Dar Al Dyafa, have terrorized the civilians, when they set checkup points at the entrance of the city, with face masks and dark window cars.

20. The governor was preparing to form a new militia under the task of protecting headquarters, it was declared that 700 elements would be recruited for this militia.

21. The Southern Transition Council declaration of recruiting 4500 fighters, meant that this new militia aims at destabilizing the province

22. There are financial and administrative violations with huge spending by the governor to buy loyalties and shake the stability in the province, something that represent a violation of the law.

Saudi Arabia is bringing in medium and heavy weapons and distributing them to extremists groups, while establishing jails and prisons that are out of the authorities' control, as well at setting Saudi military posts along the sea ports, the land crossing and airports, all, viol[ates] the least values and affirms that the local authority had accepted to be a proxy for the occupation, and is practicing terrorism.

The crime of the Fartak tunnel where two people died is a proof of protecting the killers away from justice.

It is really fearful when the land is occupied and the nation's sovereignty is absent in violation of the constitution, and Bakrit has given all prerogatives and power of the state to the Saudi occupation, which have circled the province with Saudi military positions.

Pages 14–15

Are we wrong if we demand that the state military and security institutions are granted full power, while rejecting the foreign interference and Saudi interventions? In addition to calling on the coalition to respect its pledges to support the legality and the constitution away from occupation control, which killed, tortured, harassed, jailed in violated of human rights. The Aden incident is enough proof to strongly reject the proxy militias who are keen on destroying the state institutions and replacing them with chaos.

President and members of the Presidential Committee,

We as citizens do not accept the treason against the constitution and the violation of our sovereignty and destroying the state institution, similar to what happened in our province, which had always been a land of love, peace, security and stability, it is the only province that stood away from the conflicts, thus there is not even one reason for the foreign forces to implant their militias to destabilize the province.

The civilians have the right to defend their state institutions and the legality. We hope that you will take the side of justice, and return things the way they were, and to have the only power for the state institutions ruling.

The daily violations, and painful incidents have become unbearable. The media propaganda of the local authority are lies are deceiving the public opinion, deforming the positions of the tribes who are attached to the land and reject the Saudi military occupation. The tribes are carrying on their duties, and are adherent to protect the state institutions and the laws and regulations. They are protective to safeguard the public funds, which are spent to buy the consciences and obedience, creating an atmosphere of confrontation among tribes and people. The funds of the state, which should be spend on projects, are said to be donations from Saudi Arabia, this is not true.

It is sad to misuse the potentials of the province. The corruption and breaking of the law have reached an extent that did not exist in any country. The illegal appointments have been abusing the law by hiring unqualified, out of the administrative department director people.

President and members of the Presidential Committee,

The people of Al Mahrah have renewed and reaffirmed in every protest, the respect of the constitution legality, those demands are constitutional and legal goals.

President and members of the Presidential Committee,

We have confidence in your honorable alignment to the values and principals. We are sure that you will evaluate our work as a duty initiated from our commitment to security and stability, development and national sovereignty. The tribes' rejection to have militias and Saudi military presence is a matter that needs to be supported and answered by everyone.

President and members of the Presidential Committee,

We, the peaceful protestors committee renew our demand and calls through you on our political leadership represented by Brother/ President/ Abdrabbuh Mansour Hadi the following:

1. Implementation of the demands of the people of Al Mahrah, represented by the six points.

2. The withdrawal of the Saudi forces from all Al Mahrah territories.

3. Abide with the independent boarders of Al Mahrah and Sakatra region (67)

4. Preserve the state legal institutions in the province and stop the corruption and the theft of the public funds.

5. Preserve the army and security institutions to carry out their constitutional and legal duties that ensure security and stability, rejecting any militia role under any justifications.

6. Remove Rajeh Bakrit from his position as governor and put him under interrogation.

May God give you strength for the good of our country and our precious province Al Mahrah,

Peace be with you,

Your Brothers/ members of the peaceful protest committee In Al Mahrah

Al Ghaydah–Al Mahrah 8/3/2019

بسم الله الرحمن الرحيم

البيان الصادر عن اللقاء الموسع برناسة السلطان/عبدالله بن عيسى أل عفرار رئيس المجلس العام لأبناء المهرة وسقطره المنعقد بتاريخ٢٦مارس ٢٠١٩م مع الشيوخ والشخصيات الاجتماعية بمحافظة المهرة.

(واعتصموا بحبل الله جميعا ولا تفرقوا واذكروا نعمة الله عليكم إذ كنتم اعداء فألف بين قلوبكم فأصبحتم بنعمته إخوانا)

انطلاقا من الواجب الوطني الذي يتحمله جميع ابناء محافظة المهرة في هذه المرحلة الاستثنائية التي تشهدها المنطقة بأسرها فقد أجمع كل الشيوخ وجميع الرجال المخلصين من أبناء محافظة المهرة على التماسك والاصطفاف إثر دعوة المجلس العام لأبناء المهرة وسقطره وبرعاية رئيس المجلس السلطان / عبدالله بن عيسى ال عفرار فقد تم الاجماع على ما يلي:

١-يجددون أبناء محافظة المهرة تمسكهم بالقيادة السياسية ممثلة بفخامة الرئيس/ عبدربه منصور هادي حفظه الله والتحالف العربي بقيادة المملكة العربية السعودية ودولة الامارات وفقا للاهداف المعلنة ، ويشكرون فخامة الرئيس على اهتمامه الكبير الذي يوليه لأبناء المهرة من خلال تكليف لجنة رئاسية للنزول إلى المحافظة للاطلاع على الاوضاع بالمحافظة ونتطلع منها النتائج الإيجابية بما يخدم مصلحة المهرة وأبنائها وحفظ امنها واستقرارها ووحدة أبنائها. .

٢-التمسك بالمجلس العام لابناء محافظتي المهرة وسقطره برئاسة الشيخ/ عبدالله بن عيسى ال عفرار وبرؤيته السياسية وبخيارهم المجمع عليه المتمثل بإقامة إقليم المهرة وسقطره على حدود ١٩٦٧م .

٣-التمسك باستعادة الأراضي المستقطعة من محافظة المهرة الى محافظة حضرموت وتصويب الخارطة الجغرافية الادارية الجائرة واعادة رسمها الى ما كانت عليه حدود أراضي محافظة المهرة عام ١٩٦٧م .

٤-تحريم الاقتتال الداخلي بين أبناء محافظة المهرة وتوجيه السلاح الى نحور بعضهم البعض وتغليب المصلحة العامة على المصالح الشخصية الضيقة.

٥-المحافظة على أمن واستقرار محافظتنا ووحدتنا الداخلية ونسيجنا الاجتماعي المتميز الذي ظل وضرب المثل طيلة الفترات السابقة في التآخي والمحبة والسلام.

٦-نطالب قيادة السلطة المحلية ولجنة الاعتصام بالتهدئة وعدم استحداث أي مراكز جديدة وتغليب المصلحة العليا وتحكيم العقل وإتباع الحكمة في حل النزاعات

والخلافات وعدم الانجرار الى مربع الصدام لكي لا تصبح محافظتنا ساحة لأي صراع محلي او إقليمي او دولي .

٧- الحفاظ على أراضي محافظة المهرة وثرواتها البرية والبحرية وعدم التفريط بها باي شكل من الاشكال وليس لاحد الحق في استغلا لها او استخدامها إلا بعد التخاطب مع سلطاتها وموفقتها بمشاركة أهل الحل والعقد والرجالات الوطنية ومكونه ومنظمات المجتمع المدني وفق ضوابط واسس متفق عليها وموثقة ومعلنه ليتبدد بذلك أي لبس أو مخاوف على مستقبل المحافظة وابنائها.

٨- يتمسك ابناء محافظة المهرة بمبادئ ومواد الاعلان الاممي لحقوق الانسان والشعوب الاصلية إزاء أي تهميش أو تعسف يمارس ضدهم من قبل أي جهة.

٩- التعامل بمصداقية مع حكومات وشعوب دول الجوار وغيرها انطلاقا من أخوة الدين والعروبة والحوار وتداخل العلاقات والروابط الاجتماعية وتبادل المنافع والمصالح والترحيب باي دعم او استثمار وفقا للانظمة والقوانين المنبثقة وبطريقة واضحة وشفافة للجميع.

١٠- تأييدنا الكامل لكل ما يتضمنه البيان الصادر عن الاجتماع الموسع للمشايخ والوجهاء والشخصيات الاجتماعية والشباب والمرأة بمحافظة سقطره المنعقد بتاريخ ١٩مارس ٢٠١٩م.

١١- التأكيد على ضرورة اعداد ميثاق شرف أو وثيقه وطنية وتقديمها لأبناء المحافظة بسلطاتهم الرسمية ومكوناتهم الشعبية السياسية وجميع القبائل والشرائح الاجتماعية للتوافق والتصديق عليها من الجميع .

والله الموفق ...

صادر عن اللقاء الموسع للمشانخ والوجهاء
والشخصيات الاجتماعية بمحافظة المهرة
الغيضة ٢٤/٣/٢٠١٩م

APPENDIX 6

STATEMENT ISSUED FOLLOWING A MEETING
HEADED BY SULTAN/ABDULLAH BEN ESSA AL AFRAR,
THE HEAD OF THE GENERAL COUNCIL OF AL MAHRAH
AND SOCCOTRA, WHICH GROUPED SHEIKHS AND
SOCIAL FIGURES IN AL MAHRAH PROVINCE.*

(a Quran verse)

On the bases of the national duties of all citizens in Al Mahrah province, and amid these extra-ordinary times, all Sheikhs and devoted men of Al Mahrah have agreed on unity in harmony and cohesion.
They all unanimously approved on the following:

1. The people of Al Mahrah reaffirm their commitment to the political leadership represented by president Abdrabbuh Mansour Hadi, (may God protect him), and the Arab coalition under the command of the kingdom of Saudi Arabia, and the UAE, according to the declared goals.

    They are thankful to the president's enormous attention directed to the people of Al Mahrah, by designating a presidential committee to visit the province and explore to situation. We are excepting positive outcomes for the interest of the province and its people, with security, stability and unity.

2. The Commitment to the general Council of Al Mahrah and Socotra, headed by Shiekh Abdullah Ben EssaAl Afrar, and his political vision, with his unanimous decision

---

* Translated by Suzan Haidamous.

to establish the region of Al Mahrah and Sakrata on the bases of 1967 boarder demarkation.

3. Adherence to the return of annexed lands from Al Mahrah province to Description Hadhramaut, and correction of the geographic administration map, to be back to the way it was assigned in 1967.

4. Prohibit all sorts of inter-fighting among Al Mahrah citizens, and raise the public interest over personal narrow interests.

5. Preserve the security, stability, internal unity and the unique social fabric in province, which has always been an example for love and brotherhood.

6. We call on the local authority command and the protest committee to establish calm, and refrain from setting up new positions, and have the higher interest conquer by ration and wisdom in managing crisis, thus, avoid being dragged into clashes, which will lead to local, regional and international conflicts.

7. Protect the areas of Al Mahrah, its land and sea resources, by not granting to anyone the right to exploit it before discussing with the authorities, national figures and civil societies according to restrictions that are agreed upon.

8. The people of the province are committed to the principles of the international declaration of human rights, against arbitrariness from any side.

9. Credible relations with the neighboring governments and people, on the grounds of common religion, Arabism, dialogue, and social bonds, thus, welcome any support or investments according to the laws and regulations, with clearness and transparency.

10. Full support to the statement issued following the meeting of Sheikhs , prominent personalities, social ,youth and female figures in Saktara province on March 19, 2019

11. Stress the need to prepare a pact of honor, or a national accord that would be presented to the province's people, officials, popular movements, tribes and social actors, to be agreed upon and ratified by all.

Issued by the gathering of Sheikhs and prominent social figures in Al Mahrah province.

Al Ghaythah—March /3/2019

بسم الله الرحمن الرحيم

البيان الصادر عن اللقاء الموسع برئاسة السلطان/ عبد الله بن عيسى آل عفرار رئيس المجلس العام لأبناء المهرة وسقطرى المنعقد بتاريخ 26 مارس 2019م مع الشيوخ والشخصيات الاجتماعية بمحافظة المهرة.

(واعتصموا بحبل الله جميعاً ولا تفرقوا واذكروا نعمة الله عليكم إذ كنتم أعداءً فألف بين قلوبكم فأصبحتم بنعمته إخواناً).

انطلاقاً من الواجب الوطني الذي يتحمله جميع أبناء محافظة المهرة في هذه المرحلة الاستثنائية التي تشهدها المنطقة بأسرها فقد أجمع كل الشيوخ وجميع الرجال المخلصين من أبناء محافظة المهرة على التماسك والاصطفاف إثر دعوة المجلس العام لأبناء المهرة وسقطرى وبرعاية رئيس المجلس السلطان/ عبد الله بن عيسى آل عفرار فقد تم الاجماع على ما يلي:

1- يجددون أبناء محافظة المهرة تمسكهم بالقيادة السياسية ممثلة بفخامة الرئيس/ عبد ربه منصور هادي حفظه الله والتحالف العربي بقيادة المملكة العربية السعودية ودولة الإمارات وفقاً للأهداف المعلنة، ويشكرون فخامة الرئيس على اهتمامه الكبير الذي يوليه لأبناء المهرة من خلال تكليف لجنة رئاسية للنزول إلى المحافظة للاطلاع على الأوضاع بالمحافظة ونتطلع منها النتائج الإيجابية بما يخدم مصلحة المهرة وأبناءها وحفظ أمنها واستقرارها ووحدة أبناءها.

2- التمسك بالمجلس العام لأبناء محافظتي المهرة وسقطرى برئاسة الشيخ/ عبد الله بن عيسى آل عفرار وبرؤيته السياسية وبخيارهم المجمع عليه المتمثل بإقامة إقليم المهرة وسقطرى على حدود 1967م.

3- التمسك باستعادة الأراضي المستقطعة من محافظة المهرة إلى محافظة حضرموت وتصويب الخارطة الجغرافية الإدارية الجائرة وإعادة رسمها إلى ما كانت عليه حدود أراضي محافظة المهرة عام 1967م.

4- تحريم الاقتتال الداخلي بين أبناء محافظة المهرة وتوجيه السلاح إلى نحور بعضهم البعض وتغليب المصلحة العامة على المصالح الشخصية الضيقة.

5- المحافظة على أمن واستقرار محافظتنا ووحدتنا الداخلية ونسيجنا الاجتماعي المتميز الذي ظل وضرب المثل طيلة الفترات السابقة في التآخي والمحبة والسلام.

6- نطالب قيادة السلطة المحلية ولجنة الاعتصام بالتهدئة وعدم استحداث أي مراكز جديدة وتغليب المصلحة العليا وتحكيم العقل وإتباع الحكمة في حل النزاعات والخلافات وعدم الانجرار إلى مربع الصدام لكي لا تصبح محافظتنا ساحة لأي صراع محلي أو إقليمي أو دولي.

7- الحفاظ على أراضي محافظة المهرة وثرواتها البرية والبحرية وعدم التفريط بها بأي شكل من الأشكال وليس لأحد الحق في استغلالها أو استخدامها إلا بعد التخاطب مع سلطاتها وموافقتها بمشاركة أهل الحل والعقد والرجالات الوطنية ومكونات ومنظمات المجتمع المدني وفق ضوابط وأسس متفق عليها وموثقة ومعلنة ليتبدد بذلك أي لبس أو مخاوف على مستقبل المحافظة وأبناءها.

8- يتمسك أبناء محافظة المهرة بمبادئ ومواد الإعلان الأممي لحقوق الإنسان والشعوب الأصيلة إزاء أي تهميش أو تعسف يمارس ضدهم من قبل أي جهة.

269

9- التعامل بمصداقية مع حكومات وشعوب دول الجوار وغيرها انطلاقاً من أخوة الدين والعروبة والحوار وتداخل العلاقات والروابط الاجتماعية وتبادل المنافع والمصالح والترحيب بأي دعم أو استثمار وفقاً للأنظمة والقوانين المنبثقة وبطريقة واضحة وشفافة للجميع.

10- تأييدنا الكامل لكل ما يتضمنه البيان الصادر عن الاجتماع الموسع للمشايخ والوجهاء والشخصيات الاجتماعية والشباب والمرأة بمحافظة سقطرى المنعقد بتاريخ 19 مارس 2019م.

11- التأكيد على ضرورة إعداد ميثاق شرف أو وثيقة وطنية وتقديمها لأبناء المحافظة بسلطاتهم الرسمية ومكوناتهم الشعبية والسياسية وجميع القبائل والشرائح الاجتماعية للتوافق والتصديق عليها من الجميع.

والله الموفق،،،

صادر عن اللقاء الموسع للمشايخ والوجهاء
والشخصيات الاجتماعية بمحافظة المهرة
الغيظة- 2019/3/24م

APPENDIX 7

SULTAN DECREE*

No:29/2018

Releasing the law of prohibiting the ownership by non-Omanis of land and real estate in some areas.

Qaboos Ben Said
Sultan of Oman

Following the review of the primary law of the state, issued by a Sultan decree No. 101/96.

And the law of the land issued by a Sultan decree No. 5/80.

And Sultan decree No. 5/81, which organize the use of the Sultanate lands.

And the government Land entitlement system, issued by a Sultan decree 81/84.

And Sultan decree No. 22/2004, which regulates the ownership of real estate in the Gulf Cooperation Council states by non-member states.

And Sultan decree No. 22/2006, on the regulation for non-Omanis ownership of properties in the integrated tourist complexes.

And the Omani nationality law issued by a Sultan decree No 38/2014.

And based on the public interest

We have decided:

---

* Translated by Suzan Haidamous.

First article

The ban on non-Omani ownership of land and real Estate in some places would be ruled by the attached provision of the law.

Second article

The minister of housing would issue the lists and decrees necessary to implement the provisions of the attached law after consulting with the concerned parties, until the time the lists are issued, the available lists would be used as long as it does not contradict with the provisions.

Third article

All articles that contradict the attached law would be annulled.

Fourth article

The decree would be published in the official newspaper, and would be put into practice the next day of the date of publishing.

Issued on: Nov. 11, 2018

Qaboos Ben Said
Sultan of Oman

مرسـوم سلطـاني
رقم ٢٠١٨/٢٩
بإصدار قانون حظر تملك غير العمانيين للأراضي والعقارات في بعض الأماكن

نحن قابوس بن سعيد   سلطان عمان

بعد الاطلاع على النظام الأساسي للدولة الصادر بالمرسوم السلطاني رقم ٩٦/١٠١ ،
وعلى قانون الأراضي الصادر بالمرسوم السلطاني رقم ٨٠/٥ ،
وعلى المرسوم السلطاني رقم ٨١/٥ بتنظيم الانتفاع بأراضي السلطنة ،
وعلى نظام استحقاق الأراضي الحكومية الصادر بالمرسوم السلطاني رقم ٨١/ ٨٤ ،
وعلى المرسوم السلطاني رقم ٢٠٠٤/٢١ بتنظيم تملك مواطني دول مجلس التعاون لدول الخليج العربية للعقار في الدول الأعضاء ،
وعلى المرسوم السلطاني رقم ٢٠٠٦/١٢ في شأن نظام تملك غير العمانيين للعقارات في المجمعات السياحية المتكاملة ،
وعلى قانون الجنسية العمانية الصادر بالمرسوم السلطاني رقم ٢٠١٤/٣٨ ،
وبناء على ما تقتضيه المصلحة العامة .

رسمنـا بمـا هـو آت

المـادة الأولـى

يعمل في شأن حظر تملك غير العمانيين للأراضي والعقارات في بعض الأماكن ، بأحكام القانون المرفق .

المـادة الثانيـة

يصدر وزير الإسكان اللوائح والقرارات اللازمة لتنفيذ أحكام القانون المرفق بعد التنسيق مع الجهات المختصة ، وإلى أن تصدر يستمر العمل باللوائح والقرارات المعمول بها ، بما لا يتعارض مع أحكامه .

المـادة الثالثـة

يلغى كل ما يخالف القانون المرفق ، أو يتعارض مع أحكامه .

المـادة الرابعـة

ينشر هذا المرسوم في الجريدة الرسمية ، ويعمل به من اليوم التالي لتاريخ نشره .

صدر في : ٣ من ربيع الأول سنة ١٤٤٠هـ
الموافـق : ١١ من نوفمبـر سنة ٢٠١٨م

قابوس بن سعيد
سلطان عمان

-١٨-

الجريدة الرسمية العدد (١٢٦٨)

قانون حظر تملك غير العمانيين للأراضي والعقارات في بعض الأماكن

المادة (١)

مع عدم الإخلال بنظام تملك غير العمانيين للعقارات في المجمعات السياحية المتكاملة المشار إليه ، يحظر على غير العمانيين تملك الأراضي والعقارات بجميع استعمالاتها في أي من الأماكن الآتية :

١ - محافظات كـل مـن : (ظفـار عـدا ولايـة صلالـة ، ومسندم ، والبريمـي ، والظاهرة ، والوسطى) .

٢ - ولايات لوى ، وشناص ، ومصيرة .

٣ - الجبل الأخضر ، وجبل شمس ، وأي جبال أخرى لها أهمية استراتيجية تحددها الجهات المختصة .

٤ - الجـزر .

٥ - المواقع القريبة من القصور ، والجهات الأمنية ، والعسكرية ، والتي تحددها الجهات المختصة .

٦ - الحارات الأثرية ، والقديمة ، والتي تحددها الجهات المختصة .

المادة (٢)

مع عدم الإخلال بحكم المادة (١) من هذا القانون ، يحظر على غير العمانيين - بعد العمل بأحكامه - تملك الأراضي والعقارات المخصصة للاستعمال الزراعي في جميع محافظات السلطنة .

المادة (٣)

يجـب علـى مـن فقـد الجنسـية العمانيـة ، أو أسقطت عنـه ، أو سحبت منـه التصرف في الأرض الفضاء الممنوحة له من قبل الدولة والواقعة في الأماكن المنصوص عليها في المادة (١) من هذا القانون ، ونقلها إلى شخص عماني بأي من طرق التصرف المقررة قانونا لنقل الملكية ، وذلك خلال (٢) سنتين من تاريخ فقد الجنسية العمانية ، أو إسقاطها ، أو سحبـها ، قابلـة للتمديـد لسـنة واحـدة فقط بعـد موافقـة وزيـر الإسـكان بالتنسيـق مع الجهات المختصة .

وإذا لم يقم بذلك خلال تلك المدة ، تقوم وزارة الإسكان باسترداد الأرض الفضاء ، مع رد قيمة منح الأرض .

المـادة (٤)

يجب على من فقد الجنسية العمانية ، أو أسقطت عنه ، أو سحبت منه التصرف في الأرض الممنوحة له من قبل الدولة ، والتي توجد بها إشغالات قائمة ، والواقعة في الأماكن المنصوص عليها في المادة (١) من هذا القانون ، ونقلها إلى شخص عماني بأي من طرق التصرف المقررة قانونا لنقل الملكية ، وذلك خلال (٢) سنتين من تاريخ فقد الجنسية العمانية ، أو إسقاطها ، أو سحبها ، قابلة للتمديد لسنة واحدة فقط بعد موافقة وزير الإسكان بالتنسيق مع الجهات المختصة .

وإذا لم يقم بذلك خلال تلك المدة ، يتولى القضاء بيع تلك الأرض ، وما عليها من إشغالات جبرا إلى أشخاص عمانيين ، بناء على طلب وزير الإسكان ، طبقا لقانون الإجراءات المدنية والتجارية ، على أن يعود ثمن البيع إلى المالك .

المـادة (٥)

يجب على غير العماني التصرف في الأراضي والعقارات الواقعة في الأماكن المنصوص عليها في المادة (١) من هذا القانون ، وكذلك الأراضي والعقارات المنصوص عليها في المادة (٢) من هذا القانون ، ونقلها إلى شخص عماني بأي من طرق التصرف المقررة قانونا لنقل الملكية ، وذلك خلال (٢) سنتين من تاريخ فقدانه حق التملك وفقا لأحكام هذا القانون ، قابلة للتمديد لسنة واحدة فقط بعد موافقة وزير الإسكان بالتنسيق مع الجهات المختصة .

وإذا لم يقم بالتصرف فيها خلال تلك المدة ، يتولى القضاء بيع تلك الأراضي والعقارات جبرا إلى أشخاص عمانيين ، بناء على طلب وزير الإسكان ، طبقا لقانون الإجراءات المدنية والتجارية ، على أن يعود ثمن البيع إلى المالك .

المـادة (٦)

يجب على غير العماني الذي انتقلت إليه الأراضي والعقارات الواقعة في الأماكن المنصوص عليها في المادة (١) من هذا القانون وكذلك الأراضي والعقارات المنصوص عليها في المادة (٢) من هذا القانون عن طريق الإرث أو الوصية أو الهبة ، التصرف فيها إلى شخص عماني بأي من طرق التصرف المقررة قانونا لنقل الملكية ، وذلك خلال (٢) سنتين من تاريخ انتقال الملكية قابلة للتمديد لمدة سنة واحدة فقط بعد موافقة وزير الإسكان بالتنسيق مع الجهات المختصة .

-٢٩-

وإذا لم يقم الوارث أو الموصى له أو الموهوب بالتصرف في الأراضي والعقارات خلال تلك المدة ، يتولى القضاء بيعها جبرا إلى أشخاص عمانيين ، بناء على طلب وزير الإسكان ، طبقا لقانون الإجراءات المدنية والتجارية ، على أن يعود ثمن البيع إلى الوارث أو الموصى له أو الموهوب .

المادة (٧)

يكون تنظيم عقد انتفاع أو إيجار الأراضي والعقارات الواقعة في الأماكن المنصوص عليها في المادة (١) من هذا القانون ، وكذلك الأراضي والعقارات المنصوص عليها في المادة (٢) من هذا القانون عند فقد الجنسية العمانية ، أو إسقاطها ، أو سحبها ، وفقا للضوابط التي يصدرها وزير الإسكان بالتنسيق مع الجهات المختصة .

كما تنظم تلك الضوابط عقود الانتفاع أو الإيجار للأراضي والعقارات الواقعة في الأماكن المنصوص عليها في المادة (١) من هذا القانون ، وكذلك الأراضي والعقارات المنصوص عليها في المادة (٢) من هذا القانون المنتفع بها أو المؤجرة لغير العمانيين .

المادة (٨)

على المخاطبين بأحكام هذا القانون توفيق أوضاعهم وفقا لأحكامه خلال سنتين (٢) من تاريخ العمل به ، ويجوز تمديدها لمدة سنة واحدة فقط ، بعد موافقة وزير الإسكان ، بالتنسيق مع الجهات المختصة .

المادة (٩)

يقع باطلا بطلانا مطلقا كل تصرف يتم بالمخالفة لأحكام هذا القانون ، ويكون لكل ذي شأن التمسك بالبطلان أو طلب الحكم به ، وعلى المحكمة أن تقضي به من تلقاء نفسها ، وفي جميع الأحوال يجب إعادة الحال إلى ما كان عليه قبل إجراء التصرف الباطل .

المادة (١٠)

مع عدم الإخلال بأي عقوبة أشد ينص عليها أي قانون آخر ، يعاقب بالسجن مدة لا تقل عن (٣) ثلاثة أشهر ، ولا تزيد على سنة ، وبغرامة لا تقل عن (١٠٠٠) ألف ريال عماني ، ولا تزيد على (٣٠٠٠) ثلاثة آلاف ريال عماني ، أو بإحدى هاتين العقوبتين كل من أقدم عمدا على إبرام عقد ملكية أو إجراء أي تصرف بالمخالفة لأحكام هذا القانون أو توسط في ذلك .

وتكون العقوبة السجن مدة لا تقل عن (٦) ستة أشهر ولا تزيد على (٢) سنتين ، وبغرامة لا تقل عن (٢٠٠٠) ألفي ريال عماني ، ولا تزيد على (٥٠٠٠) خمسة آلاف ريال عماني إذا استعمل الجاني في الجريمة المنصوص عليها في الفقرة السابقة إحدى طرق الاحتيال .

APPENDIX 8

LAW THAT BANS OWNERSHIP OF LAND AND REAL ESTATE TO NON-OMANIS, IN SOME AREAS*

Paragraph (1)

Excluding and not violating the ownership regulations for non-Omanis in integrated tourism compounds, the non- Omanis are banned from land and real estate ownership in the following areas:

1. The Province of Dhofar, Musandam, Al Buraimi, Dhahirah, Al Wusta.

2. Wilayat Loui, Shnas and Musaira.

3. Jabal Al Akhdar (Green Mountain),

Jebel Al Shams (Sun Mountain), In addition to any other mountains, with strategic importance that are determined by the concerned parties.

4. The islands.

5. All locations close to the mansions, security and military bases.

6. The Archeological and old sites determined by the concerned authority.

Paragraph (2)

Without violating paragraph (1), non-Omanis are banned from ownership of agricultural land in all provinces.

---

* Translated by Suzan Haidamous.

Paragraph (3)

Anyone who lost the Omani nationality, and was granted by the state any of the locations stated in the first paragraph, should transfer the land to an Omani national legally, and within two years after losing the nationality, the two years can be extended for one more year after the approval of the housing minister and concerned authorities.

If the time passes and the registration and transfer are not complete, the ministry of housing will retrieve the land and pay back the value of the land to the initial owner.

Paragraph (4)

Anyone who lost the Omani nationality, or was taken from him, and owns a land by the state, with constructions or work on this land that is located in areas of the first paragraph, should transfer the land to a Omani national according to the ownership law, within 2 years after loosing the nationality, that can expand to only one more year, after the approval of the minister of housing and the concerned authorities.

Paragraph (5)

A non-Omani, should hand over the land and real estate located in the first and second paragraph to a Omani national according to the law of ownership within 2 years, that can be expanded one more year, only after the approval of the minister of housing, in cooperation with the concerned authorities.

Paragraph (6)

A non-Omani, who inherited or was granted a land in the areas designated in the first and second paragraph, should turn them over to a Omani authority according to the ownership law within 2 years that can be expanded one more year after the approval of the housing minister in coordination with the concerned authorities.

In case this did not happen, the Omani court would sell the land and real estate to Omani nationals, at the request of the minister of housing and in coordination with the concerned authorities. The money would be given to the heirs or those under sponsorships.

Paragraph (7)

The usufruct and lease contracts in the real estates stated in paragraph 1 & 2, when losing the nationality, would be organized according to the Instructions issued by the housing minister in coordination with the concerned authorities.

Those instructions organize the usufruct and lease contracts for land and real estate in areas stated in paragraph 1 & 2 of this law.

Paragraph (8)

Those concerned with the rules of this law, should settle their situation accordingly within 2 years, that can be extended one more year, after the approval of the housing minister and the concerned authorities.

Paragraph (9)

Any act violating the provisions of this law would be absolutely null and void. Anyone related, have the right to preserve the annulment or demand a judgment, the court should look into the case, and return the situation to the way it was before.

Paragraph (10)

Anyone who concludes an ownership contract or helped in concluding it, in violation of the provisions of this law, and without violating any other strict punishment stated by another law, should be sentence to no less than three months and not more than a year in jail.

A fine should be paid no less than 1000 Omani Riyal, and no more than 3000 Riyals, or any one of those two punishments.

In case of using any method of fraud, a jail sentence would not be less than 6 months and not more than 2 years, and a fine of no less than 2000 Riyal and no more than 5000 Riyals.

APPENDIX 9

OMANI STATEMENT[*]

HIS MAJESTY THE SULTAN DISCUSSES THE WAYS OF ADVANCING THE PEACE PROCESS IN THE MIDDLE EAST BETWEEN THE PALESTINIAN AND ISRAELI SIDES.

His Majesty the Sultan received His Excellency Benjamin Netanyahu, Prime Minister of Israel yesterday at Bait Al-Barakah where they discussed the ways of advancing the peace process in the Middle East and other issues of common interest that would serve the security and stability of the region.

---

[*] Translated by Nabeel Al Nowairah, June 2020.

بـيـان

جلالة السلطان المعظم يبحث سبل الدفع
بعملية السلام في الشرق الأوسط بين
الجانبين الفلسطيني والإسرائيلي

استقبل جلالة السلطان المعظم - حفظه الله ورعاه - يوم
أمس في بيت البركة دولة بنيامين نتنياهو رئيس الوزراء
الإسرائيلي، حيث تم بحث السبل الكفيلة بالدفع بعملية
السلام في الشرق الأوسط ومناقشة بعض القضايا التي
تحظى بالاهتمام المشترك وبما يخدم الأمن والاستقرار في
المنطقة.

NOTES

1 Erin Knecht, "Qatar disowns tourism official's comments on visas for 'enemies,'" *Reuters*, May 5, 2019, https://www.reuters.com/article/us-qatar-politics/qatar-disowns-tourism-officials-comments-on-visas-for-enemies-idUSKCN1SB06O, last accessed March 17, 2020.

2 Nicole Gaouette, "Meet the 'Mad Dog' Donald Trump wants to lead the Pentagon," *CNN*, December 3, 2016, https://www.cnn.com/2016/12/03/politics/donald-trump-james-mattis/index.html, last accessed March 17, 2020.

3 McFarlane, Sarah, and Bradley Olson: "Exxon, Qatar in Talks on US Shale Deal," *The Wall Street Journal*, April 11, 2018, https://www.wsj.com/articles/exxon-qatar-in-talks-on-u-s-shale-deal-1523358862, last accessed March 17, 2020.

4 B. Michalski: "Minerals Yearbook," *US Department of Interior/ US Geological Survey*, page 189, 1995.

5 "Exxon-Mobil merger done," *CNN*, November 30, 1999, https://money.cnn.com/1999/11/30/deals/exxonmobil/, last accessed March 17, 2020.

6 "UAE-US Security Relationship," *Embassy of the United Arab Emirates in Washington, DC*, https://www.uae-embassy.org/uae-us-relations/key-areas-bilateral-cooperation/uae-us-security-relationship, last accessed March 17, 2020.

7 Allen J. Fromherz, Qatar: *A Modern History*, United Kingdom: I.B. Tauris, 2012, p. 34.

8 Ibid.

9 "Timeline of Qatar-GCC disputes from 1991 to 2017," *Al Jazeera*, June 9, 2017, https://www.aljazeera.com/indepth/features/2017/06/timeline-qatar-gcc-disputes-170605110356982.html, last accessed March 17, 2020.

10 Max Fisher, "How the Saudi-Qatar Rivalry, Now Combusting, Reshaped the Middle East," *The New York Times*, June 13, 2017, https://www.nytimes.com/2017/06/13/world/middleeast/how-the-saudi-qatar-rivalry-now-combusting-reshaped-the-middle-east.html, last accessed March 17, 2020.

11 Uzi Rabi, "Qatar's Relations with Israel: Challenging Arab and Gulf Norms," *Middle East Journal*, Volume 63, Number 3 (Summer 2009), Middle East Institute.

12 "Timeline of Qatar-GCC disputes from 1991 to 2017," *Al Jazeera*, June 9, 2017.

13 Uzi Rabi, "Qatar's Relations with Israel: Challenging Arab and Gulf Norms," *Middle East Journal*, Volume 63, Number 3 (Summer 2009), Middle East Institute.

14 Frederick Wehrey, Theodore Karasik, Alireza Nader, Jeremy Ghez, Lydia Hansell, and Robert Guffey, *Saudi-Iranian Relations Since the Fall of Saddam*, Santa Monica: Rand Corporation, 2009, p. 48.

15 Yoel Guzansky and Efraim Halevy, "Oman: The End of the Qaboos Era," *Institute for National Security Studies at Tel Aviv University*, January 13, 2020, https://www.inss.org.il/publication/oman-the-end-of-the-qaboos-era/, last accessed March 17, 2020.

16 "Arabs offer Israelis peace plan," *BBC News*, March 28, 2002, http://news.bbc.co.uk/2/hi/middle_east/1898736.stm, last accessed March 17, 2020.

17 Ibid.

18 Frederick Wehrey, Theodore Karasik, Alireza Nader, Jeremy Ghez, Lydia Hansell, and Robert Guffey, *Saudi-Iranian Relations Since the Fall of Saddam*, Santa Monica: Rand Corporation, 2009, p. 48.

19 Uzi Rabi, "Qatar's Relations with Israel: Challenging Arab and Gulf Norms," *Middle East Journal*, Volume 63, Number 3 (Summer 2009), Middle East Institute.

20 Hussein Ibish, "Qatar crisis: a regional schism that's been years in the making," *The National*, June 6, 2017, https://www.thenational.ae/opinion/qatar-crisis-a-regional-schism-that-s-been-years-in-the-making-1.76490, last accessed March 17, 2020.

21 Hussein Ibish, "The crisis is only just beginning for Qatar," *The National*, June 10, 2017, https://www.thenational.ae/opinion/the-crisis-is-only-just-beginning-for-qatar-1.35814, last accessed March 17, 2020.

22 Hussein Ibish, "To Help Settle Qatar Feud, US Needs to Understand It," *Bloomberg*, February 22, 2018, https://www.bloomberg.com/opinion/articles/2018-02-22/qatar-feud-over-terrorism-and-islam-confounds-u-s, last accessed March 17, 2020.

23 Dalia Adiqi, "Prominent US expert: Doha policies threat to whole region," *Al Arabiya*, April 24, 2018, http://english.alarabiya.net/en/perspective/features/2018/04/23/Analyst-says-Washington-should-put-pressure-on-Qatar-about-moving-Udeid-Air-Base.html, last accessed March 17, 2020.

24 "Statement by President Barack Obama on Egypt," *Obama White House*, July 3, 2013, https://obamawhitehouse.archives.gov/the-press-office/2013/07/03/statement-president-barack-obama-egypt, last accessed March 17, 2020.

25 Awadalla, Nadine, and Enas Al Ashray, "Egypt's ousted Islamist president Mursi dies after collapsing in court," *Reuters*, June 17, 2019, https://www.reuters.com/article/us-egypt-mursi/egypts-ousted-islamist-president-mursi-dies-after-collapsing-in-court-idUSKCN1TI21T, last accessed March 17, 2020.

26 Bill Law, "Egypt crisis: Fall of Morsi challenges Qatar's new emir," *BBC*, July 5, 2013, https://www.bbc.com/news/world-middle-east-23185441, last accessed March 17, 2020.

27 Simeon Kerr, "Fall of Egypt's Mohamed Morsi is blow to Qatari leadership," *The Financial Times*, July 3, 2013, https://www.ft.com/content/af5d068a-e3ef-11e2-b35b-00144feabdc0, last accessed March 17, 2020.

28 Giorgio Cafiero, "Al Jazeera in the Eye of a Storm," *Atlantic Council*, July 12, 2017, https://www.atlanticcouncil.org/blogs/new-atlanticist/al-jazeera-in-the-eye-of-a-storm/, last accessed March 17, 2020.

29 Ibid.

30 Raghavan, Sudarsan, and Jobby Warrick, "How a 91-year-old imam came to symbolize the feud between Qatar and its neighbors," *The Washington Post*, June 27, 2017, www.washingtonpost.com/world/middle_east/how-a-91-year-old-imam-came-to-symbolize-feud-between-qatar-and-its-neighbors/2017/06/26/601d41b4-5157-11e7-91eb-9611861a988f_story.html, last accessed March 17, 2020.

31 Simeon Kerr, "Fall of Egypt's Mohamed Morsi is blow to Qatari leadership," *The Financial Times*, July 3, 2013, https://www.ft.com/content/af5d068a-e3ef-11e2-b35b-00144feabdc0, last accessed March 17, 2020.

32 "Qatar: 2018 Article IV Consultation-Press Release; Staff Report; and Statement by the Executive Director for Qatar," *International*

Monetary Fund, 30 May 2018, https://www.imf.org/en/Publications/CR/Issues/2018/05/30/Qatar-2018-Article-IV-Consultation-Press-Release-Staff-Report-and-Statement-by-the-Executive-45915, last accessed March 17, 2020.

33 Saeed Azhar, "Qatar says economic growth to accelerate in 2019-2020," *Reuters*, August 15, 2019, https://af.reuters.com/article/energyOilNews/idAFL8N25B1OF, last accessed March 17, 2020.

34 Yolande Knell, "Qatar cash and cows help buck Gulf boycott," *BBC*, June 5, 2018, https://www.bbc.com/news/world-middle-east-44354409, last accessed March 17, 2020.

35 Matt Smith, "How is Qatar coping with its economic embargo?," *BBC*, January 10, 2019, https://www.bbc.com/news/business-46795696, last accessed March 17, 2020.

36 Saeed Azhar, "Qatar says economic growth to accelerate in 2019-2020," *Reuters*, August 15, 2019, https://af.reuters.com/article/energyOilNews/idAFL8N25B1OF, last accessed March 17, 2020.

37 Sigurd Neubauer, "How Qatar Seeks to Establish New Trade Routes," *The Washington Institute for Near East Policy*, 13 September 2017, https://www.washingtoninstitute.org/fikraforum/view/how-qatar-seeks-to-establish-new-trade-routes, last accessed March 17, 2020.

38 Simeon Kerr, "Qatar weathers embargo storm, finance minister says," *The Financial Times*, May 6, 2018, https://www.ft.com/content/446607ac-4fa4-11e8-a7a9-37318e776bab, last accessed March 17, 2020.

39 Jim Waterson, "Football and fat fees: questions raised over funding of sporting conference," *The Guardian*, July 16, 2018, https://www.theguardian.com/football/2018/jul/16/football-and-fat-fees-questions-raised-over-funding-of-sporting-conference, last accessed March 17, 2020.

40 Erin Knecht, "Qatar disowns tourism official's comments on visas for "enemies"," *Reuters*, May 5, 2019, https://www.reuters.com/article/us-qatar-politics/qatar-disowns-tourism-officials-comments-on-visas-for-enemies-idUSKCN1SB06O, last accessed March 17, 2020.

41 Ibid.

42 Barbara Tasch: "RANKED: The 30 richest countries in the world," *Business Insider*, March 6, 2017, https://www.businessinsider.com/the-richest-countries-in-the-world-2017-3, last accessed March 17, 2020.

43 Matt Smith, "How is Qatar coping with its economic embargo?" *BBC*, January 10, 2019, https://www.bbc.com/news/business-46795696, last accessed March 17, 2020.

44 "Energy and Resources in Qatar," *US-Qatar Business Council*, https://www.usqbc.org/energy-and-resources-in-qatar, last accessed March 17, 2020.

45 "Foreign Affairs Committee Releases Transcript of Interview with Former Secretary of State Rex Tillerson," *US House of Representatives Committee on Foreign Affairs*, June 27, 2019, https://foreignaffairs.house.gov/2019/6/foreign-affairs-committee-releases-transcript-of-interview-with-for-mer-secretary-of-state-rex-tillerson, last accessed March 17, 2020.

46 Taimur Khan, "Sheikh Mohammed bin Zayed meets Trump for talks in Washington," *The National*, May 15, 2017, https://www.thenational.ae/world/sheikh-mohammed-bin-zayed-meets-trump-for-talks-in-wash-ington-1.80250, last accessed March 17, 2020.

47 Butler, Desmond, Tom LoBianco, and Bradley Klapper, "A top Trump fundraiser took $2.5 million from Dubai before pushing an anti-Qatar agenda in Congress," *The Associated Press*, March 26, 2018, https://www.businessinsider.com/a-top-trump-fundraiser-took-25-million-from-dubai-before-pushing-an-anti-qatar-agenda-in-congress-2018-3, last accessed March 17, 2020.

48 Foundation for the Defense of Democracies, https://www.fdd.org/about-fdd/, last accessed March 17, 2020.

49 Lachlan Markay, "GOP Moneyman Elliott Broidy Enlisted Veteran Diplomat Amid Influence Campaign," *The Daily Beast*, 2July 5, 2019, https://www.thedailybeast.com/gop-moneyman-elliott-broidy-enlist-ed-veteran-diplomat-amid-secret-influence-campaign, last accessed March 17, 2020.

50 David Weinberg, "Qatar and Terror Finance (Part II): Private Funders of Al Qaeda in Syria," *Foundation for Defense of Democracy*, January 18, 2016, https://s3.us-east-2.amazonaws.com/defenddemocracy/uploads/

documents/11717_Weinberg_Qatar_Report.pdf, last accessed March 17, 2020.

51 David Weinberg, "Qatar Embraces Admitted Al Qaeda Operative," *Foundation for Defense of Democracy*, January 23, 2015, https://www.longwarjournal.org/archives/2015/01/celebrating_terror_q.php, last accessed March 17, 2020.

52 David Weinberg, "Terror Financiers "Operating Openly" in Qatar and Kuwait," *Foundation for Defense of Democracy*, 13 February 2017, https://www.fdd.org/analysis/2017/02/13/terror-financiers-operating-openly-in-qatar-and-kuwait/, last accessed March 17, 2020.

53 Mohamed Fahmy, "Qatar behind state sponsorship of terrorism," *The Star*, April 11, 2017, https://www.thestar.com/opinion/commentary/2017/04/11/qatar-behind-state-sponsorship-of-terrorism-fahmy.html, last accessed March 17, 2020.

54 Jonathan Schanzer, "Time for the US to stop Qatar's support for terror," *New York Post*, 20 April 2017, https://nypost.com/2017/04/20/time-for-the-us-to-stop-qatars-support-for-terror/, last accessed March 17, 2020.

55 Richard Miniter, "Sec. Mattis: Time to Get Though on Qatar," *Forbes*, 22 April 2017, https://www.forbes.com/sites/richardminiter/2017/04/22/secretary-mattis-time-to-get-tough-on-qatar/#5c2ef4985631, last accessed March 17, 2020.

56 Wald, Charles, and Michael Makovsky, "The Two Faces of Qatar, a Dubious Mideast Ally," *The Wall Street Journal*, April 24, 2017, https://www.wsj.com/articles/the-two-faces-of-qatar-a-dubious-mideast-ally-1493075654, last accessed March 17, 2020.

57 Husain Haqqani, "Mattis' Balancing Act: Managing America's Middle East Enemies," *The Huffington Post*, April 25, 2017, https://www.huffpost.com/entry/mattis-balancing-act-managing-americas-middle-east_b_58ff86afe4b047ce3ee27c9e, last accessed March 17, 2020.

58 Richard Miniter, "Why is our Ally Qatar Hosting Terrorists like Hamas?" *Forbes*, April 28, 2017, https://www.forbes.com/sites/richardminiter/2017/04/28/why-is-our-ally-qatar-hosting-terrorists-like-hamas/#5f5ac19a21bd, last accessed March 17, 2020.

59 David Weinberg, "Congress must press Qatar for highlighting hate preacher," *The Hill*, April 30, 2017. https://thehill.com/blogs/pundits-blog/foreign-policy/331264-congress-must-press-qatar-for-highlighting-hate-preacher, last accessed March 17, 2020.

60 Bruce Majors, "Time to get tough with Qatar," *The Daily Caller*, May 2, 2017, https://dailycaller.com/2017/05/02/time-to-get-tough-with-qatar/, last accessed March 17, 2020.

61 Ilan Berman, "How Qatar helped Hamas get its Groove Back," *The National Interest*, May 2, 2017, https://nationalinterest.org/feature/how-qatar-helped-hamas-get-its-groove-back-20454, last accessed March 17, 2020.

62 "Qatar: A good or Dubious Ally?," *The Jewish Institute for National Security Affairs*, May 5, 2017, https://jinsa.org/archive_post/jinsa-press-conference-on-the-hill-qatar-a-good-or-dubious-ally/, last accessed March 17, 2020.

63 JINSA Presser: "Press conference call on US Cooperation w/Qatar's Al Udaid Air Base," *The Jewish Institute for National Security Affairs*, May 5, 2017.

64 Dennis Ross, "Qatar needs to stop funding Islamists," *USA Today*, May 8, 2017, https://www.usatoday.com/story/opinion/2017/05/08/qatar-funding-islamism-muslim-brotherhood-hamas-column/101300766/, last accessed March 17, 2020.

65 Schanzer, Jonathan, and Kate Havard, "By hosting Hamas, Qatar is Whitewashing Terror," *Newsweek*, May 11, 2017, https://www.newsweek.com/qatar-hosting-hamas-whitewashing-terror-606750, last accessed March 17, 2020.

66 Bruce Majors, "Qatar's Anti-Christian and Anti-Semitic Policies Should Bar it from UNESCO Seat," *The Daily Caller*, May 11, 2017, https://dailycaller.com/2017/05/11/qatars-anti-christian-and-anti-semitic-policies-should-bar-it-from-unesco-seat/, last accessed March 17, 2020.

67 Ilan Berman, "The Danger of Qatar's Duality," *US News*, May 15, 2017, https://www.usnews.com/opinion/world-report/articles/2017-05-15/donald-trump-should-question-qatars-allegiance-in-the-war-on-terror, last accessed March 17, 2020.

68 Bruce Majors, "Trump's Pivot to the Middle East has Already Begun," *The Daily Caller*, May 17, 2017, https://dailycaller.com/2017/05/17/trumps-pivot-to-the-middle-east-has-already-begin/, last accessed March 17, 2020.

69 David Weinberg, "Catch and Release: Did Qatar Free a Future Al Qaeda Emir?" *The Huffington Post*, 18 May 2017, https://www.huffpost.com/entry/catch-and-release-did-qatar-free-a-future-al-qaeda_b_591e-3b27e4b07617ae4cbabe, last accessed March 17, 2020.

70 John Hannah, "Qatar Needs to Do Its Part," *Foreign Policy*, May 22, 2017, https://foreignpolicy.com/2017/05/22/qatar-needs-to-do-its-part/, last accessed March 17, 2020.

71 "Qatar says cyberattack originated from the UAE," *Al Jazeera*, July 20, 2017, https://www.aljazeera.com/news/2017/07/qatar-sheds-light-cyberattack-official-media-170720151344996.html, last accessed March 17, 2020.

72 "Qatar Communications Office confirms QNA website hacked," *The Peninsula*, May 24, 2017, https://www.thepeninsulaqatar.com/article/24/05/2017/Qatar-Communications-Office-confirms-QNA-website-hacked, last accessed March 17, 2020.

73 A. Bakir: "Divided Gulf: The Anatomy of a Crisis," *Palgrave Macmillan*, page 209, 2019.

74 Lorenzo Franceschi-Bicchierai, "The Hack that Caused a Crisis in the Middle East Was Easy," *VICE*, June 7, 2017, https://www.vice.com/en_us/article/8x9xmk/the-hack-that-caused-a-crisis-in-the-middle-east-was-easy, last accessed March 17, 2020.

75 Fitch, Aya, Nicolas Parasie, and Margherita Stancati, "Saudi Arabia, U.A.E., Bahrain and Egypt Cut Diplomatic Ties With Qatar," *The Wall Street Journal*, June 6, 2017, https://www.wsj.com/articles/qatar-calls-for-talks-to-end-diplomatic-crisis-in-persian-gulf-1496753144, last accessed March 17, 2020.

76 "Qatar foreign minister denounces "unfair", "illegal" sanctions," *AFP*, June 13, 2017, https://m.muscatdaily.com/Archive/Gcc/Qatar-foreign-minister-denounces-unfair-illegal-sanctions-5ljo, last accessed March 17, 2020.

77 https://www.youtube.com/watch?feature=share&v=vMTnX9Z_
Lrk&app=desktop

78 "Saudi king on regional tour ahead of GCC summit," *The New Arab*,
December 5, 2016, https://www.alaraby.co.uk/english/news/2016/12/5/
saudi-king-on-regional-tour-ahead-of-gcc-summit, last accessed March
17, 2020.

79 https://www.youtube.com/watch?v=kAe6a3kZZqU&fea-
ture=share&app=desktop

80 https://mobile.twitter.com/adelaljubeir/status/864526971933470721?s=12

81 "Joint Statement of the US-GCC Foreign Ministers Meeting," *US
Department of State, August 3*, 2015, https://2009-2017.state.gov/r/pa/prs/
ps/2015/08/245619.htm, last accessed March 17, 2020.

82 Edward Cody, "Arab League condemns broad bombing campaign in Libya," *The Washington Post*, March 20, 2011, https://www.
washingtonpost.com/world/arab-league-condemns-broad-bombing-
campaign-in-libya/2011/03/20/AB1pSg1_story.html, last accessed
March 17, 2020.

83 A.E. Gomati: "Divided Gulf: Anatomy of a Crisis," page 184, *Palgrave
MacMillan*, 2019.

84 A.E. Gomati: "Divided Gulf: Anatomy of a Crisis," page 185, *Palgrave
MacMillan*, 2019.

85 Eric Schmitt, "CIA Said to Aid in Steering Arms to Syrian Rebels," *The
New York Times*, June 21, 2012, https://www.nytimes.com/2012/06/21/
world/middleeast/cia-said-to-aid-in-steering-arms-to-syrian-rebels.
html, last accessed March 17, 2020.

86 Ishaan Tharoor, "3 ways the U.A.E. is the Sparta of the modern-day
Middle East", *The Washington Post*, November 15, 2014, https://www.
washingtonpost.com/news/worldviews/wp/2014/11/15/3-ways-the-u-
a-e-is-the-sparta-of-the-modern-day-middle-east/?arc404=true, last
accessed March 17, 2020.

87 "14 November 2015, Statement of the International Syria Support
Group Vienna," *United Nations*, November 14, 2015, https://www.
un.org/undpa/en/Speeches-statements/14112015/syria

88 "Note to Correspondents: Statement of the International Syria Support Group," *United Nations*, May 17, 2016, https://www.un.org/sg/en/content/sg/note-correspondents/2016-05-17/note-correspondents-statement-international-syria-support, last accessed March 17, 2020.

89 "Foreign Affairs Committee Releases Transcript of Interview with Former Secretary of State Rex Tillerson," *US House of Representatives Committee on Foreign Affairs*, June 21, 2019, https://foreignaffairs.house.gov/2019/6/foreign-affairs-committee-releases-transcript-of-interview-with-former-secretary-of-state-rex-tillerson, last accessed March 17, 2020.

90 "Trump hawks 'beautiful' US weapons to unite Muslim world against terror," *Associated Press*, May 21, 2017, https://www.wtsp.com/article/news/politics/trump-hawks-beautiful-us-weapons-to-unite-muslim-world-against-terror/441583693, last accessed March 17, 2020.

91 Sigurd Neubauer, "The Gulf Crisis isn't Beyond Hope—Here's How Washington Can Help," *The Cipher Brief*, October 13, 2017, https://www.thecipherbrief.com/gulf-crisis-isnt-beyond-hope-heres-washington-can-help, last accessed March 17, 2020.

92 Manu Raju, "Exclusive: Rice told House investigators why she unmasked senior Trump officials," *CNN*, September 18, 2017, https://www.cnn.com/2017/09/13/politics/susan-rice-house-investigators-unmasked-trump-officials/index.html, last accessed March 17, 2020.

93 Kirkpatrick, David, Ben Hubbard, Mark Landler, and Mark Mazzetti, "The Wooing of Jared Kushner: How the Saudis Got a Friend in the White House," *The New York Times*, December 8, 2018, https://www.nytimes.com/2018/12/08/world/middleeast/saudi-mbs-jared-kushner.html, last accessed March 17, 2020.

94 "Remarks by President Trump and Emir Sabah al-Ahmed al-Jaber al-Sabah of Kuwait in Joint Press Conference," *The White House*, 7 September 2017, https://www.whitehouse.gov/briefings-statements/remarks-president-trump-emir-sabah-al-ahmed-al-jaber-al-sabah-kuwait-joint-press-conference/, last accessed March 17, 2020.

95 "Qatar deports Saudi asylum-seeker to Saudi Arabia: Amnesty," *Reuters*, May 30, 2017, https://www.reuters.com/article/us-saudi-qatar-rights-idUSKBN18Q2H9, last accessed March 17, 2020.

96 "Qatar 2017 Human Rights Report," *US Department of State*, https:// qa.usembassy.gov/wp-content/uploads/sites/136/QatarHRR2017.pdf, last accessed March 17, 2020.

97 "Saudi Arabia sentences human rights activists to prison: Amnesty," *Reuters*, January 26, 2018, https://www.reuters.com/article/ us-saudi-rights/saudi-arabia-sentences-human-rights-activists-to-pris- on-amnesty-idUSKBN1FF1JV, last accessed March 17, 2020.

98 Anthony Harwood, "ON THE RUN UAE politician's wife who's hiding in Britain after sparking country's huge row with Qatar fears she'll be tortured if she's sent home," *The Sun*, January 12 2018, https:// www.thesun.co.uk/news/5328679/uae-politician-wife-hiding-brit- ain-fears-torture-qatar/, last accessed March 17, 2020.

99 David Kirkpatrick, "Emirati Prince Flees to Qatar, Exposing Tensions in U.A.E.," *The New York Times*, 14 July 2018, https://www.nytimes. com/2018/07/14/world/middleeast/emirati-prince-qatar-defects.html, last accessed March 17, 2020.

100 Ibid.

101 "Qatar 2017 Human Rights Report," *US Department of State*, https:// qa.usembassy.gov/wp-content/uploads/sites/136/QatarHRR2017.pdf, last accessed March 17, 2020.

102 "Qatar: Gulf's First Refugee Asylum Law," *Human Rights Watch*, October 30, 2018, https://www.hrw.org/news/2018/10/30/qatar-gulfs- first-refugee-asylum-law, last accessed March 17, 2020.

103 "Qatar Guarantees Asylum to Political Refugees," *Qatar-America Institute*, September 6, 2018, https://qataramerica.org/qatar-guaran- tees-asylum-to-political-refugees/, last accessed March 17, 2020.

104 Jure Snog, "Population of Qatar by nationality," *Priya DSouza Communications*, August 15, 2019, http://priyadsouza.com/popula- tion-of-qatar-by-nationality-in-2017/, last accessed March 17, 2020.

105 Manu Raju, "Exclusive: Rice told House investigators why she unmasked senior Trump officials," *CNN*, September 18, 2017, https://www.cnn.com/2017/09/13/politics/susan-rice-house-in- vestigators-unmasked-trump-officials/index.html, last accessed March 17, 2020.

106 Fitch, Aya, Nicolas Parasie, and Margherita Stancati, "Saudi Arabia, U.A.E., Bahrain and Egypt Cut Diplomatic Ties With Qatar," *The Wall Street Journal*, June 6, 2017, https://www.wsj.com/articles/qatar-calls-for-talks-to-end-diplomatic-crisis-in-persian-gulf-1496753144, last accessed March 17, 2020.

107 Karl Vick, "President Trump Says Isolating Qatar Could End Terrorism. He's Wrong," *Time*, June 6, 2017, https://time.com/4807216/donald-trump-twitter-qatar-terrorism/, last accessed March 17, 2020.

108 Interviews in Washington, D.C. during the summer of 2018 with several influencers close to President Trump.

109 McFarlane, Sarah, and Bradley Olson: "Exxon, Qatar in Talks on US Shale Deal," *The Wall Street Journal*, April 11, 2018, https://www.wsj.com/articles/exxon-qatar-in-talks-on-u-s-shale-deal-1523358862, last accessed March 17, 2020.

110 McFarlane, Sarah, Summer Said, and Michael Amon, "Oil-Rich Saudi Arabia Barrels Into the Gas Business," *The Wall Street Journal*, May 22, 2019, https://www.wsj.com/articles/oil-rich-saudi-arabia-barrels-into-the-gas-business-11558549343, last accessed March 17, 2020.

111 "Readout of President Donald J. Trump's Call with King Salman Bin Abdulaziz Al Saud of Saudi Arabia," *The White House*, 20 December 2017, https://www.whitehouse.gov/briefings-statements/readout-president-donald-j-trumps-call-king-salman-bin-abdulaziz-al-saud-saudi-arabia-4/, last accessed March 17, 2020.

112 Yousef Al-Otaiba, "Qatar Cannot Have It Both Ways," *The Wall Street Journal*, June 12, 2017, accessed https://www.wsj.com/articles/qatar-cannot-have-it-both-ways-1497307260, last accessed March 17, 2020.

113 "Pentagon: Boeing wins $6.2bn contract for Qatar's F-15," *Al Jazeera*, December 23, 2017, https://www.aljazeera.com/news/2017/12/pentagon-boeing-wins-62bn-contract-qatar-15-171223192108186.html, last accessed March 17, 2020.

114 "Saudi King Salman, Qatar's Sheikh Abdullah Al Thani discuss opening of Salwa border for Hajj pilgrims," *Arab News*, August 18, 2017, https://www.arabnews.com/node/1146686/saudi-arabia, last accessed March 17, 2020.

115 Callum Paton: "Who is Sheikh Abdullah bin Ali al-Thani, The Qatari Royal Held 'Prisoner' In The UAE?," *Newsweek*, January 15, 2018, https://www.newsweek.com/who-sheikh-abdullah-bin-ali-al-thani-qatari-royal-held-prisoner-uae-781399, last accessed March 17, 2020.

116 In September 2019, Twitter suspended Saud Al Qahtani's Twitter account over his role in the Khashoggi murder.

117 "FaceOf: Saud Al-Qahtani, Saudi Royal Court adviser," *Arab News*, June 23, 2018, https://www.arabnews.com/node/1326371/saudi-arabia, last accessed March 17, 2020.

118 Benner, Katie, Mark Mazzetti, Ben Hubbard, and Mike Isaac, "Saudis' Image Makers: A Troll Army and a Twitter Insider," *The New York Times*, October 20, 2018, https://www.nytimes.com/2018/10/20/us/politics/saudi-image-campaign-twitter.html, last accessed March 17, 2020.

119 Kirchgaessner, Stephanie, and Nick Hopkins, "US urges Saudi prince to ditch aide linked to Khashoggi killing," *The Guardian*, April 12, 2019, https://www.theguardian.com/world/2019/apr/12/us-urges-saudi-prince-to-ditch-aide-linked-to-khashoggi-killing, last accessed March 17, 2020.

120 Hadas Gold, "Twitter suspends account of former adviser to Saudi Arabia's crown prince," *CNN*, September 20, 2019, https://www.cnn.com/2019/09/20/tech/twitter-suspends-accounts-saudi-al-qahtani/index.html, last accessed March 17, 2020.

121 Madawi Al-Rasheed, "Saudi Arabia's attempt at a Qatari coup backfired - now wait for the blowback," *Middle East Eye*, August 22, 2017, https://www.middleeasteye.net/opinion/saudi-arabias-attempt-qatari-coup-backfired-now-wait-blowback, last accessed March 17, 2020.

122 "Is it Time for Change in Qatar?!," *Okaz Newspaper*, September 26, 2017, https://www.okaz.com.sa/articles/na/1575334, last accessed March 17, 2020.

123 https://twitter.com/salansar1/status/911771844646141952?lang=en

124 "Qatar condemns arrest of its citizen by Saudi Arabia," *Gulf Times*, May 3, 2018, https://www.gulf-times.com/story/591365/Qatar-condemns-arrest-of-its-citizen-by-Saudi-Arab, last accessed March 17, 2020.

125 Twitter transcript has since been deleted.

126 A. Al-Khatib, "Saudi Arabia releases Qatari citizen Mohsen Al Qurabi," The New Arab, July 22, 2019, https://www.alaraby.co.uk/society/2019/7/21/السعودية-تطلق-سراح-المواطن-القطري-محسن-الكربي, last accessed March 17, 2020.

127 "Qatari national freed by Saudi Arabia after arbitrary detention," Al Jazeera, July 22, 2019, https://www.aljazeera.com/news/2019/07/qatari-national-freed-saudi-arabia-arbitrary-detention-190722145407134.html, last accessed March 17, 2020.

128 "Bahrain sees "no glimmer of hope" for ending Qatar crisis soon," CNBC, May 27, 2018, www.cnbc.com/2018/05/27/bahrain-sees-no-glimmer-of-hope-for-ending-qatar-crisis-soon.html, last accessed March 17, 2020.

129 Stephen Kalin, "Saudi threatens military action if Qatar deploys anti-aircraft missiles: report," Reuters, June 2, 2018, https://www.reuters.com/article/us-saudi-qatar-france/saudi-threatens-military-action-if-qatar-deploys-anti-aircraft-missiles-report-idUSKCN1IY0IW, last accessed March 17, 2020.

130 A. Bakir: "Divided Gulf: The Anatomy of a Crisis," Palgrave Macmillan, page 211, 2019.

131 A. Bakir: "Divided Gulf: The Anatomy of a Crisis," Palgrave Macmillan, page 211, 2019.

132 A. Bakir: "Divided Gulf: The Anatomy of a Crisis," Palgrave Macmillan, page 212, 2019.

133 "Erdogan visits Saudi Arabia over Gulf crisis," Al Jazeera, July 23, 2017, https://www.aljazeera.com/news/2017/07/erdogan-set-visit-saudi-arabia-gulf-crisis-170722173756933.html, last accessed March 17, 2020.

134 Stephen Kalin, "Qatar says five suspects in news agency hacking detained in Turkey," Reuters, August 26, 2017, https://www.reuters.com/article/us-gulf-qatar-cyber/qatar-says-five-suspects-in-news-agency-hacking-detained-in-turkey-idUSKCN1B608L, last accessed March 17, 2020.

135 A. Bakir: "Divided Gulf: The Anatomy of a Crisis," Palgrave Macmillan, page 207, 2019.

136 A. Bakir: "Divided Gulf: The Anatomy of a Crisis," Palgrave Macmillan, page 207, 2019.

137 Sanam Vakil, "Iran and the GCC Hedging, Pragmatism and Opportunism," *Chatham House*, September 13, 2018, https://reader. chathamhouse.org/iran-and-gcc-hedging-pragmatism-and-opportunism#, last accessed March 17, 2020.

138 "GCC Condemns Iran Interference in Region," Embassy of the Kingdom of Saudi Arabia in Washington, DC, January 9, 2016, https://www.saudiembassy.net/press-release/gcc-condemns-iran-interference-region, last accessed March 17, 2020.

139 "Zarif Visits Qatar Amid Ongoing Diplomatic Crisis," *Radio Farda*, October 3, 2017, https://en.radiofarda.com/a/iran-zarif-visit-to-qatar/28771637.html, last accessed March 17, 2020.

140 S. Boussois: "Divided Gulf: The Anatomy of a Crisis," page 228, *Palgrave Macmillan*, 2019.

141 "Remarks on the Middle East," *US Department of State*, June 9, 2017, https://www.state.gov/remarks-on-the-middle-east/, last accessed March 17, 2020.

142 Manson, Katrina, and Demetri Sevastopulo, "Trump criticises Qatar for funding terrorism at 'high level,'" *The Financial Times*, June 9, 2017, https://www.ft.com/content/e9967b54-4d42-11e7-919a-1e14ce4af89b, last accessed March 17, 2020.

143 Gardiner Harris, "State Dept. Lashes Out at Gulf Countries Over Qatar Embargo," *The New York Times*, June 20, 2017, https://www.nytimes.com/2017/06/20/world/middleeast/qatar-saudi-arabia-trump-tillerson.html, last accessed March 17, 2020.

144 Patrick Wintour, "Qatar given 10 days to meet 13 sweeping demands by Saudi Arabia," *The Guardian*, June 23, 2017, https://www.theguardian.com/world/2017/jun/23/close-al-jazeera-saudi-arabia-issues-qatar-with-13-demands-to-end-blockade, last accessed March 17, 2020.

145 "Secretary of State Tillerson Travel to Kuwait, Qatar, and Saudi Arabia," *US Department of State*, July 13, 2017, https://www.state.gov/secretary-tillerson-travels-to-kuwait-qatar-and-saudi-arabiasecretary-tillerson-travels-to-kuwait-qatar-and-saudi-arabia/, last accessed March 17, 2020.

146 Tom Finn, "US, Qatar sign agreement on combating terrorism financing," *Reuters*, July 10, 2017, https://www.reuters.com/article/us-gulf-qatar-kuwait/u-s-qatar-sign-agreement-on-combating-terrorism-financing-idUSKBN19V2RV, last accessed March 17, 2020.

147 "Public Schedule—July 12, 2017," US *Department of State*, https://www.state.gov/public-schedule-july-12-2017/

148 Yousef Al-Otaiba, "Qatar Cannot Have It Both Ways," *The Wall Street Journal*, June 12, 2017, accessed https://www.wsj.com/articles/qatar-cannot-have-it-both-ways-1497307260, last accessed March 17, 2020.

149 "Foreign Affairs Committee Releases Transcript of Interview with Former Secretary of State Rex Tillerson," *US House of Representatives Committee on Foreign Affairs*, June 27, 2019, https://foreignaffairs.house.gov/2019/6/foreign-affairs-committee-releases-transcript-of-interview-with-former-secretary-of-state-rex-tillerson, last accessed March 17, 2020.

150 Taimur Khan, "Arab countries' six principles for Qatar "a measure to restart the negotiation process,'" *The National* (UAE), July 19, 2017, https://www.thenational.ae/world/gcc/arab-countries-six-principles-for-qatar-a-measure-to-restart-the-negotiation-process-1.610314, last accessed March 17, 2020.

151 Haberman, Maggie, Michael Shear, and Glenn Thrush, "Stephen Bannon Out at the White House After Turbulent Run," *The New York Times*, August 18, 2017, https://www.nytimes.com/2017/08/18/us/politics/steve-bannon-trump-white-house.html, last accessed March 17, 2020.

152 Haberman, Maggie, and Matt Stevens, "Sebastian Gorka Is Forced Out as White House Adviser, Officials Say," *The New York Times*, August 25, 2017, https://www.nytimes.com/2017/08/25/us/politics/sebastian-gorka-leaves-white-house.html, last accessed March 17, 2020.

153 https://t.co/mrhRhlApWT pic.twitter.com/DFuMu0Hew8

154 "Outrage ensues over Al Arabiya video about airspace breaches," *Doha News*, August 15, 2017. https://twitter.com/dohanews/status/897337283053060096

155 Alex Macheras, "Saudi News Channel Shows Simulated Downing of a Civilian Jet," *ThePointsGuy*," August 15, 2017, https://thepointsguy.com/2017/08/saudi-channel-simulation-downing-jet/, last accessed March 17, 2020.

156 "Emir speech in full text: Qatar ready for dialogue but won't compromise on sovereignty," *Qatar News Agency*, July 22, 2017, https://qsearch.qa/news-details/221/emir-speech-in-full-text-qatar-ready-for-dialogue-but-wont-compromise-on-sovereignty, last accessed March 17, 2020.

157 "Sheikh Tamim: Any talks must respect Qatar sovereignty," *Al Jazeera*, July 22, 2017, https://www.aljazeera.com/news/2017/07/sheikh-tamim-talks-respect-qatar-sovereignty-170721184815998.html, last accessed March 17, 2020.

158 "Remarks by President Trump and Emir Sabah al-Ahmed al-Jaber al-Sabah of Kuwait in Joint Press Conference," *The White House*, September 7, 2017, https://www.whitehouse.gov/briefings-statements/remarks-president-trump-emir-sabah-al-ahmed-al-jaber-al-sabah-kuwait-joint-press-conference/, last accessed March 17, 2020.

159 "In Full Text: The speech of Qatar Emir at the opening session of UN General Assembly," *The Peninsula*, September 19, 2017, https://www.thepeninsulaqatar.com/article/19/09/2017/In-Full-Text-The-speech-of-Qatar-Emir-at-the-opening-session-of-UN-General-Assembly, last accessed March 17, 2020.

160 Jon Gambrell, "US military halts exercises over Qatar crisis," *The Associated Press*, October 6, 2017, https://apnews.com/33d75eaedbdd4b178e9025ea8a0edc83/APNewsBreak:-US-military-halts-exercises-over-Qatar-crisis?utm_campaign=SocialFlow&utm_source=Twitter&utm_medium=AP, last accessed March 17, 2020.

161 Nick Wadhams, "Tillerson Signals Impatience with China While Vowing to Stay On," *Bloomberg*, October 19, 2017, https://www.bloomberg.com/news/articles/2017-10-19/tillerson-signals-impatience-with-china-on-north-korea-trade, last accessed March 17, 2020.

162 Ibid.

163 "Qatari forces participate in Gulf shield drill in Saudi Arabia," *Al Jazeera*, April 19, 2018, https://www.aljazeera.com/news/2018/04/qatari-forces-participate-gulf-shield-drill-saudi-arabia-180419053305193.html, last accessed March 17, 2020.

164 Joyce Karam, "Bahrain Crown Prince and Trump address Iran actions and Gulf dispute," *The National*, November 30, 2017, https://www.thenational.ae/world/gcc/bahrain-crown-prince-and-trump-address-iran-actions-and-gulf-dispute-1.680418, last accessed March 17, 2020.

165 Naser Al Wasmi, "GCC summit: Second day cancelled amid Qatar row," *The National*, December 5, 2017, https://www.thenational.ae/world/gcc/gcc-summit-second-day-cancelled-amid-qatar-row-1.681611, last accessed March 17, 2020.

166 "Readout of President Donald J. Trump's Calls with Gulf State Leaders," *The White House*, July 2, 2017, https://www.whitehouse.gov/briefings-statements/readout-president-donald-j-trumps-calls-gulf-state-leaders/

167 "Readout of President Donald J. Trump's Call with Amir Tamim bin Hamad Al Thani of Qatar," *The White House*, September 8, 2017, https://www.whitehouse.gov/briefings-statements/readout-president-donald-j-trumps-call-amir-tamim-bin-hamad-al-thani-qatar/, last accessed March 17, 2020.

168 "Readout of President Donald J. Trump's Call with Emir Tamim bin Hamad Al Thani of Qatar," *The White House*, January 15, 2018, https://www.whitehouse.gov/briefings-statements/readout-president-donald-j-trumps-call-emir-tamim-bin-hamad-al-thani-qatar/

169 "Joint Statement of the Inaugural United States-Qatar Strategic Dialogue," *US Department of State*, January 30, 2018, https://www.state.gov/joint-statement-of-the-inaugural-united-states-qatar-strategic-dialogue/, last accessed March 17, 2020.

170 "Readout of President Donald J. Trump's Call with Emir Tamim bin Hamad Al Thani of Qatar," *The White House*, February 28, 2018, https://www.whitehouse.gov/briefings-statements/readout-president-donald-j-trumps-call-emir-tamim-bin-hamad-al-thani-qatar-2/, last accessed March 17, 2020.

171 "US, Saudi and UAE hold trilateral NSA dialogue," *Press Trust of India*, March 26, 2018, https://www.outlookindia.com/newsscroll/us-saudi-and-uae-hold-trilateral-nsa-dialogue/1278125, last accessed March 17, 2020.

172 "Trump: US-Qatar ties 'work extremely well,'" *Al Jazeera*, April 11, 2018, https://www.aljazeera.com/news/2018/04/trump-qatar-ties-work-extremely-180410135820276.html, last accessed March 17, 2020.

173 Kumar, Anita, and Ben Wieder, "Steve Bannon's already murky Middle East ties deepen," *McClatchy*, October 23, 2017, https://www.mcclatchydc.com/news/politics-government/white-house/article180111646.html, last accessed March 17, 2020.

174 "US secretary of state meets with UAE foreign minister in Washington D.C.," *Xinhua News Agency*, May 15, 2018, http://www.xinhuanet.com/english/2018-05/15/c_137179745.htm, last accessed March 17, 2020.

175 "Donald Trump to meet Gulf leaders in March and April," *The National*, February 24, 2018, https://www.thenational.ae/world/gcc/donald-trump-to-meet-gulf-leaders-in-march-and-april-1.707490?videoId=5750420390001, last accessed March 17, 2020.

176 https://twitter.com/AnwarGargash/status/991302321794580481

177 "Russian president and crown prince of Abu Dhabi talks round-up," *TASS*, June 1, 2018, https://tass.com/world/1007620, last accessed March 17, 2020.

178 "UAE hosts Chinese president for talks on strengthening bilateral tie," *The Arab Weekly*, July 20, 2018, https://thearabweekly.com/uae-hosts-chinese-president-talks-strengthening-bilateral-ties, last accessed March 17, 2020.

179 Annalise Frank, "US Senate confirms Walbridge CEO John Rakolta for ambassador to UAE," *Crain's Detroit Business*, September 17, 2019, https://www.crainsdetroit.com/people/us-senate-confirms-walbridge-ceo-john-rakolta-ambassador-uae, last accessed March 17, 2020.

180 "Forum on subversive role of Qatar today," *DT News Network of Bahrain*, January 8, 2018, https://www.newsofbahrain.com/bahrain/40982.html, last accessed March 17, 2020.

181 "Al Khalifa Rule in the Qatar Peninsula: History and Sovereignty," *Bahrain Center for Strategic International and Energy Studies*, June 30, 2018, https://www.derasat.org.bh/the-al-khalifa-rule-in-the-qatar-peninsula-history-and-sovereignty-conference/, last accessed March 17, 2020.

182 Uzi Rabi, "Qatar's Relations with Israel: Challenging Arab and Gulf Norms," *Middle East Journal*, Volume 63, Number 3 (Summer 2009), Middle East Institute.

183 "Qatar informs UN of three air violations by UAE, Bahrain," *Gulf Times*, March 11, 2018, https://www.gulf-times.com/story/584604/Qatar-informs-UN-of-three-air-violations-by-UAE-Bahrain, last accessed March 17, 2020.

184 "Qatar "harassed' UAE military aircraft, general reveals," *The National*, January 23, 2018, https://www.thenational.ae/world/qatar-harassed-uae-military-aircraft-general-reveals-1.698011, last accessed March 17, 2020.

185 "Qatari jets intercept two UAE civilian planes over Bahrain," *The National*, March 26, 2018, https://www.thenational.ae/world/gcc/qatari-jets-intercept-two-uae-civilian-planes-over-bahrain-1.716360, last accessed March 17, 2020.

186 Zainab Fattah, "Countries Boycotting Qatar Want Flying-Rights Case Moved to ICJ," *Bloomberg*, June 27, 2018, https://www.bloomberg.com/news/articles/2018-06-27/countries-boycotting-qatar-want-flying-rights-case-moved-to-icj, last accessed March 17, 2020.

187 "ICAO Council rejects blockading countries' appeals against Qatar," *The Peninsula*, June 27, 2018, https://thepeninsulaqatar.com/article/27/06/2018/ICAO-Council-rejects-blockading-countries'-appeals-against-Qatar, last accessed March 17, 2020.

188 "Key questions about the Dubai port deal," *CNN*, March 6, 2006, https://www.cnn.com/2006/POLITICS/03/06/dubai.ports.qa/, last accessed March 17, 2020.

189 "US Consulate General Dubai," US Embassy and Consulate in the United Arab Emirates, https://ae.usembassy.gov/embassy-consulates/dubai/, last accessed March 17, 2020.

190 Blau, Uri, and Avi Scharf, "Mysterious Israeli Businessman Behind Mega-deal to Supply Spy Planes to UAE," *Haaretz*, August 21, 2019, https://www.haaretz.com/middle-east-news/.premium-israel-business-man-uae-spy-planes-iran-saudi-arabia-1.7696711, last accessed March 17, 2020.

191 Mahmoud Habboush, "UAE wins bid to house Irena headquarters," *The National*, June 29, 2009, https://www.thenational.ae/uae-wins-bid-to-house-irena-headquarters-1.512489, last accessed March 17, 2020.

192 "US-UAE Agreement for Peaceful Nuclear Cooperation (123 Agreement)," *US Department of State*, January 15, 2009, https://2001-2009.state.gov/r/pa/prs/ps/2009/01/114262.htm, last accessed March 17, 2020.

193 "South Korea and UAE seek cooperation beyond Barakah," *World Nuclear News*, February 27, 2019, https://www.world-nuclear-news.org/Articles/South-Korea-and-UAE-seek-cooperation-beyond-Baraka, last accessed March 17, 2020.

194 "The Anatomy of Mossad's Dubai Operation," *Der Spiegel*, January 17, 2011, https://www.spiegel.de/consent-a-?targetUrl=https%3A%2F%2Fwww.spiegel.de%2Finternational%2Fworld%2Fan-eye-for-an-eye-the-anatomy-of-mossad-s-dubai-operation-a-739908.html&ref=https%3A%2F%2Ft.co%2FtphVNJuhH8%3Famp%3D1, last accessed March 17, 2020.

195 Barak Ravid, "Exclusive: Netanyahu Secretly Met with UAE Foreign Minister in 2012 in New York," *Haaretz*, July 25, 2017, https://www.haaretz.com/israel-news/netanyahu-secretly-met-with-uae-foreign-minister-in-2012-in-new-york-1.5432342, last accessed March 17, 2020.

196 https://www.congress.gov/bill/116th-congress/house-bill/1850

197 https://www.aipac.org/learn/legislative-agenda/agenda-display/2019-oppose-palestinian-terrorism

198 Josh Gerstein, "Lawmakers push for Al Jazeera to register as foreign agent," *Politico*, March 5, 2018, https://www.politico.com/story/2018/03/05/al-jazeera-press-foreign-agent-437072, last accessed March 17, 2020.

199 https://zeldin.house.gov/sites/zeldin.house.gov/files/3.6_zeldin_gottheimer_cruz_letter_pdf.pdf

200 Raghavan, Sudarsan, and Jobby Warrick, "How a 91-year-old imam came to symbolize the feud between Qatar and its neighbors," *The Washington*

Post, June 27, 2017, www.washingtonpost.com/world/middle_east/how-a-91-year-old-imam-came-to-symbolize-feud-between-qatar-and-its-neighbors/2017/06/26/601d41b4-5157-11e7-91eb-9611861a988f_story.html, last accessed March 17, 2020.

201 "Jared Kushner on Israel-Palestine deal: Time to try something new," *Al Jazeera*, June 25, 2019, https://www.aljazeera.com/programmes/talktojazeera/2019/06/jared-kushner-israel-palestine-deal-time-190625113553537.html, last accessed March 17, 2020.

202 "Elan Carr: Global Anti-Semitism, The View from The United States," The Henry Jackson Society, October 24, 2019, https://henryjacksonsociety.org/event/elan-carr-global-anti-semitism-the-view-from-the-united-states-2/, last accessed March 17, 2020.

203 Joe Light, "Al Jazeera Target of U.A.E. Campaign in US to Hobble Network," *Bloomberg*, 11 October 2019, https://www.bloomberg.com/news/articles/2019-10-11/al-jazeera-target-of-u-a-e-campaign-in-u-s-to-hobble-network, last accessed March 17, 2020.

204 "Al Jazeera rebuts renewed push for 'foreign agent' registration," *Al Jazeera*, June 20, 2020, https://www.aljazeera.com/news/2019/06/al-jazeera-rebuts-renewed-push-foreign-agent-registration-190620155829236.html,

205 "Qatar, Money and Terror: Doha's Dangerous Policies," *Counter Extremism Project*, June 5, 2017, https://www.counterextremism.com/sites/default/files/Qatar%20Money%20and%20Terror_080519_0.pdf, last accessed March 17, 2020.

206 "HARBORS Campaign: Qatar Hosts and Assists Radicals by Offering Refuge and Support," *Counter Extremism Project*, June 6, 2017, https://www.counterextremism.com/harbors-campaign-qatar, last accessed March 17, 2020.

207 Louis Nelson, "Nonprofit urges multinational companies to shun Qatar," *Politico*, July 3, 2017, https://www.politico.com/story/2017/07/03/qatar-counter-extremism-project-companies-240203, last accessed March 17, 2020.

208 Fatah, Mohamed, and Muhammad Fraser-Rahim, "Gulf Diplomatic Crisis: Why Trump Must Label Qatar as a State Sponsor of Terrorism," *Newsweek*, June 7, 2017, https://www.newsweek.com/

trump-qatar-state-sponsored-terrorism-622398, last accessed March 17, 2020.

209 Ilan Berman, "Saudi Arabia has backed Qatar into a Corner," *The National Interest*, June 8, 2017, https://nationalinterest.org/feature/saudi-arabia-has-backed-qatar-corner-21067, last accessed March 17, 2020.

210 Joshua Block, "Qatar is a financier of terrorism. Why does the US tolerate it?" *The Los Angeles Times*, June 9, 2017, https://www.latimes.com/opinion/op-ed/la-oe-block-qatar-terrorism-syria-20170609-story.html, last accessed March 17, 2020.

211 Bruce Majors, "A New Domino Effect? Qatar and North Korea," *The Daily Caller*, June 12, 2017, https://dailycaller.com/2017/06/12/a-new-domino-effect-qatar-and-north-korea/, last accessed March 17, 2020.

212 Clifford May, "The Qatar Ultimatum," *The Washington Times*, June 13, 2017, https://m.washingtontimes.com/news/2017/jun/13/qatar-must-join-in-anti-terror-fight/, last accessed March 17, 2020.

213 "Who are the terrorists in Qatar?" *Counter Extremism Project*, June 9, 2017, https://www.counterextremism.com/press/who-are-terrorists-qatar, last accessed March 17, 2020.

214 "A decade of Hamas, the terrorist regime enabled by Qatar's deep pockets," *Counter Extremism Project*, June 15, 2017, https://www.counterextremism.com/press/decade-hamas-terrorist-regime-enabled-qatar's-deep-pockets, last accessed March 17, 2020.

215 "Qatar's hosting of Radical Brotherhood Ideologue Symbolic of Support for Extremists," *Counter Extremism Project*, June 22, 2017, https://www.counterextremism.com/press/qatar's-hosting-radical-brotherhood-ideologue-symbolic-support-extremists, last accessed March 17, 2020.

216 "The Taliban hosted in Qatar," *Counter Extremism Project*, June 28, 2017, https://www.counterextremism.com/press/taliban-hosted-qatar, last accessed March 17, 2020.

217 Richard Clarke, "We always knew Qatar was trouble, as the 1990s escape of terror mastermind Khalid Sheikh Muhammad showed," *New York Daily News*, July 6, 2017, https://www.nydailynews.com/opinion/knew-qatar-trouble-article-1.3306729, last accessed March 17, 2020.

218 Megan Wilson, "Lobby firm registers as foreign agent for Saudi group," *The Hill*, August 18, 2017, https://thehill.com/business-a-lobbying/347122-lobby-firm-registers-as-foreign-agent-for-saudi-group-feuding-with-qatar, last accessed March 17, 2020.

219 Sultan Ahmed Al Jaber, "Qatar must stop changing the subject—and start changing its behavior," *CNN*, June 20, 2017, https://www.cnn.com/2017/06/20/opinions/qatar-needs-to-change-its-behavior-opinion/index.html, last accessed March 17, 2020.

220 Khalifa Alfadhel, "How Qatar Threatens Peace," *The Washington Times*, June 21, 2017, https://www.washingtontimes.com/news/2017/jun/21/qatar-threatens-middle-east-peace/, last accessed March 17, 2020.

221 Jordan Schachtel, "Rogue Rex? State Dept demands allies back off terror-linked Qatar," *Conservative Review*, June 21, 2017, https://www.conservativereview.com/news/rogue-rex-state-dept-demands-allies-back-off-terror-linked-qatar/, last accessed March 17, 2020.

222 Jordan Schachtel, Why Trump should endorse allies demands upon terror-cozy Qatar," *Conservative Review*, June 23, 2017, https://www.conservativereview.com/news/why-trump-should-support-our-allies-demands-upon-terror-friendly-qatar/, last accessed March 17, 2020.

223 Jordan Schachtel, 'Tillerson commits US to secret deal with terror-friendly Qatar," *Conservative Review*, July 12, 2017, https://www.conservativereview.com/news/tillerson-commits-us-to-secret-deal-with-terror-friendly-qatar/, last accessed March 17, 2020.

224 Creede Newton, "Saudi lobby pays $138,000 for anti-Qatar ads in the US," *Al Jazeera*, July 25, 2017, https://www.aljazeera.com/news/2017/07/saudi-lobby-pays-138000-anti-qatar-ads-170725041529752.html, last accessed March 17, 2020.

225 https://efile.fara.gov/docs/6463-Exhibit-AB-20190701-2.pdf?utm_source=Sailthru&utm_medium=email&utm_campaign=Lobby%20update%208-9-19&utm_term=Registered%20Users

226 Dennis Ross, "Tillerson can end the Qatar Standoff," *The Wall Street Journal*, August 1, 2017, https://www.wsj.com/articles/tillerson-can-end-the-qatar-standoff-1501624470, last accessed March 17, 2020.

227 Salman Al Ansari, "How 9/11 Mastermind found safe harbor in Qatar," *The Hill*, August 5, 2017, https://thehill.com/blogs/pundits-blog/international/345437-how-the-9-11-mastermind-found-safe-harbor-in-qatar, last accessed March 17, 2020.

228 L. Todd Wood, "Restrain Qatar to counter the Shia terror hegemon in the Middle East," *Washington Times*, August 8, 2017, https://www.washingtontimes.com/news/2017/aug/8/restrain-qatar-counter-shia-terror-hegemon-middle-/, last accessed March 17, 2020.

229 Yousef Al Otaiba, "The United Arab Emirates and the Taliban," *The New York Times*, August 9, 2017, https://www.nytimes.com/2017/08/09/opinion/the-united-arab-emirates-and-the-taliban.html, last accessed March 17, 2020.

230 Tom Wilson, "Does Qatar Support Extremism? Yes. And So Does Saudi Arabia?" *The New York Times*, August 10, 2017, https://www.nytimes.com/2017/08/10/opinion/qatar-saudi-arabia-extremism.html, last accessed March 17, 2020.

231 Hamad Al Amer, "Bringing Back Qatar from open conflict with its brothers," *The Washington Times*, August 10, 2017, https://www.washingtontimes.com/news/2017/aug/10/qatars-dispute-with-arab-neighbors-hurts-everyone-/, last accessed March 17, 2020.

232 Hammond, Joseph, and Suhaib Kebhaj, "Qatar and Arab Powers are already at war…in Libya," *Washington Examiner*, August 16, 2017, https://www.washingtonexaminer.com/qatar-and-arab-powers-are-already-at-warin-libya, last accessed March 17, 2020.

233 Mutlaq Al-Qahtani, "Qatar Will Not Be Intimidated," *The Wall Street Journal*, August 13, 2017, https://www.wsj.com/articles/qatar-will-not-be-intimidated-1502660926, last accessed March 17, 2020.

234 Khalid Al Hail, "Qatar should support pilgrims, not terrorists," *The Hill*, September 4, 2017, https://thehill.com/blogs/pundits-blog/international-affairs/349126-qatar-should-support-pilgrims-not-terrorists, last accessed March 17, 2020.

235 Jamie Merrill, "A Qatari exile, a spin war, and a 'cack-handed' push for a coup," *Middle East Eye*, September 14, 2017, https://www.

middleeasteye.net/news/qatari-exile-spin-war-and-cack-handed-push-coup, last accessed March 17, 2020.

236 Kenneth Vogel, "How a Trump Ally Tested the Boundaries of Washington's Influence Game," *The New York Times*, August 13, 2019, https://www.nytimes.com/2019/08/13/us/politics/elliott-broidy-trump.html, last accessed March 17, 2020.

237 "Is it Time for Change in Qatar?!" *Okaz Newspaper*, September 26, 2017, https://www.okaz.com.sa/articles/na/1575334, last accessed March 17, 2020.

238 "Qatari Sheikh Abdullah hospitalised in Kuwait," *Al Jazeera*, January 17, 2018, https://www.aljazeera.com/news/2018/01/qatari-sheikh-abudllah-hospitalised-kuwait-180117052711511.html, last accessed March 17, 2020.

239 Hudson Institute, https://www.hudson.org/about, last accessed March 17, 2020.

240 Butler, Desmond, and Tom LoBianco, "The princes, the president and the fortune seekers," *The Associated Press*, May 21, 2018, https://apnews.com/a3521859cf8d4c199cb9a8567abd2b71/The-princes,-the-president-and-the-fortune-seekers, last accessed March 17, 2020.

241 "Enough with the rhetoric. It is time for concrete action from Qatar," *The National*, October 24, 2017, https://www.thenational.ae/opinion/editorial/enough-with-the-rhetoric-it-is-time-for-concrete-action-by-qatar-1.669954, last accessed March 17, 2020.

242 Brad Patty, "A New Way Forward in the Middle East: Nine Stratagems," *Security Studies Group*, January 14, 2019, https://securitystudies.org/a-new-way-forward-in-the-middle-east/, last accessed March 14, 2020.

243 Jim Hanson, "Is Qatar really an ally?" Security Studies Group, January 29, 2019, https://securitystudies.org/is-qatar-really-an-ally/, last accessed March 17, 2020.

244 Kyle Shideler, "Ensconced in Doha: Qatar's Resident Islamists," *Middle East Forum*, January 30, 2019, https://www.meforum.org/57690/ensconced-doha-islamists, last accessed March 17, 2020.

245 Ronald Sandee, "Hedging Radical Islam," *Middle East Forum*, January 30, 2019, https://www.meforum.org/57691/hedging-radical-islam, last accessed March 17, 2020.

246 Daniel Pipes, "Examining Qatar's Influence," *Middle East Forum*, 29 January 2019, http://www.danielpipes.org/18699/qatar-influence, last accessed March 17, 2020.

247 Jonathan Spyer, "A Cautious Alliance," *Middle East Forum*, January 30, 2019, https://www.meforum.org/57693/cautious-alliance, last accessed March 17, 2020.

248 Benjamin Baird, "President Trump and the Janus-faced Qatari Regime," *Middle East Forum*, January 30, 2019, https://www.meforum.org/57694/president-trump-and-the-janus-faced-qatari-regime, last accessed March 17, 2020.

249 Samantha Rose Mandeles, "The Three Faces of Al Jazeera: Anti-Semitism, Anti-Americanism and Exploitation," *Middle East Forum*, January 30, 2019, https://www.meforum.org/57696/the-three-faces-of-al-jazeera, last accessed March 17, 2020.

250 David Reaboi, "Qatar Hacking Scandal Illustrates How US Media Megaphones Foreign Agitprop," *The Federalist*, January 31, 2019, https://thefederalist.com/2019/01/31/qatar-hacking-scandal-illustrates-u-s-media-megaphones-foreign-agitprop/, last accessed March 17, 2020.

251 Jim Hanson, "A New Strategy for the Middle East," *Security Studies Group*, January 9, 2019, https://securitystudies.org/a-new-strategy-for-the-middle-east/, last accessed March 17, 2020.

252 Nick Short, "Post Admits Qatar Shaped Jamal Khashoggi's Writing; Experts React," *Security Studies Group*, December 24, 2018, https://securitystudies.org/post-admits-qatar-shaped-jamal-khashoggis-writing-experts-react/, last accessed March 17, 2020.

253 David Reaboi, "Khashoggi: Qatari Asset in Life; Qatari Asset in Death," *Security Studies Group*, December 23, 2018, https://securitystudies.org/jamal-khashoggi-and-qatar-in-the-echo-chamber/, last accessed March 17, 2020.

254 David Reaboi, "Qatar's Doha Forum Features Terror Supporters, Congressional Democrats," *Security Studies Group*, December 17, 2018, https://securitystudies.org/qatars-doha-forum-features-terror-supporters-congressional-democrats/, last accessed March 17, 2020.

255 Brad Patty, "The Role of Fomenting Revolutions in Qatari Grand Strategy," *Security Studies Group*, February 7, 2019, https://security-studies.org/the-role-of-fomenting-revolutions-in-qatari-grand-strategy/, last accessed March 17, 2020.

256 Tavia Grant, "Oman most-improved nation in last 40 years, UN index says," *The Globe and Mail*, November 4, 2010, https://www.theglobeandmail.com/news/world/oman-most-improved-nation-in-last-40-years-un-index-says/article1216218/, last accessed March 17, 2020.

257 Colin MacKinnon: "The Party's Over for Israeli Economic Integration Into the Middle East," *Washington Report on Middle East Affairs*, January/February 1998, Pages 20–22, https://www.wrmea.org/1998-january-february/the-mena-summit-conference-in-doha-two-views.html

258 Lori Plotkin Boghardt, "The Doha Conference: A Post-Mortem," *The Washington Institute for Near East Policy*, November 21, 1997, https://www.washingtoninstitute.org/policy-analysis/view/the-doha-conference-a-post-mortem, last accessed March 17, 2020.

259 Uzi Rabi, "Qatar's Relations with Israel: Challenging Arab and Gulf Norms," *Middle East Journal*, Volume 63, Number 3 (Summer 2009), Middle East Institute.

260 "FACTBOX: Costs of war and recovery in Lebanon and Israel," *Reuters*, July 9, 2007, https://www.reuters.com/article/us-lebanon-war-cost/factbox-costs-of-war-and-recovery-in-lebanon-and-israel-idUSL0822571220070709, last accessed March 17, 2020.

261 Nada Bakri and Alan Cowell, "Political Agreement Reached in Lebanon," *The New York Times*, May 21, 2008,
https://www.nytimes.com/2008/05/21/world/africa/21iht-lebanon.4.13105564.html, last accessed March 17, 2020.

262 "Qatar's Emir visits south Lebanon," *Associated French Press*, July 31, 2010, https://www.thenational.ae/world/mena/qatar-s-emir-visits-south-lebanon-1.547394, last accessed March 17, 2020.

263 Sultan Barakat, "Qatari Mediation: Between Ambition and Achievement," *Brookings Doha*, November 10, 2014, https://www.brookings.

edu/research/qatari-mediation-between-ambition-and-achievement/, last accessed March 17, 2020.

264 Greg Myre, "Qatar Emerges as a Mediator Between Fatah and Hamas," *The New York Times*, October 10, 2006, https://www.nytimes.com/2006/10/10/world/middleeast/10mideast.html, last accessed March 17, 2020.

265 Nidal Al Mughrabi, "Emir of Qatar to be first head of state to visit Gaza," *Reuters*, October 21, 2012, https://www.reuters.com/article/us-palestinians-gaza-qatar/emir-of-qatar-to-be-first-head-of-state-to-visit-gaza-idUSBRE89K0K420121021, last accessed March 17, 2020.

266 Jodi Rudoren, "Qatari Emir Visits Gaza, Pledging $400 Million," *The New York Times*, October 23, 2012, https://www.nytimes.com/2012/10/24/world/middleeast/pledging-400-million-qatari-emir-makes-historic-visit-to-gaza-strip.html, last accessed March 17, 2020.

267 "The "Desalination Facility for the Gaza Strip" Project," *Union for the Mediterranean*, https://ufmsecretariat.org/project/the-desalination-facility-for-the-gaza-strip-project/, last accessed March 17, 2020.

268 Sigurd Neubauer, "Gaza Water Initiative Supported By Israel, May Receive Funding From Gulf," *Foreign Policy Journal*, April 12, 2013, https://www.foreignpolicyjournal.com/2013/04/12/gaza-water-initiative-supported-by-israel-may-receive-funding-from-gulf/, last accessed March 17, 2020.

269 "Al Attiyah Meets Davutoglu and Kerry in Paris," *Qatar News Agency*, July 27, 2014, https://qatarpress.qa/al-attiyah-meets-davutoglu-and-kerry-in-paris/, last accessed March 17, 2020.

270 Akram, Fares, and Mohammed Daraghmeh, "Power-sharing deal between former foes taking shape in Gaza," *The Associated Press*, July 20, 2017, https://apnews.com/7beacaa57f014b40aa9fbc41eaef8284/Power-sharing-deal-between-former-foes-taking-shape-in-Gaza, last accessed March 17, 2020.

271 "FM Livni visits Qatar," *Israel Ministry of Foreign Affairs*, April 13, 2008, https://mfa.gov.il/mfa/pressroom/2008/pages/fm%20livni%20visits%20qatar%2013-apr-2008.aspx, last accessed March 17, 2020.

272 Simon Henderson, "Energy Discoveries in the Eastern Mediterranean: Source for Cooperation or Fuel for Tension? The Case of Israel," *The German Marshall Fund of the United States*, June 15, 2012, https://www.washingtoninstitute.org/policy-analysis/view/energy-discoveries-in-the-eastern-mediterranean-source-for-cooperation-or-f, last accessed March 17, 2020.

273 Clifford Krauss, "Israel's Energy Dilemma: More Natural Gas Than It Can Use or Export," *The New York Times*, July 5, 2019, https://www.nytimes.com/2019/07/05/business/energy-environment/israel-natural-gas-offshore.html, last accessed March 17, 2020.

274 "The Madrid Framework," *Israel Ministry of Foreign Affairs*, January 28, 1999, https://mfa.gov.il/mfa/foreignpolicy/peace/guide/pages/the%20madrid%20framework.aspx, last accessed March 17, 2020.

275 Landau, Noa, and Jack Khoury, "Netanyahu Visits Oman, Which Has No Diplomatic Ties With Israel," *Haaretz*, October 27, 2018, https://www.haaretz.com/middle-east-news/netanyahu-secretly-visits-oman-which-has-no-diplomatic-ties-with-israel-1.6594761, last accessed March 17, 2020.

276 "World Leaders at PM Rabin-s Funeral," *Israel Ministry of Foreign Affairs*, 6 November 1995, http://www.israel.org/MFA/MFA-Archive/1995/Pages/World%20Leaders%20at%20PM%20Rabin-s%20Funeral.aspx, last accessed March 17, 2020.

277 Sigurd Neubauer and Yoel Guzansky, "Why the Trump Administration Should Reconsider Oman," *Arab Gulf States Institute in Washington*, May 30, 2017, https://agsiw.org/why-the-trump-administration-should-reconsider-oman/, last accessed March 17, 2020.

278 Itamar Eichler, "Minister Katz dances traditional sword dance in Oman," *Ynet.com*, November 7, 2018, www.ynetnews.com/articles/0,7340,L-5391689,00.html, last accessed March 17, 2020.

279 El Yaakoubi, Aziz, and Rami Ayyub, "Oman to open embassy in Palestinian territories' West Bank: foreign ministry," *Reuters*, 26 June 2019, www.reuters.com/article/us-israel-palestinians-plan-oman/oman-to-open-embassy-in-palestinian-territories-west-bank-foreign-ministry-idUSKCN1TR0XE, last accessed March 17, 2020.

280 "Oman denies diplomatic ties agreed with Israel," *Associated French Press*, July 2, 2019, www.france24.com/en/20190702-oman-denies-diplomatic-ties-agreed-with-israel, last accessed March 17, 2020.

281 Guzansky, Yoel, and Efraim Halevy, "Oman: The End of the Qaboos Era," *Institute for National Security Studies at Tel Aviv University*, January 13, 2020, www.inss.org.il/publication/oman-the-end-of-the-qaboos-era/, last accessed March 17, 2020.

282 الإمارات السلطنة و أبناء دولة صاحب السمو السيد اسعد بن طارق آل سعيد متحدثا عن المشادة بين أبناء
His majesty Mr. Asaad Bin Tareq Al Saeed speaking about the argument between social media users from the UAE and the Sultanate. https://www.youtube.com/watch?v=dYX-Kd9WtaY

283 In video: the comment from the Omani foreign minister on the spying of the UAE surprises everyone, *Al Alam*, March 18, 2019. https://www.alalamtv.net/news/4120146/بالفيديو-تعليق-وزير-خارجية-عمان-على-تجسس-الامارات-يفاجىء-الجميع

284 Landau, Noa and Jack Khoury, "Netanyahu visits Oman, which has no diplomatic ties," *Haaretz*, October 27, 2018, https://www.haaretz.com/middle-east-news/netanyahu-secretly-visits-oman-which-has-no-diplomatic-ties-with-israel-1.6594761, last accessed March 17, 2020.

285 Kirkpatrick, David, and Azam Ahmed, "Hacking a Prince, an Emir and a Journalist to Impress a Client," *The New York Times*, August 31, 2018, https://www.nytimes.com/2018/08/31/world/middleeast/hacking-united-arab-emirates-nso-group.html, last accessed March 17, 2020.

286 Schanzer, Jonathan, and Nicole Salter, "Oman's Dangerous Double Game," *The Wall Street Journal*, June 10, 2018, https://www.wsj.com/articles/omans-dangerous-double-game-1528652102, last accessed March 17, 2020.

287 Nicole Salter, "Oman Needs to Prevent Iranian Weapons Shipments to Houthis," *Foundation for Defense of Democracies*, March 12, 2018, https://www.fdd.org/analysis/2018/03/12/oman-needs-to-prevent-iranian-weapons-shipments-to-houthis/, last accessed March 17, 2020.

288 Schanzer, Jonathan, and Varsha Koduvayur, "Kuwait and Oman Are Stuck in Arab No Man's Land," *Foundation for Defense of Democracies*, June 14, 2018, https://foreignpolicy.com/2018/06/14/kuwait-and-oman-are-stuck-in-the-arab-no-mans-land/, last accessed March 17, 2020.

289 Schanzer, Jonathan, and Nicole Salter, "Oman's Growing Ties with Iran Threatens its Neutrality: FDD Report," *Foundation for Defense of Democracies*, May 9, 2019, https://www.fdd.org/analysis/press_releases/2019/05/09/omans-growing-ties-with-iran-threatens-its-neutrality-fdd-report/, last accessed March 17, 2020.

290 "Oman uncovers "spy network" but UAE denies any links," *BBC*, January 31, 2011, https://www.bbc.com/news/world-middle-east-12320859, last accessed March 17, 2020.

291 https://www.youtube.com/watch?v=FQBQUZ90Tpg

292 "Spy Network Busted," *Oman Daily Observer*, January 31, 2011, https://www.pressreader.com/oman/oman-daily-observer/20110131/281526517520170, last accessed March 17, 2020.

293 Benham, Jason, and Saleh Al-Shaibany, "Oman protests spread, road to port blocked," *Reuters*, February 27, 2011, https://www.reuters.com/article/us-oman-protests/oman-protests-spread-road-to-port-blocked-idUSTRE71Q0U420110228, last accessed March 17, 2020.

294 El Nahdy, Saeed, "Oman says it has reconciled with UAE over spy ring," *The Associated Press*, March 3, 2011, https://www.sandiegouniontribune.com/sdut-oman-says-it-has-reconciled-with-uae-over-spy-ring-2011mar03-story.html, last accessed March 17, 2020.

295 Caline Malek, "Oman ruler Sultan Qaboos visits UAE," *The National*, July 12, 2011, https://www.thenational.ae/uae/oman-ruler-sultan-qaboos-visits-uae-1.422953, last accessed March 17, 2020.

296 "Hillary Clinton in Oman For Talks on Iran," *Associated French Press*, October 20, 2011, https://muscatdaily.com/Archive/Oman/Hillary-Clinton-in-Oman-for-talks-on-Iran, last accessed March 17, 2020.

297 Judith Miller, "The view from the Gulf: America's quiet go-between speaks," *Fox News*, January 31, 2012, https://www.foxnews.com/world/the-view-from-the-gulf-americas-quiet-go-between-speaks, last accessed March 17, 2020.

298 Jay Solomon, "Secret Dealings W=with Iran Led to Nuclear Talks," *The Wall Street Journal*, June 28, 2015, https://www.wsj.com/articles/iran-wish-list-led-to-u-s-talks-1435537004, last accessed March 17, 2020.

299 Richard Schmierer, "The Sultanate of Oman and the Iran Nuclear Deal," *Middle East Policy Council, 2015*, https://mepc.org/journal/sultanate-oman-and-iran-nuclear-deal, last accessed March 17, 2020.

300 McBrierty, Vincent and Mohammad Al Zubair, *Oman Ancient Civilization: Modern Nation*, Dublin: Trinity College Dublin Press & The Bait Al Zubair Foundation LLC, 2004.

301 Linda Pappas Funsch, *Oman Reborn: Balancing Tradition and Modernization*, New York: Palgrave Macmillan, 2015, p. 45.

302 "Al Azi, art of performing praise, pride and fortitude poetry," *UNESCO*, 2017, https://ich.unesco.org/en/USL/al-azi-art-of-performing-praise-pride-and-fortitude-poetry-01268, last accessed March 17, 2020.

303 "Al Azi, elegy, processional march and poetry," *UNESCO*, 2012, https://ich.unesco.org/en/RL/al-azi-elegy-processional-march-and-poetry-00850, last accessed March 17, 2020.

304 Nick Webster, "Traditional UAE poetry offered protected UNESCO status," *The National*, December 9, 2017, https://www.thenational.ae/uae/traditional-uae-poetry-offered-protected-unesco-status-1.682877, last accessed March 17, 2020.

305 Joe Gill, "Is the UAE claiming Omani traditions as its own?," *Middle East Eye*, January 22, 2018, https://www.middleeasteye.net/features/uae-claiming-omani-traditions-its-own, last accessed March 17, 2020.

306 https://www.youtube.com/watch?v=UPZL6gwAmEc

307 "Symposium highlights role of Al Muhallab," *Oman News Agency*, May 9, 2018, https://www.omanobserver.com/symposium-highlights-role-of-al-muhallab/, last accessed March 17, 2020.

308 "Ardha wins Unesco status," *Oman Daily Observer*, November 30, 2018, https://www.pressreader.com/oman/oman-daily-observer/20181130/281479277477607, last accessed March 17, 2020.

309 "The United Arab Emirates in the Horn of Africa," *International Crisis Group*, November 6, 2018, https://www.crisisgroup.org/middle-east-north-africa/gulf-and-arabian-peninsula/united-arab-emirates/b65-united-arab-emirates-horn-africa, last accessed March 17, 2020.

310 "UAE 'annexes Oman territory' on new Louvre museum map," *Al Jazeera*, January 22, 2018, https://www.aljazeera.com/news/2018/01/

uae-annexes-oman-territory-louvre-museum-map-180122060843418. html, last accessed March 17, 2020.

311 Ali Al Matani, "New decree to protect Oman's properties," *Oman Daily Observer*, November 28, 2018, https://www.omanobserver.om/ new-decree-to-protect-omans-properties/, last accessed March 17, 2020.

312 "Oman bans expat property ownership in certain areas," *Arabian Business*, November 19, 2018, https://www.arabianbusiness.com/property/408302-oman-bans-expat-property-ownership-in-certain-areas, last accessed March 17, 2020.

313 "His Majesty Sultan Qaboos bin Said issues ten Royal Decrees," *Oman News Agency*, October 14, 2019, https://timesofoman.com/ article/2067104/Oman/Government/His-Majesty-Sultan-Qaboos-bin-Said-issues-ten-Royal-Decrees, last accessed March 17, 2020.

314 Manu Raju, "Exclusive: Rice told House investigators why she unmasked senior Trump officials," *CNN*, September 18, 2017, https:// www.cnn.com/2017/09/13/politics/susan-rice-house-investigators-unmasked-trump-officials/index.html, last accessed March 17, 2020.

315 Swan, Betsy, and Erin Banco, "Saudi Spy Met with Team Trump About Taking Down Iran," *The Daily Beast*, October 25, 2018, https:// www.thedailybeast.com/saudi-spy-met-with-team-trump-about-taking-down-iran, last accessed March 17, 2020.

316 Ibid.

317 David Welna, "Mattis Aims to Curb Iran's Influence on the Arabian Peninsula," *National Public Radio*, March 12, 2018, https://www. npr.org/2018/03/12/592823591/mattiss-middle-east-priority-curbing-irans-influence-on-the-arabian-peninsula, last accessed March 17, 2020.

318 "Secretary Pompeo in the Middle East," *ShareAmerica*, January 15, 2019, https://share.america.gov/secretary-pompeo-in-the-middle-east/, last accessed March 17, 2020.

319 Linda Pappas Funsch, *Oman Reborn: Balancing Tradition and Modernization*, New York: Palgrave Macmillan, 2015, p. 21.

320 "The Economist explains: Who are the Ibadis?," *The Economist*, December 18, 2018, www.economist.com/the-economist-explains/2018/12/18/who-are-the-ibadis, last accessed March 17, 2020.

321 "Background Reference: Oman," *US Energy Information Administration*, January 7, 2019, https://www.eia.gov/international/content/analysis/countries_long/Oman/oman_bkgd.pdf, accessed March 17, 2020.

322 Michael Quentin Morton, *Buraimi: The Struggle for Power, Influence and Oil in Arabia*, New York: Palgrave Macmillan, 2013, p. 226.

323 "United States Designates bin Laden Loyalist," *US Department of the Treasury*, February 24, 2004, https://www.treasury.gov/press-center/press-releases/Pages/js1190.aspx, last accessed March 17, 2020.

324 Elbagir, Nima, Salma Abdelaziz, Mohamed Albo El Gheit, and Laura Smith-Spark, "CNN Exclusive Report:

"Sold to an ally, lost to an enemy"," *CNN*, February 2019, https://www.learnexportcompliance.com/cnn-exclusive-report-sold-to-an-ally-lost-to-an-enemy/, last accessed March 17, 2020.

325 "UAE Penetrates Socotra by Granting Citizenship to Inhabitants," *Khalij Online*, January 3, 2019. https://alkhaleejonline.net/سياسة/وثيقة-الإمارات-تتغلغل-في-سقطرى-عبر-منح-الجنسية-لسكانها, last accessed March 17, 2020.

326 Aziz El Yaakoubi, "UAE troop drawdown in Yemen was agreed with Saudi Arabia: official," *Reuters*, July 8, 2019, https://www.reuters.com/article/us-yemen-security-emirates/uae-troop-drawdown-in-yemen-was-agreed-with-saudi-arabia-official-idUSKCN1U31WZ, last accessed March 17, 2020.

327 El Yaakoubi, Aziz, and Mohammed Mukhashaf, "UAE says pauses Hodeidah offensive for UN Yemen peace efforts," *Reuters*, July 1, 2018, https://www.reuters.com/article/us-yemen-security/uae-says-pauses-hodeidah-offensive-for-u-n-yemen-peace-efforts-idUSKBN1JR1CL, last accessed March 17, 2020.

328 "Humanitarian crisis in Yemen remains the worst in the world, warns UN," *UN News*, February 14, 2019, https://news.un.org/en/story/2019/02/1032811, last accessed March 17, 2020.

329 "Full Text of The Stockholm Agreement," *Office of the Special Envoy of the Secretary General for Yemen*, December 13, 2018, https://osesgy. unmissions.org/full-text-stockholm-agreement, last accessed March 17, 2020.

330 Khalid Al-Jaber and Sigurd Neubauer, The Gulf Crisis: Reshaping Alliances in the Middle East, Gulf International Forum, 2018, page 129.

331 "Thousands of Yemenis rally in support of southern separatists in Aden," *The Associated Press*, August 15, 2019,

https://www.latimes.com/world-nation/story/2019-08-15/thousands-of-ye-menis-rally-in-support-of-southern-separatists-in-aden, last accessed March 17, 2020.

332 https://www.al-monitor.com/pulse/lobbying-2018/yemen

333 Insert photo of Hani Bin Buraik wearing Emirati cloathing.

334 https://twitter.com/HaniBinbrek

335 "Yemen: A State Torn, Not Restored," *Gulf International Forum*, August 13, 2019, https://gulfif.org/yemen-a-state-torn-not-restored/, last accessed March 17, 2020.

336 Sarah Yerkes, "Mohammed bin Salman's comeback tour," *The Washington Post*, 6 December 2018, https://www.washingtonpost.com/news/monkey-cage/wp/2018/12/06/mohammed-bin-salmans-come-back-tour/?arc404=true, last accessed March 17, 2020.

337 "Oman issues statement on Jamal Khashoggi investigation," *Times of Oman*, November 17, 2018, https://timesofoman.com/article/443405/Oman/Government/Oman-issues-statement-on-Jamal-Khashoggi-investigation, last accessed March 17, 2020.

338 Arshad Mohammed, "Saudi Arabia's al-Jubeir says crown prince did not order Khashoggi killing," *Reuters*, February 8, 2019, https://www.reuters.com/article/us-saudi-khashoggi-jubeir-idUSKCN1PX1UB, last accessed March 17, 2020.

339 "Saudi Arabia's MBS arrives in Bahrain on latest leg of Arab tour," *Al Jazeera*, November 25, 2018, https://www.aljazeera.com/news/2018/11/saudi-arabia-mbs-arrives-bahrain-latest-leg-arab-tour-181125184400479.html, last accessed March 17, 2020.

340 "Bahrain FM: Qatar has burned its bridges with GCC," *Arab News*, December 6, 2018, https://www.arabnews.com/node/1416696/middle-east, last accessed March 17, 2020.

341 "GCC still strong despite Qatar row: Gargash," *Associated French Press*, December 6, 2018, https://gulfnews.com/world/gulf/saudi/gcc-still-strong-despite-qatar-row-gargash-1.60782308, last accessed March 17, 2020.

342 Naser Al Wasmi, "Qatar's emir will not attend GCC summit in Riyadh," *The National*, December 9, 2018, https://www.thenational.ae/world/gcc/qatar-s-emir-will-not-attend-gcc-summit-in-riyadh-1.800715, last accessed March 17, 2020.

343 Tuqa Khalid, "Bahrain criticizes Qatar emir for not attending GCC summit," *Reuters*, December 9, 2018, https://www.reuters.com/article/us-gulf-qatar-bahrain/bahrain-criticizes-qatar-emir-for-not-attending-gcc-summit-idUSKBN1O80AT, last accessed March 17, 2020.

344 Emily Tamkin, "Washington Think Tanks Still Divided on Whether to Return Saudi Donations Over Journalist's Disappearance," *Buzzfeed*, October 17, 2018, https://www.buzzfeednews.com/article/emilytamkin/washington-think-tanks-still-divided-on-whether-to-return, last accessed March 17, 2020.

345 Lipton, Eric, Brooke Williams, and Nicholas Confessore, "Foreign Powers Buy Influence at Think Tanks," *The New York Times*, September 6, 2014, https://www.nytimes.com/2014/09/07/us/politics/foreign-powers-buy-influence-at-think-tanks.html, last accessed March 17, 2020.

346 Ryan Grim, "Gulf Government Gave Secret $20 Million Gift to D.C. Think Tank," *The Intercept*, August 9, 2017, https://theintercept.com/2017/08/09/gulf-government-gave-secret-20-million-gift-to-d-c-think-tank/, last accessed March 17, 2020.

347 "Government Donors," *Center for Strategic & International Studies*.

348 Jilani, Zaid, and Alex Emmons, "Hacked E-mails Show UAE Building Close Relationship With D.C. Think Tanks That Push Its Agenda," *The Intercept*, July 30, 2017, https://theintercept.com/2017/07/30/uae-yousef-otaiba-cnas-american-progress-michele-flournoy-drone/, last accessed March 17, 2020.

349 Sabrina Siddiqui, "Leading liberal thinktank will no longer accept funds from UAE," *The Guardian*, January 25, 2019, https://www.theguardian.com/us-news/2019/jan/25/united-arab-emirates-funding-center-for-american-progress, last accessed March 17, 2020.

350 "Brookings Responds to Tablet Piece on Qatari Funding," *Tablet*, October 2, 2014, https://www.tabletmag.com/scroll/185831/brookings-responds-to-tablet-piece-on-qatar-funding, last accessed March 17, 2020.

351 Nick Short, "Post Admits Qatar Shaped Jamal Khashoggi's Writing; Experts React," Security Studies Group, December 24, 2018, https://securitystudies.org/post-admits-qatar-shaped-jamal-khashoggis-writing-experts-react/, last accessed March 17, 2020.

352 David Reaboi, "Khashoggi: Qatari Asset in Life; Qatari Asset in Death," *Security Studies Group*, December 23, 2018, https://securitystudies.org/jamal-khashoggi-and-qatar-in-the-echo-chamber/, last accessed March 17, 2020.

353 Seth Frantzman, "The Antisemitic Tweets Of Murdered Saudi Writer Jamal Khashoggi," *The Jerusalem Post*, April 14, 2019, https://www.jpost.com/Middle-East/The-antisemitic-tweets-of-murdered-Saudi-writer-Jamal-Khashoggi-586820, last accessed March 17, 2020.

354 Jon Gambrell, "Powerful Emirati Crown Prince Entangled by Mueller Report," *The Associated Press*, April 19, 2019, https://apnews.com/bbdc17a88bf54f968495c1212a509a02, last accessed March 17, 2020.

355 Dan Friedman, "House Intelligence Committee Revs Up Probe Into Saudi Influence Efforts Targeting Trump," *MotherJones*, August 9, 2019, https://www.motherjones.com/politics/2019/08/house-intelligence-committee-revs-up-probe-into-saudi-influence-efforts-targeting-trump/, last accessed March 17, 2020.

356 Jon Gambrell, "Powerful Emirati Crown Prince Entangled by Mueller Report," *The Associated Press*, April 19, 2019, https://apnews.com/bbdc17a88bf54f968495c1212a509a02, last accessed March 17, 2020.

357 Ahmed Hagagy, "Kuwait ruler Emir Sheikh Sabah has returned to Kuwait: KUNA," *Reuters*, October 16, 2019, https://www.reuters.com/article/us-kuwait-emir/

kuwait-ruler-emir-sheikh-sabah-has-returned-to-kuwait-kuna-idUSKB-
N1WV0S1, last accessed March 17, 2020.

358 Steve Holland, "White House says Trump spoke to Libyan commander
Haftar on Monday," *Reuters*, April 19, 2019, https://www.reuters.com/
article/us-libya-security-trump/white-house-says-trump-spoke-to-liby-
an-commander-haftar-on-monday-idUSKCN1RV0WW, last accessed
March 17, 2020.

359 "Meeting with Emirati Foreign Minister Abdullah bin Zayed Al
Nahyan," *US Department of State*, April 18, 2019, https://www.youtube.
com/watch?v=cfXENGsh9OM, accessed March 17, 2020.

360 Boutros, Hussein, and Lee Jay Walker, "Egypt backs counterterrorism
measures in Libya: President El-Sisi meets Khalifa Hafter," *Modern Tokyo
Times*, April 14, 2019, http://moderntokyotimes.com/egypt-backs-coun-
terrorism-measures-in-libya-president-el-sisi-meets-khalifa-hafter/,
accessed March 17, 2020.

361 "Sheikh Abdullah bin Zayed Al Nahyan Begins Washington Visit,"
Embassy of the United Arab Emirates in Washington, DC, May 14,
2018, https://www.uae-embassy.org/news-media/sheikh-abdullah-bin-
zayed-al-nahyan-begins-washington-visit, accessed March 17, 2020.

362 Vahdat, Amir, and Aya Batrawy, "UAE and Iran hold rare talks in
Tehran on maritime security," *The Associated Press*, 31 July 2019, https://
apnews.com/49c6da1c33fd45bbaf1b14836ee5e2ec, last accessed March
17, 2020.

363 "Iran sanctions Washington-based FDD for role in intensifying 'US
economic terrorism,'" *Mehr News Agency*, August 24, 2019, https://
en.mehrnews.com/news/149247/Iran-sanctions-Washington-based-
FDD-for-role-in-intensifying, last accessed March 17, 2020.

364 "Iran will soon begin the process to add UANI (written in full) to
its terrorist list," *Ministry of Foreign Affairs, Islamic Republic of Iran*, 24
September 2019, https://www.mfa.gov.ir/portal/newsview/540056/
uani-موسوی-ایران-روند-بررسی-افزودن-سازمان-پوششی-آمریکایی-اتحاد-علیه-ایران-هسته-ای
را-به-فهرست-گروههای-تروریستی-بزودی-آغاز-خواهد-کرد, accessed March 17, 2020.

365 "Iran, UAE agree to boost maritime security cooperation in joint
meeting in Tehran," *PressTV*, July 30, 2019, https://www.presstv.com/

Detail/2019/07/30/602265/Iran-UAE-maritime-security-meeting-Tehran, last accessed March 17, 2020.

366 https://twitter.com/jzarif/status/1141772824086028288?lang=en

367 https://2019iransummit.splashthat.com

368 https://www.unitedagainstnucleariran.com/press-releases/uanis-2018-iran-summit-kicks-off-as-organization-celebrates-10-years

369 Gambrell, Jon, and Zeke Miller, "Trump: US locked and loaded for response to attack on Saudis," *The Associated Press*, September 15, 2019, https://apnews.com/269744b35e16422fa746b0c1504ceb4f, last accessed March 17, 2020.

370 Rory Jones, "Saudi Arabia Shows Depth of Damage to Its Oil Facilities," *The Wall Street Journal*, September 20, 2019, https://www.wsj.com/articles/saudi-arabia-displays-burned-damaged-structures-at-oil-sites-after-attacks-11568985123, last accessed March 17, 2020.

371 Fassihi, Farnaz, and Ben Hubbard, "Saudi Arabia and Iran Make Quiet Openings to Head Off War," *The New York Times*, October 4, 2019, https://www.nytimes.com/2019/10/04/world/middleeast/saudi-arabia-iran-talks.html, last accessed March 17, 2020.

372 Isabel Kershner, "El Al Sues Israel After Air India Flies Through Saudi Airspace," *The New York Times*, March 28, 2018, https://www.nytimes.com/2018/03/28/world/middleeast/el-al-air-india-israel-saudi-arabia.html, last accessed March 17, 2020.

373 Declan Walsh, "Despite Public Outcry, Egypt to Transfer Islands to Saudi Arabia," *The New York Times,* June 14, 2017, https://www.nytimes.com/2017/06/14/world/middleeast/egypt-saudi-arabia-islands-sisi.html, last accessed March 17, 2020.

374 Dov Lieber, "In first-ever Saudi interview, IDF head says ready to share intel on Iran,' *Times of Israel*, November 10, 2017, https://www.timesofisrael.com/in-first-ever-saudi-interview-idf-head-says-ready-to-share-intel-on-iran/, last accessed March 17, 2020.

375 Judah Ari Gross, "Liberman to Saudi-owned paper: If Iran strikes Tel Aviv, we'll strike Tehran," *Times of Israel,* April 26, 2018, https://www.timesofisrael.com/liberman-to-saudi-owned-paper-if-iran-strikes-tel-aviv-well-strike-tehran/, last accessed March 17, 2020.

376 Jeffrey Goldberg, "Saudi Crown Prince: Iran's Supreme Leader "Makes Hitler Look Good"," *The Atlantic*, April 2, 2018, https://www.theatlantic.com/international/archive/2018/04/mohammed-bin-salman-iran-israel/557036/, last accessed March 17, 2020.

377 "UANI's 2018 Iran Summit Kicks off as Organization Celebrates 10 Years," *United Against a Nuclear Iran*, September 25, 2018, https://www.unitedagainstnucleariran.com/press-releases/uanis-2018-iran-summit-kicks-off-as-organization-celebrates-10-years, last accessed March 17, 2020.

378 "Netanyahu: Khashoggi killing was 'horrendous,' but Saudi stability is paramount," *The Times of Israel*, November 1, 2018, https://www.timesofisrael.com/netanyahu-khashoggi-killing-horrendous-but-saudi-stablity-paramount/, last accessed March 17, 2020.

379 Josh Lederman, "Netanyahu's dinner diplomacy with a UAE envoy," *The Associated Press*, May 14, 2018, https://apnews.com/422993dcaf-c645b09025bb69558c968c, last accessed March 17, 2020.

380 "PM Netanyahu meets with US President Trump in Washington," *Israel Ministry of Foreign Affairs*, March 5, 2018, https://mfa.gov.il/MFA/PressRoom/2018/Pages/PM-Netanyahu-meets-with-US-President-Trump-5-March-2018.aspx, March 17, 2020.

381 Amir Tibon, "Israel's US Envoy Shares Dinner Table with UAE Counterpart in Rare Sign of Warming Ties," *Haaretz*, October 11, 2018, https://www.haaretz.com/israel-news/.premium-israel-s-u-s-envoy-shares-table-with-uae-counterpart-in-sign-of-warming-ties-1.6548090, last accessed March 17, 2020.

382 Kenneth Vogel, "How a Trump Ally Tested the Boundaries of Washington's Influence Game," *The New York Times*, August 13, 2019, https://www.nytimes.com/2019/08/13/us/politics/elliott-broidy-trump.html, last accessed March 17, 2020.

383 Wintour, Patrick, and Oliver Holmes, "Mike Pence chides US allies at Warsaw summit on Iran," *The Guardian*, February 14, 2019, https://www.theguardian.com/world/2019/feb/14/us-and-israel-say-confrontation-with-iran-needed-for-peace, last accessed March 17, 2020.

384 Wroughton, Lesley, and Justyna Pawlak, "US meeting on Middle East brings together Israel, Gulf Arab states," *Reuters*, February 13, 2019, https://www.reuters.com/article/us-mideast-crisis-summit/u-s-meet-ing-on-middle-east-brings-together-israel-gulf-arab-states-idUSKCN-1Q22E2, last accessed March 17, 2020.

385 "Khalid Bin Salman meets Sultan Qaboos in Oman," *Reuters*, November 12, 2019, https://gulfnews.com/world/gulf/oman/khalid-bin-salman-meets-sultan-qaboos-in-oman-1.67778812, last accessed March 17, 2020.

386 Delcan Walsh, "Persian Gulf Standoff Starts to Thaw on the Soccer Field," *The New York Times*, December 19, 2019, https://www.nytimes.com/2019/12/19/world/middleeast/qatar-saudi-arabia-soccer-al-hilal.html, last accessed March 17, 2020.

387 "GCC summit calls for unity amid hopes of easing Gulf crisis," *Al Jazeera*, December 10, 2019, https://www.aljazeera.com/news/2019/12/gcc-summit-calls-unity-hopes-easing-gulf-crisis-191210133956942.html, last accessed March 17, 2020.

388 C. Todd Lopez, "Middle East Strategic Alliance Effort Aimed at Stabilization," *US Department of Defense*, April 30, 2019, https://www.defense.gov/Explore/News/Article/Article/1829790/middle-east-strate-gic-alliance-effort-aimed-at-stabilization/, last accessed March 17, 2020.

389 Scuitto, Jim, and Jeremy Herb, "Exclusive: The secret documents that help explain the Qatar crisis," *CNN*, July 11, 2017, https://www.cnn.com/2017/07/10/politics/secret-documents-qatar-crisis-gulf-saudi/index.html, last accessed March 17, 2020.

390 Suzanne Kianpour, "Emails show UAE-linked effort against Tillerson," *BBC News*, March 5, 2018, https://www.bbc.com/news/world-us-can-ada-43281519, last accessed March 17, 2020.

391 Faisal Abbas, "Why Tillerson wasn't the secretary of state Trump needed," *Arab News*, March 14, 2018, https://www.arabnews.com/node/1265841, last accessed March 17, 2020.

392 "The end of Tillerson's ineffectual tenure comes as no surprise," *The National*, March 13, 2018, https://www.thenational.ae/opinion/

editorial/the-end-of-tillerson-s-ineffectual-tenure-comes-as-no-surprise-1.712838, last accessed March 17, 2020.

393 https://twitter.com/Abdulkhaleq_UAE/status/973543144032755712

394 "Foreign Affairs Committee Releases Transcript of Interview with Former Secretary of State Rex Tillerson," *US House of Representatives Committee on Foreign Affairs*, June 21, 2019, https://foreignaffairs.house.gov/2019/6/foreign-affairs-committee-releases-transcript-of-interview-with-former-secretary-of-state-rex-tillerson, last accessed March 17, 2020.

395 Hossein Alizadeh: "Is Oman Mediating Between Iran And Israel?," *Radio Farda*, November 12, 2018, https://en.radiofarda.com/a/netanyahu-visit-to-oman-possible-link-to-iran/29596257.html

Habib Toumi, "Bahrain hails, Iran condemns Oman's wisdom in receiving Netanyahu," Gulf News, October 27, 2018, https://gulfnews.com/world/gulf/bahrain/bahrain-hails-iran-condemns-omans-wisdom-in-receiving-netanyahu-1.2294535

396 Yousef Al-Otaiba, "Qatar Cannot Have It Both Ways," *The Wall Street Journal*, June 12, 2017, accessed https://www.wsj.com/articles/qatar-cannot-have-it-both-ways-1497307260, last accessed March 17, 2020.

397 Hussein Ibish, "To Help Settle Qatar Feud, US Needs to Understand It," *Bloomberg*, February 22, 2018, https://www.bloomberg.com/opinion/articles/2018-02-22/qatar-feud-over-terrorism-and-islam-confounds-u-s, last accessed March 17, 2020.

398 Dalia Adiqi, "Prominent US expert: Doha policies threat to whole region," *Al Arabiya*, April 24, 2018, http://english.alarabiya.net/en/perspective/features/2018/04/23/Analyst-says-Washington-should-put-pressure-on-Qatar-about-moving-Udeid-Air-Base.html, last accessed March 17, 2020.

399

400 "Bannon backs Quartet's policy on Qatar," *Bloomberg*, October 24, 2017, https://gulfnews.com/world/gulf/qatar/bannon-backs-quartets-policy-on-qatar-1.2112133, last accessed March 17, 2020.

401 Kenneth Vogel, "How a Trump Ally Tested the Boundaries of Washington's Influence Game," *The New York Times*, August 13, 2019,

https://www.nytimes.com/2019/08/13/us/politics/elliott-broidy-trump.html, last accessed March 17, 2020.

402 Sigurd Neubauer: "Bahraini FM : 'Arab-Israel Dialogue Could Lead to Normalization,'" The Huffington Post, 6 December 2010, https://www.huffpost.com/entry/bahraini-fm-arabisrael-di_b_792338?fbclid=IwAR1c_dnNPqBHHVFbKf0caCSrRKInEwjE-3UDryiBHUk-Ly38Z8sUBBWPvcjE

403 "President Trump's Speech to the Arab Islamic American Summit," The White House, May 21, 2017, https://www.whitehouse.gov/briefings-statements/president-trumps-speech-arab-islamic-american-summit/, last accessed March 17, 2020.

404 "Emir speech in full text: Qatar ready for dialogue but won't compromise on sovereignty," Qatar News Agency, July 22, 2017, https://qsearch.qa/news-details/221/emir-speech-in-full-text-qatar-ready-for-dialogue-but-wont-compromise-on-sovereignty, last accessed March 17, 2020.

405 "In Full Text: The speech of Qatar Emir at the opening session of UN General Assembly," The Peninsula, September 19, 2017, https://www.thepeninsulaqatar.com/article/19/09/2017/In-Full-Text-The-speech-of-Qatar-Emir-at-the-opening-session-of-UN-General-Assembly, last accessed March 17, 2020.

INDEX

INDEX

INDEX

www.ingramcontent.com/pod-product-compliance
Lightning Source LLC
Chambersburg PA
CBHW020333270326
41926CB00007B/170